Still through the dusk of dead, blank-legended,
And unremunerative years we search
To get where life begins, and still we groan
Because we do not find the living spark
Where no spark ever was; and thus we die,
Still searching, like poor old astronomers
Who totter off to bed and go to sleep,
To dream of untriangulated stars.

LONDON : GEOFFREY CUMBERLEGE

OXFORD UNIVERSITY PRESS

Untriangulated Stars

Stars

LETTERS OF
EDWIN ARLINGTON ROBINSON
TO HARRY DE FOREST SMITH
1890–1905

EDITED BY DENHAM SUTCLIFFE
• HARVARD UNIVERSITY PRESS ~ CAMBRIDGE ~ 1947 •

COPYRIGHT, 1947

BY THE PRESIDENT AND FELLOWS OF HARVARD COLLEGE

PRINTED IN THE UNITED STATES OF AMERICA

FOR

Sarah Emma

CONTENTS

PREFACE

WHEN Edwin Arlington Robinson died in the spring of 1935 he was called America's most distinguished poet. He was the object of critical study on the Continent and in South America; in his own country, scores of critical books and articles had celebrated his skill. He had three times received the Pulitzer Prize, had accepted honorary degrees from Bowdoin College and from Yale, and had refused many more. Close students of American literature had been aware of him since the appearance, in 1916, of *The Man Against the Sky;* after 1927 the most casual reader knew the author of *Tristram.*

Yet few men of his eminence were so little known as persons. Robinson had never delivered a lecture nor read a line of his verse in public; he had never written a popular article about himself. During the summers he withdrew to the MacDowell Colony at Peterborough, New Hampshire; in the winters he moved among a small group of intimates in Boston and New York. Even they knew little about the struggles that had elevated him from lonesome obscurity to late fame.

In 1936 a few letters of his young manhood were published by the *Yale Review;* the *Virginia Quarterly* issued a few more in 1937. But not until Hermann Hagedorn's *Edwin Arlington Robinson, A Biography* (1938) was there any wide public knowledge of his youth. Two years later some friends collaborated to produce *Selected Letters of Edwin Arlington Robinson.* Those letters were addressed to a variety of persons, most of them were brief, and few of them had been written during his youth. The present volume makes public the first major collection of Robinson's early letters. None of them has hitherto appeared in print.

During ten years, from 1890 to 1900, Robinson gave to Harry Smith such fullness of confidence as native reticence allows. To external events he most often referred obliquely; some, like the emotional crisis recounted in Mr. Hagedorn's ninth chapter, he mentioned not at all. He was always chary with names, even of persons they both knew intimately. But of his ambitions and fears he could speak to Smith as he did to few even of his early friends. Harry Smith, he said, was a man he could "take to his soul." Robinson was not, during those years, a member of the National Academy of Arts and Letters. He was a miserable young man whose poems no one cared to buy. In that misery he was discovering the major ideas and themes to which he would give expression during a lifetime of unremitting labor. They were not ideas of which he could speak to every man with an expectation of being understood, but Harry Smith, as Robinson knew, did not expect all men to be alike. He would not accuse his friend of "wearing half his life away for bubble work that only fools pursue." Hence it was that Robinson could write to him with assurance of being understood that "To be born with just one thing to live for, and that thing a relative impossibility, is to be born with certain disadvantages."

My first thanks belong to Professor William A. Jackson, Librarian of Houghton Library, for permission to prepare this text. Several of Robinson's friends have given kind assistance. Mr. Leonard Barnard, who supplied the photograph of Smith, was generous in his recollections. Mr. Louis Ledoux, Mr. Linville Robbins, Mrs. Harry de Forest Smith, and Miss Rosalind Richards have all put me under obligation. The assistance of Professor Emery Neff of Columbia University, generously given during the preparation of his own forthcoming study of Robinson, has saved me from egregious omissions.

Passages from "The Long Trail," "Ballad of the 'Bolivar,'" "Tomlinson," "An Imperial Rescript," and "Mandalay," are reprinted from *Barrack-Room Ballads,* by permission of Mrs. Bambridge, daughter of the late Rudyard Kipling, and of the publishers Methuen & Company, Ltd., of London, the Macmillan Company of Canada, and Doubleday & Company, of New York. Charles Scribner's Sons, publishers of *The Children of the Night,* and The Macmillan Company, publishers of *The Collected Poems of Edwin Arlington Robinson* (1937) and *Selected Letters of Edwin Arlington Robinson* (1940), have granted permission to reproduce brief passages from those publications. The lines on the half title are reprinted from "Octaves" in *The Children of the Night,* by permission of Charles Scribner's Sons.

One cannot undertake extensive study of Robinson without recognizing his debt to the *Bibliography* (Yale University Press, 1936) by Charles Beecher Hogan, who deserves credit for much information that appears in the Notes. My frequent reference to Mr. Hagedorn's biography sufficiently reveals my dependence upon his work. Because his book is so readily available, I have not thought it necessary to paraphrase it in my introduction. I have tried there only to mark out, briefly, the main events and ideas that held Robinson's attention during the period of the letters.

DENHAM SUTCLIFFE

Kenyon College
Gambier, Ohio
March, 1947

INTRODUCTION

In 1896 Robinson gave a copy of his first book to Joe Barstow, who knew more about shooting rabbits and cutting ice than about poetry. But Joe read *The Torrent and the Night Before,* and Robinson recorded his judgment: "There's a hell of a lot of hell in it." Joe was right. There was "not a red-bellied robin in the whole collection." Instead, Cliff Klingenhagen drank the wormwood of self-knowledge, the clerks tiered their webs of discontent, and the condemned murderer of "The Night Before" declared that

> *a happy man is a man forgetful*
> *Of all the torturing ills around him.*

To Joe Barstow, as to many later readers, the poems seemed only to affirm the inevitability of defeat. Like Harry Thurston Peck, who called Robinson's poetic world a prison-house, Joe overlooked the sustaining idealism that Robinson had distilled from a life he could describe only as "a sort of hell."

That hell was created by the clash of his ambition with the circumstances in which it must be fulfilled. For any career but a poet's, those circumstances might have seemed enviable. His father, Edward Robinson, had drawn a not inconsiderable fortune from his grain and lumber business in the village of Head Tide, Maine, and in 1870 had removed with his wife and three sons to the near-by market town of Gardiner, on the Kennebec. There he became a director of banks, a town officer, the owner of extensive properties. He was the father of three promising sons for whom, in the prosperous seventies and eighties, he might have hoped that they would repeat his industry and prosperity.

Dean, the eldest, went on to take a degree in medicine from Bowdoin College. The second son, Herman, was a handsome and universally popular boy, his father's favorite. The last and late-born, Edwin Arlington, though he had been unexpected—perhaps, even, unwanted—should have been upheld by the prosperous image of his father and the model of his brothers. Yet the child was miserable. His parents' affections were already caught up by his brothers, who were themselves too much older to share their pleasures with him. He seems never to have won conviction that he belonged in the family. Physically awkward and by temperament retiring, he early withdrew into his own wonderings. Close knowledge of his childhood is meager, yet fact and conjecture alike support the speculations of T. K. Whipple, who "pictures him, judging from his poetry, as a gloomy little boy, on his guard against the world, hostile to a hostile universe."

During only one short period of youth was he happy; at least, his reminiscence turned with pleasure only to his years in the Gardiner High School. Even then he made no easy friendships. With a few boys, apparently with no girls, he was familiar. He had no inclination to games or to the common sports of the Maine countryside, shooting and fishing. He enjoyed tobacco with a few intimates; he shared hesitantly in their social gatherings. But friends of his youth confirm the impressions of those who knew him later, that he was at ease only with two or three well-known companions. In a larger group he was silently attentive to conversation, in the midst of hilarity he was miserable.

Graduation from high school meant that he must bestir himself to adult concerns, but for those that Gardiner and America most admired he had no reverence. He knew with a fateful certainty what he wished to make of his life, and the plan included no emulation of his father and his father's friends. The loneliness of boyhood had been solaced by reading; his youthful distinction had been ability to make verses, original and translated. More than anything else, he wanted to extend his literary knowledge. That meant he must have education beyond Gardiner's offering, but Edward Robinson, then nearing seventy and no longer in complete self-command, had no thought of sending his youngest son to college. He had been too severely disappointed by the results of education as he saw them in his eldest, for Dean, now a narcotic, could no longer attend his medical practice.

Balked though he was in his scheme of education, the youngest Robinson boy did not strike out for himself in the sawmills, in a store, in some steady and manifestly useful job. He returned to high school for a post-graduate year. For a part of one winter he worked on the wind-swept ice of the Kennebec; for a month or two of one summer he carried the transit for workers on the River Survey. But getting a job, he said, or merely "doing something," is not always the salvation of a man, and for the most part he sat at home, reading and—secretly—writing. If Gardiner noticed him at all, it might have remarked that the Robinsons had gone from shirt sleeves to shirt sleeves in two generations.

Gardiner was a small town, dependent upon shipyards and paper and lumber mills, and especially upon the thick, clear ice of the Kennebec which it harvested by millions of tons and sent from the world's largest icehouses to Boston, Baltimore, or Calcutta. It was not, despite its manor house and two or three patrician families, a town of wide social distinctions nor of eccentricities less familiar than a skirt-crazed drunkard or a reclusive spinster. A Gardiner man was expected to earn an honest and, if possible, comfortable living. If he didn't, everyone would know it and talk about it. It was not, more than any other industrious New England town, a place where a healthy young man could conscientiously write verses while he lived on an aging father's diminishing income. Yet the young man was determined to do just that and to pay unsmilingly the cost of a tortured conscience and galling loneliness.

Actually it is improbable that Gardiner was more aware of Win Robinson than of any other youth, but his preternatural sensitivity convinced him that it was. He fancied himself the object of general scorn for laziness and incompetence. He felt miserably dependent at home, worse away from it. Still, whatever the humiliation of asking his mother for every dime he spent, it was scarcely worse than plodding the dull road of a job, following the blatant horns of Success. He was disgusted by the "diabolical dirty race" after dollars and could give no admiration to the "excruciatingly active and practical men" that Gardiner offered as models of virtue. He cherished an uneasy conviction that despite his being "different" his life was not to be altogether a fiasco.

More than anything else, perhaps, he needed companionship. Most of his high school friends had drifted away, some to college, others to jobs and marriage. Sonnet-writing Dr. Schuman, who lived near by, could encourage the young poet but not befriend the young man. There was not yet a girl. "My girl," Robinson wrote to Arthur Gledhill in the fall of 1889, "is still designated by the character (x)—unknown quantity, doncherknow." He enjoyed the roughly genial friendship of Joe Barstow, but Joe, for all his good nature, could not understand why Rob spent his days translating Virgil or scouring the town library. Fortunately, one man could. Harry de Forest Smith, says Rosalind Richards, "was born for learning. He foamed to it, as a stream rushes down hill." Smith's father, whose farm lay on the rocky slopes of Iron Mine Hill a mile or two outside the town, had taken an attitude quite opposite to Edward Robinson's and had put all he had, both labor and money, into his only child's education. Robinson had made Harry's acquaintance rather late in Smith's days at the high school, having been impelled to it by a shared affection for Latin verse. When Smith left the high school in 1887 to go to Bowdoin College, acquaintance had become warm affection. Harry Smith, Robinson told Gledhill, was a man he could "take to his soul." During every lonesome winter, Robinson looked forward and back to the grateful summers when Smith's vacation allowed them to spend long afternoons under the trees on Iron Mine Hill, reading, smoking, shaping their critical ideas. In the interim, he found his only solace in letters.

The letters at once reveal his greatest need: to justify to himself and to the world his conviction that "the invisible powers" had destined him for something else than business. He knew, or imagined, what people must be saying about his apparent shiftlessness; he knew that rhyme could not silence "the calling of loud progress and the bold incessant scream of commerce." But neighborly inquiry after his "plans" sent him into a flurry of impatience, for his ambitions were of a kind that even less reticent men are slow to reveal. Despite the seeming stagnation of his life, he could not forego the wish for education nor believe that his years of reading and composition had been wholly wasted. When he was suddenly required to go to Boston for extensive treatment of his diseased ear, his father was persuaded to let him enter Harvard as a special student. The belated opportunity to go to college, though characteristically he shunned enthusiasm, seemed a confirmation of his faith.

The first unnerving weeks at Harvard did not strengthen his assurance. He sprang at once to the conclusion that his progress did not justify the cost, that he would flunk out and become the butt of Gardiner's jokes. He even had trouble with the mechanics of registration. Loneliness in Cambridge, he discovered, was not less painful than in Gardiner, and he resumed his ruminations upon high school days. Those troubles overborne, he began to anticipate the sorrow of leaving, as he expected he should, at the end of the first year. He had discovered new friends and ambitions. He wanted to know William Vaughn Moody and the literati; a visit from Robert Lovett aroused naïve faith that he could join the select group on the *Harvard Monthly*. A professor's party stirred a wish to learn the social graces, though they bored him. He found a conviviality he had never known before. Leonard Barnard of Gardiner was at the Massachusetts Institute of Technology, Dexter Whitney was at Boston University, Dr. Schuman frequently came down from Gardiner, there were students who would discuss Matthew Arnold. He discovered beer, the theater, and the opera. The *Advocate* accepted two poems, grades on the first examinations were encouraging, and by the time he went home for the Christmas vacation he could look forward with pleasure to his return to Harvard.

Of course he found new worries. His innate feeling of insecurity transformed the words "special student" into a mark of isolation and he boggled over the phrase "since I came—er—to college." He could not forget the eyes of the world. A bad photograph appalled him with fear of what people might think; news of a minor undergraduate scandal must not be breathed in Gardiner lest it stimulate gossip about the Robinsons. He convinced himself that he had chosen the worst possible course of study and that his incorrigible "dreaminess" doomed him to failure in a practical world. Nevertheless, he reaffirmed faith in his destiny and at the same time resolved to forego his pessimism.

That in some degree he succeeded is apparent from the letters of his second and final year at Harvard. True to his resolution, he studied more, played less. He had friends still, and went as usual to the theater with them, but he forbade himself the little excesses of the first year. He published no more verse, gave more time to his courses and to his desultory reading. Even an operation on his ear and an attack of shingles did not fully arouse his tendency to hypochondria, and only occasionally did he wonder whether life is a dubious joke and whether his years at college, like all the years before, had been futile.

This brief attendance at Harvard was the great experience of his young manhood—even, it may be, of his life. Robinson was a country boy. He had been a solitary writer, unaccustomed to an audience wider or more critical than a few secretive friends. He had never known a learned man. It is doubtful if he took to Harvard any clear notion of university life; certainly he could not have foreseen what changes two years would make in his life and thought. He went to Cambridge with no more definite objective than a wish to extend his "literary knowledge" and to push back the horizons of life in Gardiner. He returned with an unquenchable thirst for literary recognition. "I wonder more and more," he once said, "just where I might have come out if I had never seen Harvard Square as I did . . . There was something in the place that changed my way of looking at a good many things."

Academic Harvard of course wrought some of those changes. Charles W. Eliot had become president of the University in the year of Robinson's birth and had revolutionized American education by introducing the elective curriculum. For one special student, whose sole interest was literature, that system was ideally suited, and he plunged eagerly into his first formal study of literature. From Lewis Gates he learned what it meant to undertake close examination of texts that hitherto he had read for casual pleasure. The study of German and especially of French opened new literary avenues that led him to moderate his youthful scorn of realistic literature. Josiah Royce is commonly invoked as an influence upon Robinson's thought; the comments in these letters will not support the inference. But Charles Eliot Norton inspired him with ideals of taste and conduct; he revered, if he could not emulate, the learning of Kittredge; A. S. Hill added vigor to an existing predilection for niceties of language. As Robinson later said, "it was not in the nature of things" that he should take full advantage of all his opportunities for learning. His domestic troubles made his college life "about one-fourth as pleasant as it would have been otherwise." But the man who returned unhappily to Gardiner in the spring of 1893 carried with him an impetus to study that did not flag during four years more of solitude.

More important, he carried a memory of friends who had taught him what in Gardiner he had begun to doubt, that he could win the esteem of men who shared his standards of achievement. They had not changed, they had established, his conviction that the poet's function is an honorable one and that he would not be making a fool of himself if he tried to fulfill it. Latham, Saben, Tryon, Burnham, Ford, Butler, Hubbell, Johnson were closer names in his memory than even Norton's, the only Harvard man to whom he would give the epithet "great."

With these friends he had heard the chimes at midnight, and the echo would not leave his ears. Without those men, Gardiner was a "town of banishment," and his return to it in the spring of 1893 could only confirm his suspicion of futility.

His widowed mother was beset with troubles, and he burned with shame of what Gardiner must think of the third Robinson boy, whose "college education" had not changed his queer ways. He was utterly without friends. Ed Moore had married, Art Gledhill was in Massachusetts, Smith was teaching in Rockland, Maine, and was at home only during the long vacations. "To live week after week without a soul to speak to on any congenial topic is hell for a man of my nature," he wrote to Smith. His letters to Gledhill were in the same key: "A good friend or two here in Gardiner would make all the difference in the world." His nostalgia turned always to Harvard. "It was there that I met, with one or two exceptions, the friends of my life." He longed for the freedom of his college room, for the joy of shared pipes and ideas. At Harvard he had felt less of that torment which at home he suffered from his "almost unnatural pride." His "failure to accomplish anything or to be anybody," his fear that Gardiner derided him, and a nagging suspicion that his ideals were out of tune with the world kept him permanently out of sorts.

Above all, he was tortured by the situation at home. Pride forbade him to speak openly, even to his closest friends, but he could not wholly exclude despair from his letters. For the most part he limited himself to New England understatement: "I had considerable to contend with." But there were days when he was impelled to speak almost plainly: "All my life at home has been a kind of hell." He was saying the same to Gledhill: "My great trouble is that I have so many things to contend with outside my regular work that that is really the smallest part of the strain that comes on my poor gray matter." He could not help wondering how much he was himself to blame for his "failure in life." Almost anything would have been better for him after Harvard than this anticlimactic return to Gardiner, once more—as he supposed—to be snickered at by the "dear friends" who "felt so much for his welfare." Although he refused to foresee a life of failure or to deny the "Palladium" that ruled his life, the long struggle between faith and doubt reduced him at times to utmost despair.

Whatever "quaint esteem of self" was left to him was shattered in the spring of 1894. At the end of January he began to tutor "a young lady" preparatory to her entering Wellesley College, and he clearly expected the lessons to extend through the summer. They ended in April, and he was plunged into gloom. "You may interpret this as you like," he said to Smith, "but I fancy you will not get far out of the way in your conclusions." He found singular irony in Willie Butler's present of *Ships that Pass in the Night.* In Beatrice Harraden's tale of thwarted love he found a sincerity "which appeals to anyone who has ever had any great trouble—especially trouble of a particular sort that comes to us mortals now and then." He suffered a "horrible dose of the blues" for a long time, and when at the end of May he sent ambiguous congratulation upon Smith's engagement he allowed himself an unusually forthright statement: "I am not (now) engaged to be married, I am not happy, and the world and the future look so dark and gloomy that I look mostly into the past." Soon afterward he spoke of his "separation from the one who is and always will be a part of my daily life." This last assurance of his incapacity for normal life made it "an absolute necessity" to give his feelings "some kind of more or less literary expression."

Believing that fiction was his proper medium, he wrote for two years without selling a page. He planned a volume of short stories and collaborated with Smith in a translation of the *Antigone.* Neither project succeeded. He turned once more to verse, but he was in his twenty-sixth year before the stream of "declination blanks" was interrupted by a check. He gave a year to preparing a volume of poems that, like everything else, was rejected by the publishers. As years passed, suspicion grew upon him that he had made "a giant blunder" in trying to become a writer. He was penniless, with neither prospects nor hope; he was a failure both by his own and by the world's standards. Yet it would require more courage to jettison his ideals than to fail in his effort to realize them, and he kept on. He dared to feel "the splendid shame of uncreated failure."

Robinson had always had "a clambering idea that there is another architect behind ourselves" and had come to an early conviction that no man can fulfill himself in defiance of the master plan. Solitude had bred in him a quick sympathy for failure "where fate had been abused and self demoralized," and had led him to attribute success to a man's willingness

to comprehend
The strangeness of his own perversity.

It became the great object of his life, as it was to be the major theme of his verse, to discover what his destiny was.

"How the devil is a man to understand things in an age like this," he cried, "when the whole trend of popular thought is in the wrong direction—not only that, but proud of the way it is taking?" It made him "positively sick to see the results of modern materialism" as they were revealed in Gardiner. Like many another heart-sick American, he looked to Europe for evidence that artistry was not dead.

The more he read, the more was he convinced that the English novelists—he was reading Hardy at the moment—had "a finish that the American writer lacks . . . They may lack a certain freshness and sparkle that characterizes the novelists of our country but there is a certain element of completeness—rhetorical ease that more than balances the other." With America's obtuseness and the taste reflected in our magazines he contrasted England's "undeniable ability to tell a good thing and not be deceived by outward show." In the best American reviews he saw only feeble imitation of English models, and American newspapers he thought vastly inferior to the French. The manners of American shopkeepers proclaimed our inferiority in taste as Dvořák's "New World" Symphony revealed our artistic poverty. He longed for the comradeship of men whose goddess was not engraved on a silver dollar.

This impatience with the spirit of the age was abetted by the comparative isolation of his life in Gardiner. It encouraged his aloofness—what T. K. Whipple has called his "inability to make healthy, normal, fruitful contacts with his environment." It produced an unconcern with contemporary affairs that led Granville Hicks to say, "much of his poetry is cold and remote, and some of it has no significance at all for Robinson's America." Robinson could never, like his friend William Vaughn Moody, have found matter for poetry in the annexation of the Philippines. He could not, indeed, find sufficient interest in the Spanish-American War to make it the subject of a letter. The financial panic of 1893 and the bitter presidential campaign of 1896 caught little more of his attention. Though his revulsion from the life of business is everywhere apparent, it seems not to have shaped his political views; he gave cool allegiance to McKinley and at the same time judged Bryan in a nonpartisan spirit.

Critical custom sets Edwin Arlington Robinson among the rebels who transfused the anemic literature of the genteel tradition. The same impulses are attributed to him as made Masters and Frost turn to homely subjects and daily speech; as sent the Imagists in quest of new patterns; as produced the new realism in fiction. He is variously regarded as a pioneer realist, a partaker in the new disillusion, as a social satirist. Yet the letters of his young manhood blow no self-conscious trumpets of rebellion. He admired Thomas Bailey Aldrich sufficiently to send him a copy of *The Torrent* and to quote him frequently. Longfellow was more congenial than the *avant-garde* spirit of *The Yellow Book*, and he more gladly read Dickens and Thackeray than Zola. The bolder French insurgents—Mallarmé, Rimbaud, Baudelaire—he never mentioned; the work of Maupassant, Mendès, and Gautier he castigated as "matchless trash," a willful confusion of love and lust. He preferred Coppée's "healthy naturalism" and the Dickensian pleasures of Daudet. Romancers like F. Marion Crawford, Richard Blackmore, and William Black he read faithfully while *Madame Bovary* stood unopened on his shelf. Among poets his early favorite was Matthew Arnold; Cowper, Wordsworth, and Tennyson were not for him outmoded, and the last of them he could read "over and over again without tiring of him." His one reference to William Butler Yeats was scornful. The young man who had plunged enthusiastically into Lewis Gates's courses in eighteenth and nineteenth century prose had too keen a sense of his own ignorance to throw bricks at the temple of tradition.

Neither does it appear that in his religious thinking he was engaged by any coherent revolt. He thought of himself as "liberal in such matters" but there is small evidence that he gave much thought to formal doctrines. In youth, as throughout his life, he endeavored to come to terms rather with himself than with a doctrinal God. He read the Bible, but his doubts prevented reverence. Still, if he rejected the solace of Congregationalism it was for nothing more freshly rebellious than Emerson and Carlyle. He briefly felt the fascination of the new cult of Christian Science, but rationalism withheld him from acceptance of its faith just as his desperate idealism prevented him from accepting modern materialism.

Marxism he might never have encountered, so far as the letters indicate. For all his dislike of business, he was content to be "a gold man" and to follow traditional Maine Republicanism without caring much about it.

Gardiner had no literary and political coteries to stir young artists to consoling frenzy. The town's most successful author was Laura E. Richards, wife of a paper manufacturer, near relative to the wealthy Gardiners, writer of books for children. Schuman, the defeated homeopath, was satisfied to tinker with his *villanelles*. If the workmen of Gardiner grumbled, it was against a concrete foreman, not an abstract economic system. The young man who cried "business be damned" and "Oh, for a poet" spoke for himself, and only in our retrospect as one of a literary "movement." He did not, like the exotics of France and England, proclaim his superiority over the bourgeoisie nor assert the claims of an art without form or meaning. Accepting traditional morals and traditional forms in poetry, he called for only one revolution: overthrow of the delusion that self-fulfillment is self-indulgence and that man's best accomplishment is to draw "the breath of six percent." He knew that "the stopped ears of the strong" do not hear the cries of broken hearts and spirits; they "keep the tune as it has always been," and attribute others' failure to perversity. Most men plait a "two-fold screen of innocence" to hide the truth of themselves from the world, and from themselves. Robinson, revolting from the common arrogance, gave his first sympathy to the inferior wraiths. He tried to understand, not scorn, the skirt-crazed reprobate; in his short studies of character he tried to tell "what kind of good was in Alexis and Evander."

As the years of his exile dragged on, he withdrew farther and farther into himself. Smith, who had fulfilled the requirements for an M.A. while he was teaching at Rockland, had married and had followed thousands of other young Americans to graduate study in Germany. He returned to study at Harvard, to an instructorship at Bowdoin, and then, in 1901, to a distinguished career as Professor of Greek at Amherst. Gledhill was married, and Butler. Ford was prospering at the Phillips Academy in Exeter, and Latham had found a congenial life in teaching. These friends who earned their keep and held a respectable place in the world filled Robinson with shameful despair. On fall nights he shambled along the frozen ruts to the Smith farm and listened to Harry's father talk about sharks. He walked back again to his room. Next day he read some more, wrote some more, and that—apart from correspondence—was his life.

Almost anything else would have been better for Robinson than his return from Harvard to Gardiner—but America might have lost a poet. In his isolation and despair he discovered "a patience that is not averse to the slow tragedies of haunted men," and he won a conviction that could not be stifled by "the groanings of world-worshippers." Partly he came to it through his voluminous reading, unpatterned though it was and so much concerned with popular romances. Partly he was helped to it by Jones, an otherwise unnamed Christian Scientist, who revealed to him the meaning of Emerson. But chiefly he found it in his own misery. If he, the unachieving, could not believe himself a failure, perhaps other men had done the same. Such speculations brought him to an ideal of achievement that was alien to the standards of Tilbury Town. However small a man's range, he might, if he truly knew its boundaries, move freely to triumphant self-fulfillment or to reconciliation in defeat. Such a one, having discovered what he really was, and having accepted that knowledge, would not then destroy himself in vain pursuit of the unattainable; he would not accuse the "Scheme" of a disorder that belonged only to himself.

Out of this conflict between his apparent failure and his conviction that the only important thing was the utterance of what he believed to be the truth, he developed his philosophy of "optimistic desperation," his faith that the "Scheme" is essentially good if hard to discover. What he was after was "the courage to see and to believe that his present life was the best thing for him, and that every man has it in his power to overcome whatever obstacles may be in his way." Toward the end of his years in Gardiner, though he cried out against the hell that was his life, he was able to say that now and then he got a "glimpse of the real thing through the clouds of time." It was that glimpse that made him want to "live and see it out." It was that glimpse that Joe Barstow failed to discover in The Torrent and the Night Before.

What is called "Fate," Robinson had come to regard as character. He saw how men foredoom themselves and then complain of the world's injustice; how they wall themselves off from love, and then cry out against their loneliness. "The willingness 'to be a child again,'" he said, "comes hard—so hard that it will never come to many who are in the world today. That is not what they are here for." Sometimes, as in "Dear Friends," he scorned the impercipients. He mocked the hollowness of conventional success by sending the rich man home to shoot himself. But more frequently he wrote in the spirit of "The Miracle":

> God's anodyne
> For human hate is pity; and the wine
> That makes men wise, forgiveness.

He knew that he was "inclined to be a trifle solemn" in his verses, but, he told Smith, "I intend that there shall always be at least a suggestion of something wiser than hatred and something better than despair."

That description may be applied to all he wrote in the nearly forty years that followed his first publication. All his major characters, from Captain Craig to King Jasper, are brought to see "how much of what men paint themselves Would blister in the light of what they are." All look into the blinding eyes of self-knowledge, thereby to "make magnanimous advance through self-acquaintance" or to be reduced to their essential dust. Those who accept self-knowledge can with a glad release confess their crimes or go serenely back to making pumps; the others have no recourse but to put bullets in their heads or, like Bartholow's wife, to slip into the river.

> There is no cure for self;
> There's only an occasional revelation,
> Arriving not infrequently too late.

* * *
* I *

BUSINESS BE DAMNED
(September 27, 1890 ~ September 27, 1891)

Dear Smith,—

I believe I told you that I would write you something when
you left Gardiner so here goes: I have read your (or rather Henry
De Long's) *Kreutzer Sonata* and I have come to the conclusion
that Wannamaker did about right in suppressing the same.
There is altogether too much low-necked truth in it to be circulated among the young idea; it would have a tendency to "teach
them how to shoot" without taking a fair aim. But then, taken as
a picture of humanity as a whole, I cannot help thinking that it
is open to considerable criticism. We are not all rakes, and there
is such a thing in the world as a good woman, excluding those
angular spinsters who preach about woman suffrage and diseased
ballots until they rope in honest men's wives and teach them to
desert their families and husbands until the poor devils get drunk
out of sheer disgust. (God never intended man and woman both
to wear pants). And yet taking the sentiment expressed in the
Sonata as the natural outburst of the individual telling the story
the book is quite another thing: the question is, did Tolstoi intend it to be applied to the whole human nest or did he simply
essay to show the condition to which a man may bring himself
by his ungodly actions? In this book the wife would have been
a very decent sort of a woman if her husband had not "married"
so promiscuously in his younger days and so been led to believe
that they were all alike. I understand that Tolstoi has written
another book in conjunction with a Russian peasant, elaborating
the same ideas. That seems to me unnecessary.

For the past week I have been following Danforth, the engineer, with an axe and an armful of stakes together with a level-

ing rod and a corn-cob pipe. By this work I was enabled to join the River Survey gang and will go to work to-morrow morning. There will be about a month of it. I must confess that I would rather smoke the pipe under a tree in August and read Virgil, but the trouble is the Roman gentleman pays such devilish slim wages that before you know it you have no tobacco for your pipe. Dollars are convenient things to have, De Smith, but this diabolical, dirty race that men are running after them disgusts me. I shall probably outgrow this idea, but until I do I shall labor quite contented under the delusion that [there] is something to life outside of "business." Business be damned. Write when you get a chance.

Gardiner
October 12, 1890

I have been intending to purchase Fitzgerald's translation of Omar Khayyam's quatrains for some time but have never quite come to it; they are published in a very neat form by Houghton Mifflin and Co. for one dollar. I think I shall have to get them before it grows too cold to take them "underneath the bough" and peruse them to a nicotine accompaniment. As to the "jug of wine" and "thou" I am afraid I shall have to do without them. Can you imagine a man of the nineteenth century striking for the woods with a damsel, a book of verses, a loaf of bread and a two-quart jug? Perhaps the jug makes the paradise. "Oh, wilderness, etc." And yet though it be true that a little reality applied will completely knock the bottom out of the old verse-makers, we find a sort of satisfaction in reading them that is wanting in the alidade or transit, even though we are paid for lugging them and must read our verses at our own expense.

Did you ever read any of Keats' sonnets? They are great. To my mind they are the greatest in the English language. Take for instance "Kosciusko," "On Reading Chapman's Homer," "Homer," or if you like something peppered take this one:

"I cry your mercy—pity—love—ay, love!
Merciful love that tantalizes not—
One thoughted—never-wandering, guileless love—
Unmasked, and being seen—without a blot!
O! let me have thee all,—all—all—be mine!
That shape, that fairness, that sweet minor zest
Of love, your kiss—those hands, those eyes divine,
That warm, white, lucent, million-pleasured breast,—
Yourself—your soul—in pity give me all—
Withold no atoms atom or I die
Or living on, etc."

There are five or six about like this but many of them are on old, solid subjects. In the one "On the Nile" he says—

> *" 'Tis ignorance that makes a barren waste*
> *Of all beyond itself."*

If his works are in the library at Brunswick (and of course they are) get them and see if you do not agree with me.

I have not done a great deal of reading lately except *The New-comes*. I hammered away at that for a month and finished it a short time ago. Big thing, but a little tedious at times, like everything else that amounts to much—that is speaking of fiction and other extended works. I took up *The Journal of Marie Bashkirt-seff* the other day but failed to be impressed. Of course it is a wonderful book, considering the age of its author, but there are too many "O God!s" and "I love hims."

I can say today with more or less truth, *"Cras ingens iterabimus aequor."* We have been sounding the river for the past week and will probably keep at it through the month; a devilish cold job it is too. At times I don't care a cahoot whether the river is one fathom deep or forty, as long as there is water enough to take us home. I try to put my better self—if I have any—to the front, that he may brush away all idle fancies and gather in the dollars; and I tell you what it is, old man, that he hates to stay there. "When I do count the clock" from eight o'clock till four, and mark down soundings to the second, an hour seems a week. The only redeeming feature of the job is that Forney (the boss) does not put in very long days.

Well, be good to yourself and the world and read some of K's sonnets. Write next Sunday and tell me what you think of them. They are calling me to dinner and I am already murmuring again —"Oh, wilderness"—.

Gardiner
November 9, 1890

As long as I am not in Brunswick today I suppose that the least I can do is to sit down and try to write something to take the "cuss" off, to use a mannerism of polite society. Nothing would have pleased me better than to have carried out your proposition, but circumstances would hardly permit it this week, though I may possibly come down and see you next Saturday A. M. if agreeable. Please let me know as soon as you get this, as I should feel like a strayed reveler to go without hearing from you and find you had gone to a Sunday-school convention or a mill-pond baptism.

This is about as mean a day as the Lord ever made. The sky is about the color of a dirty shirt and the air is impregnated with a sort of frigid clamminess that is anything but bracing; and what with the fact that I am blessed with a "whoreson" cold in the head and that the Bros. Barstow are at Oxbow (so that there is no one for me to smoke a pipe with) renders the state of my mind anything but amiable. Longfellow assures us that "Behind the clouds is the sun still shining," but there is little consolation in that while we can't see him (the sun) and feel his grateful rays crawl down the back of our neck. Poetry is a good thing, provided a man is warm enough.

Do you have a chance to read the *Atlantic* where you are? If so I think you would like an article on William Tell in the November number. It seems to make William a nonentity, and reveals him a myth with his counterpart in the folklore of a dozen countries. Nor can the genealogists find any Gessler that could possibly have had the position of the one in the legend: the whole story (to use another mannerism) goes to pot. Besides this article there is a translation of the 4th canto of the *Inferno* in the original terza rima. It is a fine thing and must have taken a world of time, patience and rum on the part of the translator. At times the meter is a little shaky and identical rhymes are a little too frequent, but considering the nature of the work we can easily overlook these defects. Frank R. Stockton's *House of Martha* also begins in this number and bids fair to be a good thing.

My fingers are as cold as proverbial charity and I feel that, if I have any desire to behold the glimmer of another summer, I had better stop writing and shake myself. There is a barrel of cider in the barn, but I have no desire to tamper with it. This will prove to you that my indisposition is no affectation. Write and let me know if you care to harbor me over next Sunday and I will try to come if you feel that you need me.

Gardiner
December 5, 1890

How do you like this:

> *"The skies have sunk and hid the upper snow*
> *(Home, Rose, and home, Provence and La Palie),*
> *The rainy clouds are filing fast below,*
> *And wet will be the path and wet shall we.*
> *Home, Rose, and home, Provence and La Palie."*

You will find it in the poems of Arthur Hugh Clough entitled, "Ite Domum Saturae, Venit Hesperus." The refrain "Home, Rose, etc." runs all through it and makes a mess quite pleasing to the ear.

I have been expecting a letter from you ever since I came home from Brunswick but my expectations have thus far failed to materialize, so I see no other way but to write something myself. I have led a very innocent existence since I saw you and with the exception of the tube (*videlicet* the pipe) have indulged in no manner of dissipation save reading occasional episodes in *Don Juan*. And by the way did you get the decorated tobacco box I sent you a while ago. I think if you take the prescription *saepissimum* as ordered you will derive most prodigious benefits. I think that the judicious use of tobacco is to be commended—especially to students: it makes them strong (that must be a joke) and if they use it freely it "sicklies them o'er with the pale" saffron of nicotine which quite takes the place of the "pale cast of thought" and leaves marks of the midnight oil upon their very raiment.

"Sublime tobacco! . . .
Divine in hookas, glorious in a pipe.
When tipped with amber, mellow, rich and ripe"—The Island.

If there is an "h" in hooka (h?), you can put it in yourself.

I have about come to the conclusion that I shall take a year at Harvard next fall. I shall never be satisfied unless I go away somewhere to school for a year or so and it seems to me that Harvard would be the best school for a special course. If this should come to pass, as soon as I get settled I shall invite you up to my room, read you "The Future," give you my biggest pipe and tell you to spit in the stove. All of which would be duly pleasing and edifying. I sat down here with the intention of writing a letter but my room is so devilish cold that I shall have to stop.

Write and let me know what you are doing.

Gardiner
January 25, 1891

I received your letter a few days (or rather about two weeks) ago and will now take up your literary vein and advise you to read *John Halifax* if you have not already done so. It is a novel after the old school but yet there is more of the modern realism in it than you generally find in books written forty or fifty years ago. It will show you the difference between great and small writing in a most impressive manner.

Outside of this I have not done much reading since I saw you; in fact I have read nothing save a book of Bret Harte's short stories and about half of Rudyard Kipling's *The Light that Failed*. I think upon the whole the former is the greater writer, although there is a certain "queerness," as you say, about the latter's work that is rather attractive. I think Kipling's poetry is better than his prose. Are Rossiter Johnson's series of Little Classics in the Bowdoin Library? If they are, take out the one on Exile and read Harte's "Outcasts of Poker Flat"; in some ways I think it is the best short story in the English language. This may sound a little loud, but read it yourself and write me what you think of it.

I am still dragging along in the same old rut, and occasionally someone says, "Well now, Robinson, what do you intend to do?" This makes me mad. I cannot tell what I shall do. I have said that I thought I might go to Harvard in the fall for a year or two but as I am not sure of it I do not say so when these pleasant people question me, so you see all I have to do is to tell them that I do not know, which is about like pulling teeth. I suppose it does look a little queer to see me practically doing nothing at my age, but at present there is no getting out of it. Someone must be at home to run the place. I am not getting rich but I try to console myself with Blackmore's lines:

> "The more we have in hand to count
> The less we have to hope for."

There is a good deal in that if you will stop to moralize a little; but the devil of it is, while we are moralizing someone else gets what we hope for. This is a sad world, Smith, where the under-dog gets his neck chewed. Sometimes I think I shall go into the missionary business and teach the chattering Hindoos how to read the *Police Gazette* and *Town Topics*. They never would take the trouble to barbecue me, my bones are too large.

Speaking of the books I have read, I omitted Chas. Dudley Warner's *My Summer in a Garden*. It is a good thing, and contains much valuable information. Here is an extract from the "third week":—"The striped bug has come, the saddest of the year. He is a moral double-ender, iron-clad at that. He is unpleasant in two ways. He burrows in the ground so that you cannot find him, and he flies away so that you cannot catch him . . . The best way to deal with the striped bug is to sit down by the hills and patiently watch for him. If you are spry, you can annoy him. This, however, takes time. It takes all day and part of the night. For he flyeth in darkness, and wasteth at noonday."

I suppose I shall have another garden to make in the spring and a general spell of "clearing up." I think after that, a trip to Harvard would be a glorious contrast.

I trust that this letter will be a warning to you never to use a stub pen. I have used one for three or four years and this is the effect of changing over. Perhaps you will be able to read it and perhaps you will not. It is enough to make a man weep. I think I shall have to go back to the stub with my hand tipped over upon one side. Then writing is no great hardship to me; but to write this way after so many months is hell itself. Keep away from the stub.

Gardiner
February 8, 1891

It has just occurred to me that it would be no more than common decency to answer your last letter. Upon going to my desk I find that my stationery has given out, and consequently I am obliged to resurrect this somewhat ancient foolscap. You will doubtless discern a certain fringe of ante-diluvian saffron upon the same, but I trust the discovery will awake no other emotion than that of reverence. I have read that this is the kind of paper that most of the famous English novels and histories have been written upon. Doesn't it wake strange thoughts within your dreamful bosom to think that a man should be gifted with the stamina to cover ten or twelve hundred of these pages in carrying out a single narrative? Think of this, and take down one of Dickens' or Thackeray's novels. Think of the "ink and the anguish," and the golden gallons of midnight oil! I tell you what it is, old man, we poor ungifted devils of the common herd know little of the bull-dog persistency and enthusiasm required to bring forth a thing like *The Newcomes* or *Our Mutual Friend*. Dickens would cover more paper in calling a cab than I have covered thus far; and Thackeray would slap the whole human race while I stop to swear at my pen. You will probably swear also when you attempt to read this, but I shan't hear you and so will feel no remorse.

Speaking of novels makes me think of one I have just read. For some time I have been intending to try something of Thomas Hardy's but never came to until a few days ago, when I borrowed *The Mayor of Casterbridge*. It was a revelation to me. I never would suppose that a writer of such power could achieve so little popularity (in the general sense of the word) as he has done. The book in question is a novel of something less than three hundred pages, but when you come to "finis" you have the impression of having read a whole history—the history of a quiet pastoral neighborhood which leaves in your mind the odor of an enviable rusticity. (Perhaps "odor" is hardly the word to use here, but you may supply what you will). In the main, the book is loaded with a certain drowsy elegance which tends to make the reader a little sleepy; but it is never tedious, as there is enough incident to keep one well on the lookout for the story as well as the wonderful style in which it is written. At times it is disastrously pathetic; and I am perfectly willing to confess that my *fons lachrymarum* was tapped once or twice to a troublesome extent during my perusal of it. I do not mean that the brine took the stiffening out of my collar, but that a certain unpleasant haze clouded my sight, —I guess you understand me—if you do not, read Bret Harte's "Outcasts of Poker Flat." I think I have mentioned it before.

I have also skimmed over Wilkie Collins' *Heart and Science*. In this volume the author evidently attempted to add one more to his list of wonderful male characters (Sergeant Cuff in the *Moonstone*, Bishopriggs in *Man and Wife*, Count Fosco in *Woman in White*, etc.) but in my opinion has hardly made a success of it. This time the eccentricity is a doctor, to whom he assigns the somewhat startling appellation of Benjulia. His hobby is vivisection, together with an unconquerable propensity for tickling a little girl named Zoe. Almost his last words (before he committed suicide in his disappointment) were, "I wish I could tickle her once more." There is a sort of a diabolical humor about the story that is in a way attractive but after you have read it you cannot but feel that your time has been wasted. This is not the case with the *Mayor of Casterbridge*. I would write out the main ideas of the plot, which is rather unique, but I am afraid that I have already given you enough to decipher as it is. I think I shall have to purchase a typewriter. Write when you get a chance and let me know what you are doing and reading.

Gardiner
March 10, 1891

Atwood told me yesterday that you had been in Gardiner over Sunday. If I had known it at the time I should most surely have taken a constitutional in the direction of your domicile and held some converse with you on certain matters of a literary and educational nature. I am reading Carlyle's *Sartor Resartus* and am completely soaked with its fiery philosophy. It is just the book for you to read, as, in the midst of your philosophical and psychological moonings you will find it a most welcome guest. There is a certain half-diabolical humor running through that renders it all the more readable. The general tone is cynical, but never morbid. Here is an extract from Book II—Chap. IX: "Now consider . . . what a fund of self-conceit there is in each of us,— do you wonder that the balance should so often dip the wrong way, and many a Blockhead cry: 'See there, what a payment; was ever a gentleman so ill-used!' [sic]—I tell thee, Blockhead, it all comes of thy vanity . . . Fancy that thou deservest to be hanged (as is most likely) thou wilt feel it happiness to be only shot; fancy that thou deservest to be hanged in a hair halter, it will be luxury to die in hemp.—So true is it, what I then said, that the Fraction of Life can be increased in value not so much by increasing your numerator as by lessening your denominator. Nay, unless my Algebra deceive me, Unity itself divided by Zero will give Infinity. Make thy claim of wages a zero, then; thou hast the world under thy feet."

I am not sure that I quite see the meaning of the talk about hanging and shooting, but I think I have some idea of what he is driving at; I have given the book and chapter so you can read the passage yourself to a better advantage by procuring the book. I am willing to confess that there are many passages that I entirely fail to understand; but in the main it is intelligible and entertaining,—instructive, and I think upon the whole, elevating. The introduction states that he had a most doleful experience in finding a publisher; this seems to be the case with nearly all great literary efforts.

There is an article in the last *Arena* by Albert Ross, entitled "What is Immoral in Literature?" I have not read it but probably you have. It seems to me that, from a commonsense standpoint, there can be no possible defense for that gentleman's fiction (or perhaps we had better say, truth). It is the simplest thing in the world for a person with the gift of writing to concoct a slimy tale after the fashion of *Sapho, The Pace that Kills, Thou Shalt Not,* etc. and conclude it with what it pleases the author to call a moral, but so doing does not detract from the book's filthiness or pernicious influence. The first two books named above do not make the rather ghastly moral pretensions of the latter, but I consider them quite as [un]pardonable. Do not think that I am setting myself up for a Saint Anthony (Comstock) for I am not; but I will say that the recent deluge of literary nastiness that has poured for the past two or three years from the soul-sewers of six or eight half-penny writers without any special literary excellence to aid them in their obviously mercenary mission has been a disgrace to American letters. Neither Ross nor Saltus are literary artists, and their books are only bought by an itching gullible public whose mind is too shallow to realize its shallowness. Perhaps, though, I am a little too hard with Saltus, for some of his essays are said to be, in a way, fine. In a recent criticism the *Atlantic* remarked that his philosophy "shows some insight into his subject, but the light thrown upon the manner is chiefly a cigarette light." This is enough to prove that there is something in them worth reading (the essays); but I was only speaking of his novels. If a man must have something essentially filthy, why can he not satisfy himself with the work of the ancient and venerable Moses? Verily, man's demand for the foul is insatiable! Here is the book—or Book—which we are all told to peruse, and in it lies enough offal to choke the throats of millions; and still they must have fresh carrion or literature will be a dead issue except to a select and torpid few who know no better than to read Thackeray and Carlyle. If all worldly creatures could realize that there is enough rottenness in their several systems already without enhancing it by the means of scrofulous novels, the reading public would be wondrously elevated. But why dream of such a condition of things? The sooner I break from this strain, the better.

Let us talk of other things; let us go to college and be learned. If my little plan should work and I should find myself in Harvard next September I wonder if I should make a fool of myself —if I should only waste good time and money? I cannot think so; and yet, when a fellow sees no definite object in view it is natural that he should hesitate. But there is one thing that is unquestionable: throw aside the subject of books and education (that is education in the popular sense), the experience of a year among new forms and faces would do me a world of good in more ways than one. I am a little rusty, naturally, as I have spent all my days in Gardiner and never shone as a society star or "one of the boys." I have no desire to shine as either, but there is a place about midway between the two toward which what little common sense I have seems to lean.

By the way, I went to the library the other day and took out Omar Khayyam. It is rather grim philosophy but rather attractive. As you say, some of the tetrasticks are "quite pleasing": the following for instance:

> "Why," said another, "Some there are who tell
> Of one who threatens he will toss to Hell
> The luckless Pots he marred in making—Pish!
> He's a Good Fellow, and 'twill all be well."

Considerable thought in that, it seems to me. Write when you get a chance and let me know what you are driving at.

Gardiner
March 22, 1891

It is Sunday and raining like ten thousand devils; I don't seem to feel in the mood for reading, so I will take this opportunity and strike off something in reply to your last letter.

Did I say anything in my last epistle about William Black's latest novel, *Stand Fast, Craig-Royston!*? I do not remember of mentioning it [sic], so will say a few words now at the risk of repetition. The book is great in a small way—that is, the author has made a work of art of a rather tame, threadbare story: The same old anguish and loss of useful flesh and strength; the same young man and the same—no, I can hardly say the same young woman, for in many welcome respects she is an exception to the general run of frowzy confectionery heroines. Mr. Black devotes very little space in this book to the usual amplexo-osculatory demonstrations so necessary to the mushroom novelist of today, but he gives us all that we can reasonably demand of the most amorous lugubriousness. (I do not know whether there is such a word as "lugubriousness" in the dictionary or not, but it seems to convey the meaning). But the most attractive character in the story—from a psychological point of view—is the girl's (Maisrie) father: he is a curiosity. I will not attempt to anaylze him here, but will leave you to read the book for yourself. The story goes on in a masterly manner until we reach the closing chapter, when the author seems to me a trifle inconsistent. The hero has passed through months of the most harrowing anxiety, and one day receives a letter from the long absent damsel asking him to come to Scotland (he is in London) immediately. He goes, and meets her in the doorway, with the conventional literary happiness glowing in her eyes. To be sure, the illness of her grandfather—I should have said grandfather above—renders her somewhat sad, but that is no excuse for what follows, or rather what does not follow. He takes her by the hand and asks her if she has any better news for him. That is all. Might not the reader naturally ask for something a little more spirited upon such an occasion? Here, if anywhere, would seem to be the place for a little sacchariferous hugging.

I am now reading Thomas Hardy's *The Return of the Native*. Hardy is really greater than Black, but he lacks a certain naturalness that characterizes the former's (excuse me, latter's) writings. The *Native* is one of his quiet stories of English country life for which he is noted.

You must make some allowance for my giving all my space for the discussion of literary matters, as you are aware that I have little else to write about, situated as I am. I hope you will succeed in getting a commencement part, for I think you could make it rattle. But before you go on the stage you had better read "The Future" once or twice for enthusiasm.

Gardiner
April 30, 1891

I will now seize the opportunity, upon a full stomach, to answer your last letter. When you were at home sick I started out one Sunday afternoon to see you, but met "Gib" on the way and he told me that you were sick in bed. Upon hearing that I turned and went home, thinking that if that were the case my room would be more desirable than my company. I afterwards learned that I might have called and had a session with you as well as not. So you will see that my feelings were all right, though a false report spoiled my chances of meeting you. You had been in the store nearly a week before I knew that you were in town.

Speaking of Rudyard Kipling, I must say that I am tired of him. There was a time when I thought that he was booked for something great, but my ideas have changed since, considering the feverish notoriety he has received and the fulsome praise that has been showered upon him by the great and small alike, in the light of what he has really done for literature. I don't think five years hence will hear a great deal of Rudyard; but of course I may be wrong. What I have seen of his verse I like better than his prose. It is a relief to turn from him to Mr. Thomas Hardy.

I have just finished *A Pair of Blue Eyes*. Why the author should have given such a love-in-a-cottage title to a really great novel, I cannot understand; nor can I understand how it is that Hardy has failed to become popular. I think the book just named is really the best one I have read by him. It has not the quiet pastoral finish of *The Mayor of Casterbridge* nor *The Return of the Native;* but the character analysis is deeper than in either, which, by the way, is saying a great deal.

My time is now pretty well taken up with farming, and I am

raising giant harvests of cucumbers, cauliflowers, onions, and God knows what more, in the prolific garden of my mind. That is the only garden in which I have succeeded in raising anything thus far during my life, but I have hopes that I may plant a seed before long that will take root and bring forth something, if no more than fifty cents a week, provided I am to some extent contented with the soil. I am not grumbling, but it is impossible for a fellow to keep on as I am doing now and not be discontented at times. However, I shall stick to the dirt this season, at least, and trust in Providence. It is becoming painfully apparent that I am not in the mood to write a letter, and I think the best thing that I can do is to stop. Burn this thing up when you get it and I will try to do better next time.

Gardiner
May 21, 1891

Perhaps I shall find no better time than now to write you a few lines, so I will improve the opportunity. I would go down in the stable and have a smoke, but as I am out of tobacco, I will try to console myself with a short season of composition. I think my coming to Brunswick this spring is rather doubtful, but will let you know in time. There is considerable work to be done around the place, and as I am laying my plans to go to Cambridge the first of July, I must gauge myself accordingly. I was talking with Schuman the other day concerning Harvard when he made the remark that the whole damned institution ought to be wiped out. I can hardly agree with him, although I think myself that it is the root of a world of unlicensed deviltry; but for that matter, who can name a place of any considerable size that is not? The matter seems to me something like this: the college is there with its corps of instructors, and the student has his choice as to improving the opportunities placed before him or not. If a fellow goes there and spends all his time raising the devil, it does not seem exactly a fair thing to lay the whole burden of blame upon the college. If a man should find a dollar and a dogtird side by side in the street would it be the fault of the dollar should the finder choose its less resplendent neighbor for his reward? (As a rule I do not approve of vulgarity, especially in friendly correspondence, but as I desired to make myself clearly understood I trust that you will take no offence at my example).

I think I told you that I would copy off the ode of Horace, and I will do so upon another sheet. You will find it rather too literal for a poetical translation—a little prosy in places. I have not tried Horace since and I doubt if I ever do again. It is too much work for the pay. I have never seen an English translation of Horace that seemed satisfactory to me; perhaps I am over particular, but I doubt if the thing can be done to catch the spirit of the original. Horace is Latin, or nothing. For example, make a poetical translation of *"cras ingens iterabimus aequor,"* or *"Integer vitae, scelerisque purus."* Bulwer says, "Tomorrow again the great sea-plains," but it sounds rather far-fetched to me. His translation of the odes and epodes is a rather unique one, however, and it would pay you to examine it if you have never done so. He attempts to reproduce the ring of the different metres in different styles of English blank verse, mostly of his own invention I should say. If I remember rightly he renders *"dulce loquentem"*—"her the sweet-talking"—objective of course.

Well, I think I shall have to paddle down street through the rain after a plug of tobacco and have a smoke. I will copy that ode and take this letter along with me.

Please excuse the dimness of the type: there is evidently a scarcity of ink.

Horace: Book I., Ode XI.

I pray thee not, Leuconoe, to pore
Upon forbidden things—what end may be
By destiny allowed for you and me—
Nor blind Chaldea's starry page explore.
'Twere better, oh! far better, if you bore
Your lot contented: whether Jove decree

More winters yet to come, or whether he
Assign this one whose worn, wave-eaten shore
Shatters the Tyrian sea to-day the last—
  Be wise, I pray; and rack thy wine, nor fill
    Thy bosom with large hopes; for while I sing
    The envious close of time is narrowing:
  So seize the day, be merry ere 'tis past,
  And let the morrow come for what it will.

E. A. R.

Gardiner
June 10, 1891

When the latter part of the month of June comes around I always begin to feel queer; and I suppose that the queer feeling is wholly due to the approaching graduations and commencements, although I take no active part in any of them. A kind of sympathy, no doubt, causes me to take a quiet interest in such things. At any rate, when I received your invitation the other day (and you will please accept my most sincere thanks for the same) I experienced a strange sensation as if the world had lost something, —as if Time had taken an unseemly swath with that diabolical scythe of his in fields where he had no business. Perhaps a mind like yours will understand me, though I am not confident that I understand myself; but I have a vague idea that I am trying to define an exit from a school as a dividing point in a life. Mine was thus divided three years ago, but it seems to still linger around the old gash, which somehow is rather slow in healing. It is curious to note the difference in people about such matters: some leave school and think no more about it; they "get a job" and are happy, as the word goes, and their school-days are a thing of the past and they are well rid of them. Upon the whole I think this is, in most cases, the better way to be constructed; but what the deuce is a man to do if he happens to be compounded differently? I am well aware that memories and ruminations occupy altogether too much of my time, but when I behold one of these excruciatingly active and practical individuals, the same awakens no feeling of awe or admiration within me. This is undoubtedly wrong, but still I have a presentiment that my life is not to be altogether a fiasco. I may be disillusioned, but I shall have the satisfaction of knowing that I am a "drop of the eternal spring" and consequently not made in vain, as Coleridge says. When you come home I will pass the hat.

Now nothing would give me more pleasure than to be in Brunswick on Class Day; but circumstances render it impossible. Do not take this as a formal declination, but believe me,

Yours sincerely,

Gardiner
June 21, 1891

I am in receipt of your last letter and you may be sure that I will seize the opportunity of writing you once more as you have requested. I have been in a rather uncomfortable frame of mind for the past week but am gradually getting out of it, I think; it is all on account of idleness, I suppose, though I cannot feel that I have altogether wasted the past three years. Getting a job is not always the salvation of a man, and knowing as I do that I should never have been satisfied had I taken up with some work with the sole incentive of "doing something" and given up the idea of a further literary knowledge, my hopes for the future are not as dark as they might be. If I am ever fortunate enough to secure employment in some publishing house or in the office of some one of the higher grade of newspapers, I shall be perfectly satisfied. Sometimes I look with envy upon the editor of a popular local paper—E. W. Morrell, for example. Of course to fill such a position one must go through the dirty work and learn the ropes, and then the chances are small for the realization of a great income; but the editor is eminently his own boss and lives as it were in a little world of his own. All this you will of course understand as nothing more than a kind of contemplation, but it will give you an idea as to the current of my thoughts and reflections. I think it is a misfortune to be too ideal in these times; what I mean by ideal is the fixing of one's desires too strongly upon the attainment of some end not generally reached. Successful local papers are far more scarce than we would naturally suppose, and the gaining of a livelihood through literary labors of any kind is, to quote from Thomas Hood, "at best a sorry game." But I suppose I shall have to try it or else live the rest of my days in a state of general dissatisfaction.

I hardly think you will find any difficulty in getting a school this fall—and while I think of it, the position of first assistant in the G. H. S. is open for an applicant; but as a lady generally takes the chair it may not be of any interest to you. I think you could give Prof. Wright a few points in teaching Virgil. Don't you think you could turn an occasional dollar by tutoring this summer if you should strike the right place? There are always three or four ad's in the Boston *Journal* of private tutors for the Massachusetts colleges and it is rumored that they receive celestial prices for their services; but you of course know more of such matters than I, and it will be better for me to talk of something of which I am not absolutely ignorant. I could give you a dozen pages on garden truck, but it hardly seems the time for considering such matters.

As I realize that this is in all probabilities the last letter I shall ever write you as a Bowdoin man, my thoughts naturally are led into a rather different channel than heretofore: our correspondence has been the source of much pleasure to me, not so much for the written words in themselves perhaps, as for the sentiment and friendliness of the thing. I have about come to the conclusion that friends are scarce; I can easily count mine upon the fingers of one of my hands and still have fingers to spare. You will understand that I am speaking of friends in the higher sense of the word. I never thought so much of having a host of acquaintances, and in fact my nature is not one to acquire it if I so desired. Once in a great while I meet with a person in whom I find certain elements that strike a sympathetic chord in my own spiritual anatomy: thus, it gave me a certain kind of satisfaction when I read your remarks upon Mr. Black and his little piper at Castle Dare. I myself have a weakness for the "skirl" of the bagpipe even if it be played by an Irishman or an unctuous Italian. I have always considered *Macleod of Dare* a great novel; consequently I like to read lines in its praise. I do not care so much for the gloomy ending, as I look upon such a book more as a work of art than as a story. The closing is, to say the least, magnificent; there is genius in the last sentence.

In closing I will ask you to send me a programme of the class-day speaking. I shall not be able to hear it myself but will be much obliged if you will find time [to] do me the favor. I was very glad to hear of your success in obtaining a part though it be "nothing to boast of." I think however that there would have been a disappointed Smith in Brunswick about now had things turned the other way. I should be glad to have you write a line or two if you send the programme, and when you come we will have a big pipe in the forest.

Gardiner
September 13, 1891

As there will be no "bower" today I will take out my machine and endeavor to thump a few sentences for your benefit. It seems strange to think that you are not in town, and that I would not find you if I went over the hill; but I suppose it is all so, and I will stay where I am and try to be sensible. I am glad for you, but it is devilish lonesome for me.

I shall have a change soon, however, as my application to Harvard has been accepted and I shall probably leave Gardiner about the 27th. I expect it will seem rather odd at first, but I trust I shall get used to the new life in a few weeks. As I am not subject to "swelled head" and have no idea of overturning the faculty, I see no reason why I should not be an "eddy of the mighty stream" and pass with the multitude. His erudition, M. Frederic

Cesar de Sumichrast will be my adviser, and I shall be obliged to hold a parly with him before I enter upon my course. Entering as a special student is far from satisfactory, but it is better than nothing. It will give me a taste of the college atmosphere and cause me to mingle with people of all sorts and conditions—a thing which I sadly need. The truth is, I have lived in Gardiner for nearly twenty-two years and, metaphorically speaking, hardly been out of the yard. Now this is not right; the process tends to widen one's thoughts, or rather sympathies, to an unwholesome extent. This may be a new theory, but I firmly believe it to be the truth. Solitude (in the broad sense of the word) tends to magnify one's ideas of individuality; it sharpens his sympathy for failure where fate has been abused and self demoralized; it renders a man suspicious of the whole natural plan, and leads him to wonder whether the invisible powers are a fortuitous issue of unguided cosmos, or the cosmos itself—"The master of the show," as Omar Khayyam says. In short, this living alone is bad business; and I have had more than my share of it.

But here the old question comes up again, Why have I not done differently? I cannot conscientiously say that it has been necessary that I should stay at home as I have; and the more I think it over, the more am I convinced that the fault lies with myself. But how about the unseen powers? The old buffers (no offence to them) will smoke their pipes and cut their coupons and tell us all about how the world is what we make it, and how every man is the architect of his own fortune, etc. It is good to hear them, but I sometimes have a clambering idea that perhaps there is another architect behind ourselves. This is probably moral cowardice, and the chances are, ten to one, that the element is but an outgrowth of objective inactivity.

You are now in a position where you will have a glorious chance to study into this matter; so when you write next Sunday, let us have a word or two on the subject of free agency. Now I will smoke a pipe and wonder whether I have made a fool of myself in writing what I have.

This is a day for the gods, and it seems wicked that there is no one to spend it with. The Barstow Bros. are both upstream and you are beyond reach. So you see there is nothing for me to do save sit still and think it over. The idea that I shall leave for Harvard tomorrow morning does not seem to affect me much, but I have a vague presentiment that I shall rather enjoy it after I fairly learn the ropes. I expect that I shall entertain some queer thoughts en route to Boston and shall doubtless smoke more cigars than my system requires; but then, life is short, and a man may be pardoned for an occasional over-indulgence in so small an evil as tobacco. I have an affinity for the smoker when I travel—I feel more at home there.

This pen is a kind of a parody on a Roman stylus, and if you ever succeed in reading what I have written you will be thankful that I have nothing to say. Some days I can write a letter and some days I cannot. This is one of the latter. I wish you would write me a letter so that I can receive it next Sunday. Address #166 Putnam Ave., Cambridgeport, Mass. After I get settled I hope we may keep up a regular weekly correspondence. It will be "good for the ghost." I will send you those books as soon as I can do so with anything like convenience.

II

THE FRIENDS OF MY LIFE
(October 6, 1891 ~ June 21, 1893)

Your most welcome letter has been received and in response I will make this proposition: If you will write next Sunday I will do the same. I have been so stirred up for the past week, and in fact am still, that I hardly find time to swear. When I write I will let you know how I feel and what I am doing.

According to agreement, I will now try to inform you what I am doing and how I am feeling. I have been feeling by turns hopeful and blue, for the past two weeks; it is the change, more than anything else, I suppose. But the fact is, I am not fixed upon the firmest footing possible; I am where I have no business. This is what I mean:

When I came to Harvard, the idea of a special wishing to take courses primarily intended for upper class men and graduates, with nothing to show but a diploma from a second rate high school, rather dazzled the faculty; and the result was, that at half past ten o'clock Thursday A. M. (registration closed at 1.00) I was no nearer entering Harvard College than I was when we were talking it over in the "bower." But when I succeeded in fully convincing them that I had no idea of entering as a special with the intention of gaining an A.B. in a year or two by jumping to one of the upper classes, they looked more favorably upon my case. I succeeded in registering about 12.45, but I do not feel easy yet. Prof. Lathrop, or rather Mr. Lathrop, who has charge of the English A division (Composition and Rhetoric), has an abnormally swelled (swollen?) head; and I am in that division merely on trial. If I were dropped, I do not know how it would be about my keeping on in the other studies.

This is my program:

English A Tu, Sat. 12 (Sander's Theater)
 (This class numbers over 500).
English 3 (Anglo-Saxon) Mon, Wed, Fri. at 11. { Prof.
 " 10 (Shakespeare) " " " " 10. { Child.
English 9 (Prose writers 19th century) Friday at 3.30 Mr. Gates.
French A Mon. Fri. at 1.30—Dr. Marcou.
 " " Tu. at 3.30—Prof. de Sumichrast.
English A (written work) Upper Dane—Th. at 11. Prof. L. B. R. Briggs.

I was obliged to give up the idea of taking German, as it would make a general split in the time-arrangement. My eyes are troubling me, too. As to Anglo-Saxon, the rudiments are hellish. (I know you will pardon me; I dislike profanity in correspondence as heartily as any man, but this is the only adequate adjective I can think of). The Shakespeare is of course fine and Prof. Child is the man for the place. You have doubtless heard of him. French seems to come quite easy. At the end of the year I shall be expected to take up an ordinary French novel and read it without any idea of translation. I hope it may prove true.

The "Prose Writers of the 19th century" means work; I am beginning to wish that I had not taken it. Four recitations a day are too many for a man who has done no compulsory studying for over three years. To be candid, I am working about three times as hard as I expected to. It will probably be of no injury to my system, but it is a most decided surprise. When I get fairly at work, however, things may look differently and come easier.

By the way, I submitted the White Ship ballade to the *Advocate* the other day and received a card of acceptance yesterday morning. *"Sic itur ad astra* (!)" I have the idea of a ballade with a refrain, "When Themes are due on Friday next." If I ever work it out I may spring it on the *Lampoon.*

Upon the whole I am living a tolerably comfortable life and am probably a deal more fortunate than I realize. I shall probably begin to thoroughly enjoy myself about next May—just before I leave. I think some of taking a private class in penmanship to pay for my tobacco.

Trusting that I shall receive a letter from you tomorrow. . . .

> 717 *Cambridge St.*
> *Cambridge, Mass.*
> *October 18, 1891*

Your letter has made me quite uneasy; it seems to me that I am not as anxious that the Columbia business should turn out all right as you can be yourself. I have always had an idea that you were intended for something above the common herd, and shall continue to think so for some time to come. Write and let me know how things are looking in that direction.

I have fallen into quite a nest of Bowdoin boys, though of course I do not know them. Hubbard ('90) has the next room to mine. He is the only fellow in the University that I am any way acquainted with, thus far. They are a devilish queer lot. I have of course had some conversation with quite a number but I have not yet seen one that I have [been] at all attracted by. This is my nature, and it will probably play the very devil with me all through my life. But as for cultivating familiarity with Tom, Dick and Harry, wherever one may be, it is out of the question in my case. I shall probably come across someone after a time, with whom I can smoke a pipe and talk of Matthew Arnold, Andrew Lang and Co., but he has not appeared yet. My "ballade" is in the last *Advocate,* will get one tomorrow and send it to you. This is your own request, remember.

I do not think the college papers are very well patronized here. It is a rare thing to meet a fellow with one in his hand, and the very fact of my contribution being accepted and printed within two weeks of my coming here would go to prove there is no great deluge of manuscript submitted to the editors. I have subscribed for the *Advocate* and the *Monthly,* but I doubt if I ever appear in the latter. It seems to be a medium for airing the work of its editors. There is not an article in prose or verse (excepting the alumnus' opening paper on Dumas, *fils*) that is not contributed by one of the staff. However I think I shall spring something on them pretty soon, to see how it will work.

Here is a pleasant quatrain (barring the rhyme) from the *Lampoon:*

> *In Boston town her sons may drown*
> *Their cares in sweet oblivion;*
> *But coppers here swipe kegs of beer*
> *And at the station divvy 'em.*

I have come to the conclusion that it will be for my interest to drop Anglo-Saxon, for two reasons: First, because it will take at least ten hours work every week that could be spent far more profitably upon French and English.

Second, because my eyes are going back on me and the less glossary-hunting and grammar consultation I have to do, the better. And more than that, I think I am practically wasting time, considering the fact that I am to have but one year in college. But the question is: can I drop it? I shall know by tomorrow night, I hope.

I have just read three pages of *L'Abbé Constantin.* I have to guess at half the words and all the tenses, and for that reason do not make very startling headway; but I think in a few weeks I shall surprise myself. At least, that is what Marcou and Sumichrast say—to the class, not me.

I have got to write an essay on Sydney Smith, English as I have been taught, and on the first two chapters of Hill's *Rhetoric* before next Saturday. It has been so long since I have written anything like a theme that I feel a little anxious about these first three. Sydney Smith is a gentleman for whom I have no particular regard, and I anticipate a rather dry job. As for the other two, I had ought to make something from them.

We have almost finished the first act of *Hamlet* and I have a better idea of the characters (especially Horatio) than I ever had before. I am anticipating great sport in this course, though there will be a good deal of hard work combined with it. Prof. Child is a curiosity. I cannot conceive of a man's head being so packed with erudition as his. The only trouble is that he is old and hard of hearing. And speaking of ears, I went to see Dr. Greene yesterday. He thinks it is looking a little better and gives me a little encouragement. There is a possibility that the operation may not be necessary. If it is so, it will mean a good deal to me, I can tell you. The idea of not syringing it out in the morning for a week to come makes me want to dance.

Rum was rampant last night. The very buildings and trees were drunk. There will probably be some hot times here before spring, and if the Parietal Committee mind their business they will be sadly afflicted with compulsory insomnia.

It may be an insult to write such a scrawl as this, but I will start in to write a sentence with something like care, and forget all about it in ten seconds, relapsing into my customary jerkiness. If you do not read it you will live quite as long as if you had. My Muse is drowsy.

717 Cambridge St.
Cambridge, Mass.
October 25, 1891

I have just been having a quiet spell of thinking, the while I have smoked my new bull-dog. This thinking is bad business for a man, but sometimes he falls into it in spite of all he can do. I fear that I do so altogether too often. If you care to know what I have been thinking about, I will say that I have been wondering what the deuce I am here for. This is an old story and you are doubtless heartily sick of it; but to be honest, I cannot get over the

* 33 *

idea that I am wasting time and money. To be sure I shall be able to read a French novel—unless I fail in the course—by next June, but I might have done that without leaving Gardiner. I cannot understand how a text-book can be so lucidly written as Chardenal's *First French Course* is. Any person with ordinary ability could take it up of his own accord and read ordinary French with comparative ease after six months of regular application. The pronunciation is of course another matter. I called on Prof. de Sumichrast Thursday evening and found him in his library with his two dogs. "That gentleman," he said, pointing to a Yorkshire pup asleep in an easy chair, "is apparently satisfied with worldly existence." At the same time he was holding a snow-white terrier of some breed or other in his arms. I had a great time with the Prof. for about an hour, and when I left he came to the door lugging the pup in his arms. He advised me to drop Anglo-Saxon, as Prof. Child did, and I shall probably have no difficulty in so doing. Then I shall have a little time for breathing.

I have got to read one of Scott's novels for English 9. Think I shall take *Guy Mannering*, as it is the only one I have with me, and is one of the shortest that Sir W. has written. A very little of Scott will go a great way with me. I shall have to write an essay on some subject dealing with him before next Friday.

I have just written one on "Sydney Smith: his character as displayed in his writing." It is a somewhat marvelous production, I expect, though it may never immortalize the writer. Shakespeare is going on finely and there will be the devil of an examination before long on *Hamlet* and Shakespeare's life and times. I shall have to do considerable reading before it comes off, but I do not apprehend much trouble. A fellow can generally do something with a subject that interests him.

I am moving rather slowly through *L'Abbé Constantin*, as it comes hard when one is absolutely ignorant of French grammar. De Sumichrast is beginning to conduct recitations in French, but I guess I told you so last Sunday. I have not sent any more contributions to the *Advocate* yet but think I will sometime next week. The number I sent you is not a fair sample of the periodical; you have probably seen enough of them to know that. And you will also see that the editors spoiled my ballade in the mechanical punctuation they adopted. This letter is rather personal, but I trust you will overlook that and let me know what you are doing, and how the Columbia scheme is going on. Shall look for a letter tomorrow noon.

> *717 Cambridge St.*
> *Cambridge, Mass.*
> *November 2, 1891*

I shall have to crave your pardon this week for a break in the order of our correspondence. I felt so mean yesterday that I knew it would be of no use to attempt writing you, though I managed to get a few lines to the folks at home.

I rec'd your letter this morning and you may be sure that I was more than glad to do so. I have been rather blue for the past week, and am not at all confident of remaining here as long as I hoped. Following a course of prescribed study seems to [be] almost an impossibility. Sometimes I plug for three or four hours without any apparent benefit. I have been trying to drop Anglo-Saxon for the simple reason that I have not the brains to carry it, and do anything in French and English 9. I tell you what it is, Smith, I have had enough conceit taken out of me, in a passive manner, since I came here, to fill a Saratoga trunk. Do not infer by this that I have been in any way imposed upon, for nothing of the sort has happened. I was not even guyed when I called the cooperative society the "cō-ŏp" instead of the "Coop," in the presence of a sophomore and two juniors. Everything is quiet and each man minds his own business. But I am so grievously rusty that sometimes I am afraid that January may find me working on the ice in Gardiner. Exams are coming on this week and next and I am three themes behind in English 9. The subjects are these: William Godwin's Delineation of Character in *Caleb Williams,* Lord Jeffrey's Pessimism, and Miss Edgeworth's Realism. Not very jovial topics, are they? But they do not worry me any; the trouble is coming with the little points I have not remembered or taken down in lectures. Prof. Child has an exam in Shakspere next Friday at 10.00 A.M. It will be a "stinker."

I seem to be doing very well in French, and I ought to get out all right. As to Eng. A (Comp. and Rhet.) I have no idea what it will be like. In short, I am feeling rather down in the mouth. If I were discharged, I don't know as I would have the nerve to go back to Gardiner. Upon the whole I think I should try to hunt up some job in Boston where I could get enough to pay my board and lodging until the year is up. That would be better than being at home for everybody—my "dear friends"—to cast their remarks at and hold up as an example. But this may be due to my being "out of sorts" generally. By next Sunday I shall have taken most of the examinations and will be able to tell you something definite, perhaps. I feel that I am doing about twice the work necessary to carry my courses but cannot seem to improve matters any. All the reading I have done since I came here is *Guy Mannering*—prescribed in Eng. 9. Wrote an essay on Domine Sampson. Would give five dollars to smoke a pipe with you in the "bower."

P. S. It seems to me that you and the Prin. are having a devil of a time with those two "young lady friends." I am beginning to think you may have found that ideal you have been seeking so long. How is it?

Cambridge, Mass.
November 7, 1891

As I shall not have an opportunity to write tomorrow I will take the time now. Since writing last I have taken two examinations: Eng. Rhet. and Comp. and Shakespeare. The latter was positively awful. I probably made a failure of it, but that fact may not be vital. Exams are due in Eng. Prose Writers of the XIXth cent. and in French. The former comes next Friday, and I shall have to grind in order to meet it. I have an idea, in fact I know, it will be more of an historical than a literary test, and if there is any one thing that I cannot learn it is biography. If the questions were to be of an essentially aesthetic character I should have but little fear as to the result; but as it is, I am a little nervous.

I have succeeded in dropping Anglo-Saxon at last, but it has taken me three weeks to do it. With the four studies I now have, I find but little time for outside work or diversion. The trouble is I have forgotten, if I ever knew, how to follow a system of prescribed study. I have not read a book outside of the prescribed work since I came. There are a few that I want to read very much; for instance, F. Marion Crawford's *Khaled, Witch of Prague, Cigarette-maker's Romance;* Thomas Hardy's *Laodicean, Group of Noble Dames;* Andrew Lang's *Helen of Troy* (poems) and his philosophical and religious books.

I rec'd a letter from Gledhill a while ago; he seems to be the leading spirit in Canton "University," is taking eight courses and is a great club man. Well, Art always had the faculty of making himself popular. He is a good fellow and I wish him all success.

In the last *Scribner* you will see a poem by William Vaughn Moody; he is a Junior here. I am not acquainted with him, but as soon as I get fairly straightened out, if I ever do, I purpose to make a strong attempt to get in with the *literati* of Harvard. My ballad may help me out a little and it may not. I sent my "Villanelle of Change" into the *Advocate* a day or two ago, but have not yet heard from it. I have a long meter triolet in my mind, dealing with passion and death (that is the stuff we need) and when it is materialized I shall try to get it published. I have an idea that it is a fairly good thing in its way.

I have not written those essays on Godwin and Jeffrey yet, but will have to before next Friday. I wrote one yesterday on "Miss Edgeworth and Sir W. Scott." English 9 is a splendid course, but it requires a good deal of time for preparation. Mr. Gates is a man to be envied. He is a proctor in Matthews Hall, and instructor in English. Only has one course. He may not get a princely salary, but the surroundings and the honor will easily make up for a good deal.

It is later than I thought. I have to go to lecture in eight minutes. Will have to jump. Excuse errors, as I have no time to read it over.

717 *Cambridge St.*
Cambridge, Mass.
November 15, 1891

I am beginning to feel at home and am in a better frame of mind than when I wrote you that half lugubrious epistle telling you of my woes and uncertainties. Of course there is some uncertainty now, and will be until after the mid-years, but I am not going to trouble myself any more about it. "Sufficient unto the day, etc."

Whenever I think of a teacher's life I think of teachers' meetings, or conventions, whatever you call them. They must be purgatory to anyone save to [a] damned fool. Perhaps that is a little too strong, though, as our late preceptor G. A. Stuart, revels in them. It was he who once on a time at New [?] Portland affirmed that in the sentence, "The trees stand thick on the mountain," the adjective referred to the thickness of the wood and not to the number of the trees. I guess he was right, as "thickly" would be required to express numerical quantity. He must have blinked most jovially to himself, and poked that lead-pencil along his right cheek in secret satisfaction of his intellectual prowess over the untaught knaves of northern Maine. They all hooted him but he heeded them not. He felt upon his immortal head the crown of individual supremacy and doubtless went home and talked it over with his wife. By the way, do you know anything of the whereabouts of that youthful prodigy, Freddy?

I was never able to learn what Giles thought of me, though I have an impression that he considered me a hopeless case. When he caught Gledhill and I in the settee business his heart was well-nigh broken. So was mine, for that matter, and I always feel

* 38 *

cheap when I think of it. His veracity, or their veracities, Walter Swanton and Billy Gay blew on us, and the consequence was that we lost our good character and four dollars. I think we regretted the latter more than the former, at the time, but now I would willingly give as many dollars as I could conveniently muster if the whole thing could be forgotten by all parties concerned.

Here is an examination I took yesterday:

—English 9.—

(Spend 40 minutes on I and twenty on II)

I

1. Give your impressions of any two of S. Smith's essays.
2. What are the characteristics of Jeffrey's style?
3. What dates (from 1750 to ——) have seemed to you best worth remembering? Give reasons.

II

4. *Caleb Williams* as an attack on "things as they are."
5. What can you say of the origin of the great Reviews?
(either 4 or 5)

I wrote a steady hour on it but cannot yet tell you how I came out. But I am fairly confident that a bad mark can only result from a failure in expressing myself clearly. In English A. (Comp. and Rhet.) I managed to get a "B," being one of about eighty in a class of 500. Better than I expected, though it does not amount to anything. The course doesn't, for that matter.

Last evening I went into town to see the Russell Comedy Co. in the *City Directory*. I think it is a little the flattest thing I ever witnessed on any stage. I cannot understand how the Athenians can support such stuff. Cheap farce-comedy is undermining the whole dramatic scheme and God only knows what we shall have in a few years to come. Richard Mansfield plays *Dr. Jeckyll and Mr. Hyde* next Sat. evening and if nothing happens I shall be on hand to see it.

Last Wednesday, Dr. Schuman came to see me and I went in to see him in the evening. Beer, oysters, pipes, cigars, and literary conversation were in order. It was the most thoroughly Bohemian evening I ever passed and one of the most satisfactory. The Doctor "uttered nothing base" during the whole time. I wished you were with us more than once; you would have enjoyed it.

For some reason or other I cannot take any particular interest in Harvard athletics, though I am as much a member of the University as any Senior. And I will say here that there is remarkably little feeling between the students of different grades. I am on comparatively good terms with a Senior, a Soph and two or three Specials. They are all alike, and all seem to be fellows of good common-sense. The "fast set" we hear so much about is not a fictitious body, but they keep themselves severely away from the common herd. I can generally tell one when I see him, and he is not much to see either.

The Professors are gentlemen; but when some upper-class man is temporarily promoted to some petty office like superintendent of exams, or assistant registrar, then authority is agonizing. They are harmless, however, and I rather enjoy watching them after I get used to their ways. I might do the same thing myself, unconsciously, should the opportunity present itself. But it will not.

There are eight bowling courts in the gym, and I am quite a fiend for that rather antiquated sport. As to the other appliances, I have not touched them. I fear I am not an enthusiast on the subject of physical culture, though I am an excellent subject to [be] experimented with. My stooping shoulders are disfiguring, but I cannot bring myself to a regular course of training. In fact, I cannot find the time.

Expect a letter tomorrow.

The banners of Harvard are still crimson, but the air is blue—in a double sense. You could not well picture a more melancholy gang than came home from Springfield Saturday night. There was no enthusiasm, no yelling, and practically no drinking. Sorrow was drowned in thought rather than in booze. I am drowning mine in self-hatred, for this reason:

I was fool enough to sacrifice the Springfield game for *Dr. Jeckyll and Mr. Hyde*. It was Mansfield's only performance of the play in Boston this season and I was determined to take it in. *Hinc illae,* etc. The play was totally disappointing. Beyond the transformation scenes it does not amount to much anyway; and much to my surprise and disgust, the stage was in total darkness whenever they took place, and all the time that Hyde was personated. It might as well have been performed by an usher, as far as scenic effect was concerned. Of course we had the voice, but that was hardly satisfactory.

Just now, as I am writing, the Sabbath stillness is broken by a gang of four fellows riding by in a carriole yelling "Ya-a-ale! Ya-a-a-le!" It seems surprising that a Yale man should be in Cambridge today and perhaps they are only friends of the New Haven boys. They are making noise enough, whoever they are. If I could have the money that has changed hands through the game I should invite you down for a year or two. It would have done your soul good to see the scramble for tickets. As high as twenty and twenty-five dollars was paid for seats on the Harvard Side. I might have bought a seat in the centre section for three dollars Saturday morning, but I was set on *Dr. Jeckyll.* In consequence, I am now in a fierce humor for having made such an unconscionable fool of myself. Read the Sunday *Herald* and judge for yourself what I missed, while I might have taken it in as well as not. Experience is no doubt a good thing but I hate to think of spending a whole life in acquiring it.

I am beginning to feel blue already, thinking that I have but one year in Cambridge. And yet it is a little strange that I should feel so. I have made no intimate friends, in fact I have not yet met a single soul to whom I have been in any manner drawn. Literature is at a discount here, but I may find some damned fool yet who will read and smoke with me. The satisfaction I derive is doubtless due to the absolute change and the college atmosphere, which is enormous. I think of the old gray-headed buffers who have climbed the stairs of Massachusetts and Harvard Halls, and dream of a room in classic Holworthy. This is foolishness, but there is no great harm in it.

I took an examination last week in English 9 but will not hear from it till a week from Thanksgiving. And by the way, I am invited out on Thanksgiving evening to Mrs. de Sumichrast's. This, I suppose, is the fruit of my calling on the Prof. There will probably be ten or a dozen fellows there, and I am some concerned as to how the man from Maine will carry himself. There are some great bloods here and their style may squelch me; but I shall not worry about it. A "society man" is something I can never be, and never wish to be; but it is not pleasant to feel one's self a stick. The Prof. himself, is a fine man; this I know. If his wife matches him they must be a rather remarkable pair. I only wish that the English professors held up their end with the others. Outside of Prof. Child, Prof. Briggs, and Mr. Gates the instructors in my mother tongue seem to be little better than failures. Perhaps I am over critical, but I cannot think so. I am fully convinced that the course in English Rhet. and Composition is conducted to the least possible advantage to the student. It practically amounts to nothing. If a fellow is well posted, or thinks he is, on the subject, he is disgusted; if he is ignorant, he is not in a way to gain a great deal of facility in writing. As to the text of rhetoric, there is altogether too much time wasted on it by a course of rather watery lectures. I cannot quite understand how it is kept up as it is. To tell the truth, my experience in the XIXth century Prose course has been of twice the value to me in com-

position that Eng. A. has. I have to write an essay next week on
Jane Austen. I should have written it this week but for some rea-
son did not get around to it. I am still behind on Godwin and
Jeffrey, and I may not write on them at all. No blood will flow if
I do not.

Without wishing to give offence, I will say that your last letter
was a little unsatisfactory. It is evident that that girl of yours is
getting the upper hands of you. When you want congratulations, let me know; I will write a hymeneal sonnet that will lift
your soul to Paradise. I have not heard from the Villanelle I sent
to the *Advocate*. It is no good, and I doubt if they print it.

> 717 *Cambridge St.*
> *Cambridge, Mass.*
> *November 29, 1891*

I am a little anxious to learn how that young lady friend of
yours is getting along. If Rudyard Kipling should be the means
of uniting two young souls in eternal bliss by means of his indifferent consideration of such matters I should feel under ob-
ligations to write him a letter. I see that he has come to America
to wipe out the publishers who have been stealing his works.
Have you read *Life's Handicap,* and that story in the *Century?*
It seems to me that that magazine is making some startling innovations. Rudyard and Bill Nye will make quite a change in the
list of its contributors. It strikes me that they are making a mistake in admitting the latter, unless he changes his usual tone; but
then, I may be prejudiced against him with no adequate reason.
It always struck me, though, that he is a trifle coarse for such a
periodical as the *Century* holds itself up to be. In the Sunday
Herald or *Globe* we naturally look for that kind of a thing; we
can stand it there and rather enjoy it; but when he jumps into the
higher regions of literature, one feels doubtful as to the result.
His friend James Whitcomb Riley was probably the indirect, or
direct, means of getting him there.

F. Marion Crawford begins a new serial in the January *Atlan-*

tic. It will, of course, be a good thing, and I shall try to peruse it. I have not decided whether to subscribe another year or not. I do not find much time for reading outside of my prescribed work. Jane Austen has been taking up my time of late. Have read *Pride and Prejudice, Mansfield Park* and most, or to follow Prof. Hill's precepts, *almost* all of *Persuasion.* I suppose I have spoken of this before; I cannot remember over night what I have written in a letter; so when you find a repetition, deal gently with me.

I went to Mrs. de Sumichrast's reception last Friday evening. Had a rather comfortable time upon the whole. Found a young Law Student right from England. He knows all about Andrew Lang, Philip Bourke Marston, *et al.* and has invited me to call on him. Shall go sometime this week. I also fed an Annex girl on chocolate and bilious cocoanut cakes. I did not eat any myself, though she urged me to most earnestly. After that I wheedled her off into the Prof's library and we talked for an hour on French novels. She thinks they are shocking in their immorality and hopes I will not read them. They will injure me. This society chatter is something that I was not made for. I can handle one person very well, but when I am to make myself agreeable to the multitude, I feel like a lost orphan. There were a dozen or so in the library working the same dodge (so to speak) so I was not lonesome. Her simplicity and innocence, or mine, was startling. I do not think she was trying to seduce me, however; her eyes were too large and earnest. I do not remember her name, but she was apparently growing quite fond of me when I left her. She seemed to have a sisterly regard for me that gave me a "temporary feeling of safety for the time being." Her nose was a trifle one sided and she carried a whole arboretum on her bosom.

Shall be in G. in three weeks.

> 717 *Cambridge St.*
> *Cambridge, Mass.*
> *December 8, 1891*

I suppose about this time you are wondering where in the devil my letter is; and in view of this state of things I will explain. Last

Sunday I was (to use a worldy expression) sick enough to kill. I did nothing but lie around my room and feel blue and nasty. If I had written a letter I should probably [have] put the pessimism of our friend Omar Khayyam completely in the shade; so I concluded to let it go till I was in a better humor. I trust I am now and will try to make up for my failure to keep up the agreement.

This is the first opportunity this evening I have had a chance [sic] to write, though I have been intending to do so since I came out of Memorial from dinner at six o'clock. As soon as I got settled for a ruminative smoke in walked Mr. H. A. Cutler, business manager for the *Advocate,* and a rattling good fellow. He had the proof of my latest poetical (?) effusion,—a rondeau entitled "In Harvard 5." The subject is Shakespeare and you will see it in due time. I have not sent the last number containing the "Villanelle of Change," as I was hoping to send you a copy of the *Monthly* with one of my productions; but in this my hopes were blasted. After Cutler left, my cousins from Cambridgeport came and staid till nine o'clock. Then came a knock at the door; and at my yell of "Come!" in stepped Robert Morss Eliott, perhaps the leading spirit of Harvard outside of athletics. Of course Capt. Trafford and his crew are with the immortals. Eliott is a Senior and in many respects a remarkable man. Without any "gushing," I actually felt honored to receive a call from him, being a Special and a first year man at that. He is editor in chief of the *Monthly* and brought back the manuscript of my sonnet on Thomas Hood. At a meeting of the board of editors it was weighed in the balance and found wanting. (Perhaps I have some foolish opinions of my own, but they are of no value in this case). We talked of college papers and kindred matters for about half an hour, when he left with a request for another contribution—which I have decided to make—and an urgent request to call on him. If I succeed in getting in with such fellows as that, college life will prove most agreeable. I think the best way to do it will be to keep silence on the matter of contributions. I may change my mind but these are my feelings at present. I was sailing along in such elegant shape, putting whatever I chose into the *Advocate*, that I must confess this declination put a slight "damper" on me; but Mr. Lovett (I wrote Eliott before by mistake—must have been thinking of the President)—showed himself to be such a gentleman and "white man" that I could not feel offended. If I am a little foxy I may get in with the whole gang, which will be rather more pleasant than my present situation. Of course I have found some good fellows—but you will understand precisely what I mean. I will send you the *Advocate* with Villanelle tomorrow with this letter. Perhaps I have tired you with talk of my own affairs, but you know that I am prone to enter into confidence with now and then a fellow spirit [sic]. Of course I need not ask you not to mention anything that I have written.

Our blue books in French came due today, and as I was badly prepared I shall get a low mark. But will work up in the review and ought not to get into trouble. The courses here in elementary French are conducted in a rather peculiar manner, and in my own poor opinion call for much unnecessary work on the part of the student; but I foresee good results in the future if I half do myself justice. My rank on the last blue-book was 9—, scale same as G.H.S. That was not bad, but quite a number got 10. The exams go by letters—A-B-C, etc. I have not yet heard from my English 9 exams. At last I am through with that most estimable lady, Jane Austen. Next week we go to work on the essayists—Hazlitt first, then Lamb and Leigh Hunt. When DeQuincey and Carlyle come, there will be trouble. They are two writers of whom I am absolutely ignorant. I have read *Sartor Resartus,* but should hate to be called upon to write a review of it.

I am afraid that this letter will prove rather dry picking. I am sure it would to anyone *but* you, and feel a little guilty as it is. Rec'd a letter from Gledhill today. He is going on swimmingly and is apparently one of the "big guns" of St. L. University. That is one advantage, as I have said before, of a small college. For the leaders it is clover, but for the others it cannot be so pleasant if they are at all sensitive. Here at Harvard there is less of the real college spirit, but there is more equality. I have been treated first rate by everyone I have seen and have tried to do the same myself. Lovett said that my sonnet was about the first contribution on record by a first year man to the *Monthly*. I have an idea that that fact was instrumental in its restoration to its "inventor."

I have been writing for three quarters of an hour, and begin to feel sleepy. Will have a little smoke and turn in. Wish you were here with me.

> *717 Cambridge St.*
> *Cambridge, Mass.*
> *December 13, 1891*

This time I will endeavor to be prompt in my weekly letter and give you a page or two of my usual drool so that it may reach you the first of the week. I also hope to hear from you, as usual. Your letters form no inconsiderable item in my college existence. A letter from a human being who realizes the fact that there is some breadth to human sympathy, and that all men are in a way themselves, is a matter not to be disregarded. I think you give me much credit when you tell me that I know a different Smith from that popularly regarded as "Smithy"—at least that was the former title you bore. At present you are Mr. Smith, of Rockland, and as such I send you greeting. By your permission, or I suppose more properly "with your permission," I shall make you a Christmas present in the form of Wm. Hazlitt's essays. Some of them will please you—if they don't you need not read them. You may be amused at my freedom in this announcement, but you must remember that Robinson is writing and Robinson sometimes says strange things. I think that the Annex girl has some such an idea. I have not seen her since and do not expect to.

Last night I went to the "Globe" with Barnard to see Agnes Huntington in *Captain Thérèse*. Agnes was well enough but the opera was painful in its vacuity, if I may use the word. We left at the end of the second act, and repaired to Herr Engelhart's beer shop where [we] spent the remainder of the evening quite pleasantly and I think profitably. If you could come up here for a week or so this spring I should be more than happy; and I think you would manage to enjoy yourself too. Harvard University is a great place to set a man's thoughts going. Yesterday I watched two able-bodied men spreading fragrant New England dung on the campus. I began to wonder if they were not deriving quite as much benefit from Harvard as some of its more scholarly inmates. I think they were, and I have an idea that I felt a kind of envy for their lot. There is a kind of poetry in scattering dung —if the dung is good—that must needs awaken a fine sentiment in the mind of a man of any imagination. The excrement gives the increment to the emerald grass, etc., and when the spring zephyrs begin to blow the transformation becomes apparent. It is great stuff, and the faculty are obviously poets. They use no prepared fertilizer whatever, but cling to the mushy manure of our, and their, ancestors. And shades of Cincinnatus, doesn't it stink! The odor made me homesick, I think; never before have I realized what a real countryman I am. No man of feeling can smell the odors of his native land two hundred miles from home without experiencing a tender surge of emotion within his breast. In the play of *Alabama* just closed at the Tremont Theatre there is an artificial odor of magnolia raised by burning something or other. It affects the Southern students wonderfully. So you see that it is only a natural consequence that the frank sincerity of the odor I have mentioned should turn my thoughts towards Maine. There is no counterfeit about it.

Well, perhaps I have gone far enough with this subject. If I keep on, the letter will smell so that you will not dare to open it. If it were earlier I would go out and get a nip of the substance and mail it to you; but you might not appreciate it, so I will not.

I cannot tell you the author of that quotation, though the expression "infinite manslaughter" sounds familiar to me. Will see you before long. Vale, for a time.

717 *Cambridge St.*
Cambridge, Mass.
January 18, 1892

You must excuse me for not writing to you yesterday, as my time was pretty well taken. I plugged all the forenoon and took lunch at 1 P.M. At three o'clock Whitney, Drew, and Barnard came around with a dozen of beer and we had a very pleasant time for the remainder of the day. The smell of the "innumerable pipes" has not yet left my room. I was wishing that you could be here with us; you would probably have enjoyed it. There is a sociability about pipes that I cannot explain. They seem to bring us nearer to each other and I think upon the whole that the world should be thankful for the weed—so called.

Saturday night I went to the Museum with my friend Johnson, from Kentucky. He is a great blood, and has a wilderness of "lip," but for all that is a very good kind of a fellow—as fellows go. These Saturday nights are about the only real outing I get and I enjoy them. The expense is a little unpleasant at times, but I am not a very wild youth. I have discovered one thing, however, and that is that I shall never get through my year here for eight hundred dollars unless I scrimp like the very devil. Comparatively speaking, I am virtuous and prudent (*sic*) and yet my expenses are uncomfortably large. Twelve hundred dollars, or a thousand at least, is a fair allowance for all the expenses of a year at Harvard. If a fellow has that rare faculty of living on his companions he can get through for less, but he is generally found out before long. As you have said, one cannot be a hypocrite for four years (not often for one) without being discovered. And again, of course one of these prospective self-made men can go through for very little beyond the necessary $350 or $400; but I am not of those, and I am damned glad of it.

Here is a little doggerel song that amuses me immensely. Can you tell me what there is about it that is attractive?—

'There wás an old sóldier and he hád a wooden lég,
But he hád no tobácco and tobácco couldn't bég.
There wás an old sáilor who was cúnning as a fóx,
And he álways had tobácco in his óld tobácco-bóx.'

'Said the sóldier to the sáilor, "Will you gíve me a chéw?"
Said the sáilor to the sóldier, "I'll be dámned if I dó!
Just leáve alone your drínking, and sáve up your rócks,
And you'll álways have tobácco in your óld tobácco bóx." '

You can get the tune from the words.

717 Cambridge St.
Cambridge, Mass.
January 23, 1892

I received your rather extended epistle about a week ago, and
you may be sure that it was welcome. It struck me at about the
right time. I needed some such medicine, and it was a great relief for me to be assured that the writing of long confidential letters was not a lost art with you. It reminded me of the ones I used
to receive from Bowdoin. I am afraid if the letters I received
from you when you were at Brunswick were to be compared with
those you have received from Harvard, my candle would shine
with a poor light. I do not know what is the matter with me, but
somehow I have not been able to write a decent letter to anyone
since I came—er—to college. That doesn't sound just right, does
it? I suppose I am as much a college man as anyone here, and
yet, when I think it over, I cannot reconcile myself to the fact.
Specials are not regulars, to be sure, but if you could see some of
the latter class that hang around here you would not for a moment question the equality of the matter. Sometimes I almost
think that special students who do good work attract particular
attention on the part of the instructors. I am not speaking of myself now, God knows, but I really believe that some of the bright-
est men in Harvard are not in the undergraduate dept. The elective system is a godsend to the fellows who really wish to pursue

certain branches, and when people condemn it, they don't know what they are talking about. Of course it is the means of many people getting through with less work than they would under a prescribed course, but I have about concluded that it does not require a genius to get an A.B. from most any college in the country. At Harvard, the case is just this: every opportunity is offered for a man to get what the world calls an education; and it lies with him entirely whether he does it or not. There is no question but that one can go through and do but little work, but no one with any pride could stand the continual warnings and low marks that attend such a course.

The mid-years are close at hand and for sport I will make a prophecy as to the marks I get. Keep these and compare them with the real ones which will come in about a month. Of course this is all guess-work as I have no idea what the exams will be like. However, here goes:

Eng A (Comp. and Rhet.) say B
"   2 (Shakespeare)   B minus (B—)
"   9 (19th cent. prose)   B—
French A   C

B plus or minus counts a B on the records, so with the other letters. I do not seem to have much use for A's; and in fact, have not met with many who do. They are shadowy ideals and in my opinion do not really signify much. B, and in that vicinity, is a very comfortable and safe place to hang. Then there are no warnings and no fear from a reasonable amount of cutting, if you care to cut. I pulled a B in all the hour-exams last fall, but it may not occur again. I am not much alarmed, though, as C's will carry me through all right. Good night.

717 Cambridge St.
Cambridge, Mass.
February 3, 1892

My memory has played me a little trick this week that almost startles me. To come to the point, I cannot remember whether

I wrote you a letter last Sunday or not; my impression, however, is that I did not, and taking it for granted will "let 'er go" now for a few minutes. And I will say to begin with that I have about as much business writing you (or anyone else) a letter now as I have painting my belly yellow. My midyear examination comes tomorrow morning and I am just about half prepared to meet it. The subject is Shakspere (pardon my English spelling of the word—I prefer it) and you cannot possibly have an idea of the confounded mess that it will be. Prof. Child is a demon for details and has an unpleasant penchant for odd usages of words—prolepses, adjective-adverbs, etc.—and takes delight in setting a bewildering row of them before the student's eye to be explained and illustrated by examples. This, with interpretation of hard passages and historical points relative to Shakspere and his works, I think will constitute the greater portion of the paper.

My experience of last Monday evening and Tuesday morning has kept me within doors tonight. You see Geo. Barstow is in Boston and I went in to see him. There was a season of about three hours in the "Old Elm" and of course there were innumerable pipes and frequent beers. The man who is bloody fool enough to do that kind of business the night before a midyear in Eng. Rhet. and Comp. deserves no sympathy, I suppose, but sympathy or no sympathy, I felt like a lamb being led to the slaughter the next morning. Whether I drank too much beer or whether the consciousness that I was doing unwisely rendered my nerves unsteady, I cannot tell, but for a time it seemed impossible for me to sit at a desk for three mortal hours in a hot room in the upper story of University Hall. I did it, though, but I cannot tell the result. It will come in about three weeks. I believe I prophecied a B or a B— in one of my letters, but I am afraid I flew too high. A "C" will be quite up to my expectations.

After Shakspere comes Eng. 9 (Friday); then there will be a rest for a week before French. That week means hard work for me but I do not anticipate any great difficulty. Have about given up the idea of getting "fired." You may think that my talk on that subject was all chaff, but I can assure you that it was not. There were three hundred and seventy odd students who took the mid-year in Eng. A. last year and out of this number ninety-five were dropped. So you see that a good mark is a very comfortable thing to have. Without intending to blow my own horn in the least, I think that the "B" I rec'd on the hour-exam in that course together with my written work in Eng 9, which for some reason seems to have been a little above the average, may help me out on the mid-years and make partial amends for the bad head I had Tuesday morning. I hope you will not infer from this that I was in any way "full"—that would grieve me and blast my character.

I read your last letter riding into town Monday afternoon and felt thankful that I had the pleasure of so doing. I think you squelched me forever as a correspondent but I enjoyed it none the less for that. It is a pleasure to receive a letter from a friend who can write of something [except] the old stereotyped topics and who can appreciate the natural variance of human nature. I know I have said this half a dozen times in past letters, but it is a matter worthy of considerable notice. Every day that I live I realize more and more the existence of several elements or characteristics in my make-up that, unless they are put down, will be of decided disadvantage to me in the future. In the first place, I am and always was too much of a dreamer; I have no sympathy with the cold, matter-of-fact, contriving nature that has made the fortunes enjoyed by multitudes all around us (by fortunes, I mean the possession of enough to make a man and his family comfortable and happy) and this is a dangerous state to be in. I used to think that I was a kind of pessimist, but I have outgrown that idea. The world as a whole is surely growing better and better, but there is yet an enormous field for improvement. Another thing that troubles me is the knowledge that I am lacking to a considerable extent in self-confidence:—not exactly that, either—perhaps I had better say that [the] sight of success awakens a feeling painfully approaching envy, and I am inclined too much to look upon its achievement as a kind of destiny. But I am glad to say that I think that this is leaving me gradually, and [in] time I hope to have a fair chance of growing sensible. Whether the accepted theory of life and success is the true one or not, it is at present the practical one, and biting off one's nose will not help the matter in the least.

Well, I will say good-night now, and look for a second edition of your last letter on Tuesday next.

1691 Cambridge St.
Cambridge, Mass.
February 21, 1892

The weather is rather depressing outside, and I am afraid that it has affected my disposition; so if what I write be grunty you must attribute it to the elements, not to me. I will start off, however, with Julia Marlowe, and so try to keep clear from any gloomy or complaining subject. Have seen her four times and [would] like to see her in a dozen more pieces. The first piece was *As You Like It.* It was produced magnificently, and Jacques mimicking the fool moralizing on time was well worth the admission fee, which, by the way, is always fifty cents for me. The whole thing was about as fine as it could be, and was by far the finest thing that I have ever seen on any stage. I next saw her in *Romeo and Juliet,* which was excellent but not so satisfactory. Then came *Twelfth Night,* which was simply "out of sight." Sir Andrew's duel was great, and Sir Toby was a fairy. Last Thursday evening I went in with the Kentuckian (Johnson) to see *Cymbeline.* This play is something of a rarity nowadays and brought forth Boston's "culchau" to the theatre's full capacity. The play was very large. You have read it, of course, and know the character of it; and you will doubtless wonder how it can be produced with anything like fidelity to the text. The answer is this: they study their parts and recite them. Of course, the most pointed passages are omitted, but enough is retained to answer all ordinary purposes. Yet with all the suggestiveness of the thing it is not really objectionable. Female virtue is displayed in such a glorious light that one forgets all about the other side. The bedroom scene created a little tittering on the part of some gallery gods and goddesses, but that soon quieted down. It must have been a little embarrassing for the fair lady in bed, though. But that all goes in society, and they are devilish glad to get it.

There was quite a jovial time at Saben's room last night. There were nine of us, including Whitney and Barnard and two of the Cambridge police, who came around later and took quite an active part in the festivities. I retired about 1.30 A.M. and arose at eight, trying to decide whether to write a twenty-page thesis on Lamb and Leigh Hunt. It will be something of a task but I have about concluded to do it, or try to. I shall also include Hazlitt, making the famous trio of essayists. This is how it came about. Mr. Gates has offered to excuse anyone from the hour-examination in April who will write a thesis on any subject coming under the course. That part (the excuse from the exam) does not amount to much, but I think it may be for my interest to write the thesis—both for getting into Gates's good graces, and for my own benefit. It means a heap of work, but I think I can get through it after a fashion.

How about your coming up here in March? That month will soon be here, and you could not find a much better time to come. The theatres will be showing some of their best attractions then, and I think you will find Harvard a place well worth seeing. Write and let me know what you think about it. Please note change of address.

1691 Cambridge St.
Cambridge, Mass.
March 1, 1892

I find I am at my old tricks again and as usual owe you a letter. But this time there is an excuse.

You know when I wrote last I mentioned casually a small gathering held in Saben's room which passed off quite successfully, assisted by two of the Cambridge police. Well, it has been further assisted by the Faculty, and the skies are a little cloudy. I have been awaiting developments, so that I could give you full particulars. But I cannot, and will write what I know. It is rather a bad mess, I am afraid, and Saben is practically expelled from Harvard. This is quite interesting, you see, and consequently your friend is feeling a little anxious. The worst part of the whole matter is that we did nothing to warrant such action. The madam of the house complained to the police and they went to the Faculty. (I use a big "F" for the reverence I entertain for that austere body). I have no doubt, in fact Prof. de Sumichrast practically told him as much, that Saben's trouble lies chiefly in his damnably low marks. Fortunately I do not carry such an unpleasant burden, and as far as I know, they are not aware of the fact that I was present at the festivities. As things are now it could not possibly help Saben if he gave us away, so he gives us strict orders to keep our mouths shut for our own good. He would not peach if they put him on the rack, but of course we would not let him suffer if confession would do any good. I do not have any fear of expulsion, but a reprimand might be sent home and that would be nasty. The gullible public have some queer ideas concerning Harvard methods. The fact is that it does not take but a very little to get a man into trouble, and one is not obliged to murder more than three professors to get his walking ticket. This will doubtless surprise you somewhat, but it is a fact. Here is a case which happened during mid-years. One ingenious Freshman decided that the exam. in English A would be a little too much for him. So he invited a friend to take his place, thinking that in a class of 500 he would be safe. But they discovered the trick, and out they both went—for good, too. They are not only expelled from Harvard, but from any other college that amounts to anything. About a fortnight ago two fellows were "fired" for playing poker in a dormitory room. This is the way they do things at Cambridge, and woe be unto the man who gets caught.

But I will change the subject and say a few words about mid-years. I have heard from three of them, and here is the result:

```
Eng.  A        B+
 "    9        B—
French         C
```

I was a little disappointed in French but as a whole the marks are more than good. If things should come to a crisis they stand me in good stead. But I hope I have [heard] the last of the matter.

By your last letter I infer that you will be in Gardiner soon and I will ask you not to mention this affair to *anyone*. Of course this is unnecessary, but it might slip out before you thought. You know how rumor travels and it might make an elegant stink at home. You understand. Next week I hope my mind will be easy.

[P.S.] Have you read *David Grieve?* It's immense.

Boston
March 18 (?), 1892

I have come in from Cambridge this afternoon and am now sitting in Whitney's room, smoking his tobacco and using his paper. He has a note on his table telling anyone who comes in to wait until 5.00 P.M. If he comes on time the gentleman from Maine will appear in about ten minutes.

From your letters I should say that you are turning "society-man" in a way that will leave me all in the shade. I have been to two or three receptions at Mrs. de Sumichrast's but will not attend any more. I was not made for that kind of thing and had better keep out of it. It [is] fairly a mystery to me how a fellow can mix himself with a roomfull of strangers and enjoy himself. According to my ideas of pleasure the thing is an impossibility, but my ideas are probably wrong. I don't know but they always are. There is one thing, however, that I do know, and that is that passing through one of these "at-homes" here in Cambridge— they are very informal, too—is like passing through Hell to one who dislikes it. When I watch these "polished young gentlemen" floating around from one girl to another, keeping their tongues wagging all the time and saying things that no man or woman that God ever made could remember five minutes, I begin to realize the difference in humanity. I must confess that I envy them their powers to a certain extent: such accomplishments are convenient in emergencies. No, the truth is that I never enjoy myself so much as when I am with one or two congenial souls talking on some congenial subject, and smoking the pipe. This is a misfortune, but the truth may as well out.

There is (to change the subject) something very rotten in the department of English Composition here at Harvard. There is a system of "third hour exercises" in English A that is a curiosity. Every Thursday at 11 A.M. I go to Upper Dane and there write a theme (!) on some topic generally assigned after I enter the room, and have from fifteen to twenty-five minutes to write it in. The next week they come back with decorations in red ink. These decorations are very interesting. Sometimes my paper will have none at all (which [is] a rather unusual thing, by the way) and again they will be so covered that I am hardly able to make out the original. This all comes from their being examined by different instructors, who are something better than boys. If there is any course where the best instruction should be received, it is in the department of Eng. Comp. I pulled a B+ somehow but do not consider it of any more account than a D as far as showing the real value of my work is concerned. In English 9 I expected an A— and got a B—. That barely excuses me from the hour examination to be held the Friday before the Easter recess. If I ever get that thesis on *Pendennis* written, it may raise the mark a little. It may surprise you that I care so much for marks—but then, I think I have explained how they may be of value.

Saben has a room at #16 Hancock St., and is enjoying life to its utmost. He spends his time in reading, smoking cigars, and buying books. I don't think I could take things so easy under his circumstances—I surely hope I could not.

Last Monday evening I went to see Sothern in the *Dancing Girl* at the Hollis St. I think it is one of the strongest plays that

I have ever seen. It is rather disagreeable in plot, but one hardly notices it on account of the fine acting and sparkling dialogue which is continually inserted to lighten the gloom. I have half a mind to go again tonight. Rather think I shall be fool enough to pay three dollars to hear Patti in *La Traviata* next Thursday evening—that is if I can get a seat. That is the only grand opera excepting *Trovatore* that ever interested me much. The music is great, as you doubtless know. Farce comedies have been the ruling amusement here this winter, and I would like to see a law passed rendering the composition of one of them a capital offence. If there is anything pertaining to the drama more disgusting or degrading, I have yet to see it.—Well, Whitney does not seem to appear, and while I am at the bottom of the page I think I may as well stop. Please excuse the ultra or super-colloquial tone of this mess, and write as often as you find time.

1691 Cambridge St.
Cambridge, Mass.
April 17, 1892

According to the agreement I will now try to write you something to take the place of a letter, though I am afraid that I am not in a very good mood for it. I have been loafing around my room all day and cannot seem to get over chronic Sunday laziness. I have longed for most everything that I cannot have, including that patch of woods behind your house in Gardiner, and the pipes. I had my own pipe, to be sure, but it tasted lonesome. I have an idea that that is figurative language, but I did not intend any poetry. I do not feel like it. I have made a little verse today, however—part of a sonnet beginning:

> "*I make no measure of the words they say*
> *Who come with snaky tongues to me and tell*
> *Of all the woe awaiting me in Hell*
> *When from this goodly world I go my way, etc.*"

Eventually I shall go on to say how the appearance of a good wholesome white-haired man who never told a lie or drank Maine whiskey impresses me, and how I draw a lesson from the unspoken sermon of his own self and begin to realize the real magnificence of better things—the which I have an idea will make the closing line. I shall spring it on the *Advocate*. They may object to the morality of it, though, and throw it out. If they do I have another for them beginning:

> *"There is a drear and lonely tract of Hell*
> *From all the common woe removed afar,—*
> *A flat sad land where only shadows are*
> *Whose lorn estate no word of mine can tell, etc."*

I don't know how long this Hell business will last, but I may sigh out two or three more. It is a damned cheerful subject and my muse is merry whenever she gets into it. Sometimes I think that Hell may not be such a bad place after all. If there is brimstone, it may be a little unpleasant, but otherwise I do not think a man need be afraid of it. Think of the company he will have. Who knows but you and I may sit upon a red-hot boulder and read Daudet and Zola? That would not be so bad after we got used to the caloric.

By the way, how does that picture come on? I have been expecting it for the past day or two, but came to the conclusion that it would probably come with your letter. I have an idea that I cut a classic figure perched on that rock, sucking your pipe. It will make an ornament for my mantle and cause my landlady to think I am growing to be a man when she sees it. I know that she loves me, for she has made a new table-covering for me: red felt with blue and yellow ribbons woven into the ends. Very aesthetic and possibly an invitation for me to keep my pipes and ashes on my desk—or somewhere else. But that is an unkind thought and I will banish it immediately.

I am writing this upon what is left of my thesis block. I

handed the thing in last Friday and felt as if I had dropped an elephant. As it is the first thing of the kind I have ever written I have some doubts as to its merits. All I know is that it contains about 7000 words and bears more or less upon the subject dealt with. I shall smoke my pipe and hope for a B+. If I get it, so much the better; if I don't, I suppose the world will continue to spin just the same. A man is not such an important thing after all. We all live in a world of our own and wonder what it is to others. They wonder what it is to us. And yet, if we were all to go down tomorrow, she would keep right on rolling and never feel the difference.

Well I guess I have said enough of this, and will stop before I make a complete ass of myself. Hope to get a letter Tuesday.

> *1691 Cambridge St.*
> *Cambridge, Mass.*
> *May 2, 1892*

I have received your letter and the picture. The latter seems to me a jag idealized. If you have kept a copy for yourself, destroy it for God's sake and mine. Do not think that I am finding fault with you—nothing of the kind. Besides the underdevelopment of the negative I remember that I was looking into the sun. The natural consequence was that I squinted. Hence that diseased droop about the under eye-lids. At least that is a part of it. If I had that look naturally upon the day the thing was taken, you ought to [be] shot for not saying so. There is an appearance of a painful attempt to look very tough, also, which I never anticipated. I showed it to Johnson and he said, "Good God, Rob, you must have had a hell of a good time in Maine." I have always regretted that you did not photograph those cows. Then there would have been no insinuations.

I have been reading Fielding's *Amelia* lately. It is rather startling at times, but undeniably tedious. More than that, the type is criminal. I shall have to read *Middlemarch* right away to prepare myself for the finals. I expect that Gates will require a liberal spew upon the work of that talented woman, and so I had better be ready. I also have a big mess of Carlyle to read; likewise Matthew Arnold and W. H. Mallock. Have you ever seen his (Mallock's) *New Republic?* I do not know just what it is like but have [heard] it spoken of a good deal since I came here. By the way, have you read any of Hamlin Garland's stories? He has two running now—one in the *Arena* and one in the *Century*. I hear that they are very good things in their line. There is a book just out by the author of *Dead Man's Rock*—published by Cassell. The title is *I Saw Three Ships, and other Winter Tales*, by "Q." *Dead Man's Rock* is a roarer, and I think I shall buy this to see what it is like.

I have just written four pages on the character of Silas Marner, and seem to have exhausted my abilities in that direction. You will have to excuse this thing, but as I have said a score of times, [I] will try to do better next Sunday. I don't quite understand what is the matter with me. I never could write a letter, but lately I cannot write an apology for one. Expect to find one from you tomorrow morning.

1691 Cambridge St.
Cambridge, Mass.
May 9, 1892

I wrote you a letter Sunday but I was feeling so generally "out of sorts" that I concluded not to send the stuff that I wrote. I may not do much better today, but at least I hope to write in a little better vein than I did before. There is great excitement here now on account of the class games. '94 and '95 have each won two games and I expect the finishing one will be great sport for those who enjoy that kind of a thing. One of the games I saw had something like the following mechanical aid for rattling the players. For the Sophs. there were two or three cornets, a trombone, three or four drums, guns, cannons, revolvers, etc. The Freshmen had eight drums, four bugles or something of the kind, seven or eight fish-horns, guns, pistols, etc., six pairs of kettle-covers, two dagos with hurdy-gurdies, and a German band. It was good fun at first, but I soon sickened of [it]. Men like W. V. Moody and R. M. Lovett seemed to enjoy it, however, so I am probably at fault. I suppose the great trouble [is that] my sympathies are not strong enough with either side. Of course it makes no difference to me which wins. I am working up quite an excitement over the coming games with Yale, and wish you could be here to see one of them. The general impression is that we are going to "do" them. I will enclose with this a clipping from the Sunday *Herald* describing the Princeton game. From what the fellows say who saw the game, the action of the Princeton men was painfully suggestive of that upon the part of the classes here. Of course these class games are made as wild as they can be; but it seems to me that in an inter-collegiate contest such demonstrations are not particularly edifying. It did not amount to anything, either. Yale was downed again by Holy Cross as you will see by today's paper.

Last evening I attended the French play given in Brattle Hall. It was put on in very good shape and was rather a pleasant affair. It was intended to be exceptionally funny, but did not always succeed. The parts were all taken by men, and perhaps the most successful burlesque of the evening was the skirt-dancing. The Turkers' ceremony in the 4th act (*Le Bourgeois Gentilhomme*) was altogether successful, and a good point was made by slowly changing the weird music with which the scene opens into "Annie Rooney" and concluding with "ta-ra-ra-boom-de-ay."

It is perfect torture for me to write with this pen, and I guess I had better not try to cover another sheet. These fountain pens are at the best rather uncertain things, though I think the "Wirt" is the best of all of them. I rec'd your letter Monday night.

1691 Cambridge St.
Cambridge, Mass.
May 11, 1892

I rec'd your card this noon but will not be able to give you a very satisfactory answer. The Cooperative Society cannot legally import the book and they tell me that the only chance I have of getting it is either to ask the Harpers to import a copy or to send the money to England myself. I do not know just how the new copyright law works and cannot seem to find out. The book is published by James R. Osgood, McIlvane and Co., 45 Albemarle-Street, London, W. *Tess of the D'Urbervilles*, 3 vols. octavo, cloth, 31s 6d. This seems to be the regular price of English three-volume novels.

The expurgation of Harper's editors consists of one complete chapter, which it is said does not materially affect the book. I should advise you to buy it, together with Emile Zola's *La Terre*. The latter will make up for the missing chapter.

1691 Cambridge St.
Cambridge, Mass.
May 23, 1892

At last I have settled myself and will try to write you a letter. Yesterday I could not get a chance. Since 7.30 this evening I have attended a lecture on *Sir Gawain and the Green Knight* by Prof. Kittredge, read some of *Middlemarch* and smoked a pipe. The lecture was peculiarly interesting—much more so than the subject would lead one to think. He first read a translation (his own) of the more prominent portions of the poem and concluded with comments, historical and critical. In his translation he endeavored to keep the tone and flavor of the original as far as possible and, as far as I am able to judge, succeeded admirably. If you have ever read any of *Piers Plowman* you can have some idea of the alliterative swing of the story. It is supposed to have been written somewhere in the latter half of the fourteenth century, but the author is unknown.

There was something fascinating in the Prof's version of it. He clung to Saxon words almost exclusively and some of the lines were, to say the least, unique. Here is one in particular that I remember: " 'Twas the cursedest kirk he ever had entered." The only unsatisfactory feature of the affair was the small audience. Sever 11 seats about five hundred people and I should not think there could have been over fifty or sixty there at the most.

As to *Middlemarch*, I regret to say that I am unable to appreciate the transcendent beauties of Geo. Eliot's character analysis. To me, she makes more of human character than life itself warrants. Thackeray is to me the ideal student of human nature. To be sure, his creatures are to some extent types but not in the sense that those of Dickens are. Dickens deals almost exclusively in exaggerated characteristics; Thackeray with definitely drawn and coherent characters; while Geo. Eliot's works are a study of formative influences and psychological results. In my opinion she stands below Jane Austen though she deals less with complex destiny. I may reveal my uneducated taste in making this confession of my opinions, but a fellow may as well tell the truth.

A rather interesting thing happened in my room this afternoon. Two friends of mine happened to call upon me, who are at swords' points, so to speak. I watched them pretty closely and could see that they both felt rather uncomfortable and looked very foolish at times. After a time the course of the conversation compelled them to speak to each other occasionally, and at 1.30 I left them together and went out to a French recitation. When I came back they were still in my room as good friends as they were before the difficulty. They saw me grin as I entered, and one of them immediately had an engagement.

This little incident made me think how foolish more than half of the enmities in the world are, after all. The fact is, life is too short to nourish such things profitably and a few words at the right time and in the right place might destroy hundreds of petty "spats" every day. I am not setting myself up for a professional peace-maker, but I honestly think that in this case I was the indirect means of bringing two people together who might have otherwise hated each other to the end of their lives. I was glad to see the thing take place but I must confess that I felt a kind of unchristian pleasure in watching them.

The other day my friend Latham, of New York, was in my

room and after a silence of some minutes he made a statement that startled me a little. From the lips of some fellows I should not have thought much of it but I would have as soon thought of Walter Swanton's addressing me in such a manner, as his doing so.

"Robinson," he said, "I can't see what this life of ours amounts to anyway. What is the object of it? What are we here for?" I could not give him a very definite answer, so I blew a stream of Bull Durham smoke into the air and shook my head. I guess we talked for an hour on the subject and then went to dinner. It is not such a foolish question to ask, after all, when we think it over. If we throw aside the gilded Paradise theory, it *is* a question what life really amounts to for more than three quarters of the world. I am very sure that what I have had thus far would not warrant my living it over again if I had the chance. Of course, there are portions of it that I shall always remember with pleasure, but when I consider what a small part of the whole they compose, I am quite willing to let things stand as they are.

Sometimes I get rather blue in thinking over the fact that I should now be a much different person from what I am had I come to Harvard three years ago as a Freshman. I might have done it, if I had laid my plans. With no offence to the smaller colleges, I do not think that they have much in common with the elective privileges open to students here. I am just beginning to discover what kind of a place Harvard is and what a consummate ass I made of myself in my choice of courses this year. I am satisfied with two of them; the others have been practically a waste of time.

Next year I shall do better, but that will be the end of it.

[P. S.] If you are not able to read this you can say to yourself that your friend has been getting off four pages of his guff with the best of intentions, and throw the stuff into the fire. By the way, I wish you would tell me honestly whether you can read my writing or not. Compared with yours it seems a kind of imposition.

I did not get a chance to write you a letter yesterday so I will write an apology for one now. The fact is, the day is so damnably hot that it is positively laborious to move a pen; so you must excuse me if I am brief and dull. About all I have to say is that I am hard at work on stuff that I neglected in Eng. 9. and my time is pretty well taken up. Been grinding today on Geo. Eliot and Cardinal Newman. That Oxford movement has given me more trouble than a little, and I am far from sure of it now. I have a vague idea of what it was, and that is about all. The subject does not interest me, to begin with, and that makes it doubly dry. I have no sympathy with the Tractarians and have to strain my imagination to its utmost to make myself believe that Cardinal Newman was a great man—outside of his scholarly attainments. I had better not say so in my examination book, though. I fear that Gates would not appreciate my individualism. I called on him the other day to get some special reports I handed in some time ago and he received me quite kindly. He is a dreamy sort of a devil and went off into a long monologue upon the Spenserian Revival and finally ended up with the classic French drama. He told me that I was "impressionistic—if I would excuse the euphuism." I excused it inwardly and went out and bought a box of Turkish (?) cigarettes. I have contracted a habit of smoking those things which I must stop. They make a man dull and sleepy, but there is a fascination about them that is hard to describe. I suppose they are loaded. Peters hit it about right when he said each puff from them feels as if it were killing you.— Went to see the *Foresters* (Tennyson-Daly) Sat. evening with Dr. Schuman. Drank more beer than I have for a month past, but did not feel any ill effects from it. Guess I will try it again. I think I told you that I bought *Tess of the D'Urbervilles*. Have not read it yet.

There is a game here this afternoon between Harvard and

Brown. Guess I will go down and see the end of it. If Hell is any hotter than Cambridge a man will do well to behave himself here on earth. Will see you in two weeks anyway, but hope you will be here at the game. The seats are all sold but we can get in early and lie under a tree.

1716 Cambridge St.
Cambridge, Mass.
October 1, 1892

I suppose you are beginning to think that it is about time to hear from me, and I must confess that it is. But if you have not already condemned me for a jay I will now try to make up for my negligence and hope that you will pardon me.—I am in new quarters now and am immeasurably better satisfied with them. Nature never intended Mrs. Fox and I to live in the same house for more than a year. My present room comes very near to my ideal. There is a first rate desk, a most seductive couch, window-seat, easy chair, open coal-grate, etc. The people are first-class but there is a quiet understanding that there will not be a great deal of celebrating and the like in the house. That does not interfere with my plans, however, as I am here this year to work and for no other reason, that is, primarily. And work enough there is for me to do: here is my program:—

	9	10	11	12	1.30	2.30	3.30
Mon	French	German				Phil.	
Tues	"	F. A.					German
Wed	French	German			Phil		
Thursday	French	F. A.					German
Friday	"	German			Phil		Eng. Lit.
Saturday		F. A.	French				

I have mixed the hours a little but you can see the courses. Fine Arts III (Ancient Art) is under Prof. Norton and promises to be a great thing. At the opening the Professor waxed humorous. "Gentlemen," he said, "this is a sad sight." You [see] the course is immensely popular as a "snap" and Saturday morning over 500 men walked in to take it. A good many will be thrown out; I may be one of them, though I hope not. In Phil. I we begin with logic under Prof. Palmer. I think you heard him read some of his *Odyssey* at Bowdoin. As a lecturer he is fine. The worst course I have is French 1a. It is nearly all composition and we have to commit one of La Fontaine's fables every month and deliver it before the class. That is bitter work for me, but we have to take things as they come. No man is obliged to take the course, so he cannot kick.

I have been ransacking the periodical shelves in the Library and have come to the conclusion that we do not want the *Athenaeum*. It is rather entertaining to look over a pile of them, but I am afraid we would be sorry if we subscribed for it. The *Spectator, Observer,* and *Academy* are much the same. Of course the *Critic* is all right and by the way I will send you one with this containing a review of Prof. Hyde's book which may interest you. I cannot suggest anything better to take the place of the *Athenaeum* than the *Atlantic*. It makes no difference to me which I keep at the end of the year, if you have any preference. Of course I only suggest this—shall expect to hear your views in your next letter. I have "blown" myself on a fancy edition of Jules Verne's *L'Ile Mystérieuse,* shall have it bound in half Levant with gilt top.

I am feeling rather better than when I left home and trust I shall continue so. To tell the truth I was not in very good condition this summer. I am not smoking much now. Tomorrow I begin on the non-diurnal plan. Shall only smoke evenings. If I carry out my plan this year I shall read about thirty French books of various sizes and about twelve in German. In truth I am starting in as a sort of short-haired grind; but the long hair will come. Have been here a week and have drunk but one beer. Not very bad, that. But then it is not much to my credit as I care but little for the stuff.

Give me your opinion about the magazines as soon as possible

and we will start the thing going. I can probably get quite a re-
duction—or you either, for that matter. Trusting that you have
written me today, I remain. . . .

1716 Cambridge St.
Cambridge, Mass.
October 9, 1892

Well, here it is Sunday evening, and there seems to be nothing more sensible for me to do than to write you a few lines according to the agreement, which you may be filling at your end
at this same time. I fear I am not in the mood to flourish any
masterly rhetoric this evening so will ask you to pardon all sole-
cisms and the like which may meet your eye. Last evening I indulged in a rather varied form of self-entertainment. You see
I thought I would stay in Cambridge Saturday night for once in
my life to economize. Well, about half past seven I took a little
walk down to the square and dropped into McNamee's book store.
The first thing I knew I had blown in four dollars and a half and
I thought it about time to get back "into my hole." So I went
back and sat up until midnight reading Plato's *Apologia* (Cary's
translation) and Rudyard Kipling's *Barrack-room Ballads,* both
volumes being the fruits of the night's economy. Between the
books above named, a copy of the *Advocate,* a mess of roasted
chestnuts (which, by the way, gave me a villainous pain in my
bowels) and divers pipes of Golden Scepter tobacco (which I
will say, incidentally, is about the poorest smoke I ever had—if
you were here I would throw the box at your head) I managed to
murder the time in a rather satisfactory manner. It would have
been quite so, but for the aforesaid pain and a smarting tongue
caused by the glorious mixture you were so fond of eulogizing.
But then, I do not lay it up against you that I bought it. I did it
quite out of curiosity. One thing is certain, as the French say,
and that is that the firms that make the stuff know how to advertise. That ancient gentleman lying (literally and figuratively) in
his dingy room took me right by the hair; i.e., hit me in the neck.
But I shall know better hereafter and cling to "Pride of Virginia."

I think I shall acquire a liking for German after a time, though it seems to me now that it must be about as hard as Latin. But when I look around me and see the multitude who have apparently been successful with it, I feel encouraged and hope for the best. Shall begin reading in about a week—Grimm's *Fairy Tales.*

I am sorry to say that I have neglected to see about those periodicals. As to the *Atlantic,* I suppose it would be more sensible to wait until January, and so get a complete volume. But after all, wouldn't it be more satisfactory to have two weeklies? How about *Harper's?* or the *Mahogany Tree?* I will send you a copy of the latter and let you see what you think of it. If you have not seen it, I think it will strike you as something of an oddity, and also exceedingly well fitted for a companion to the *Critic.* I must confess that I think it about the best thing of its kind (if there is anything else) that I have ever seen. It's a dollar more a year, making $7.00 in all—something less if we can get club rates. If you are willing to split on the expense, I will take the *Mahogany Tree* at the end of the year and you [take] the *Critic* if you prefer it. Let me know next week.

Here are some stanzas from Kipling:

Seven men from all the world, back to Docks again,
Rolling down the Ratcliffe Road drunk and raising Cain:
Give the girls another drink 'fore we sign away—
We that took the 'Bolivar' out across the Bay!
("The Ballad of the 'Bolivar.'")

The Spirit gripped him by the hair, and sun by sun they fell
Till they came to the belt of Naughty Stars that rim the mouth of
*   Hell:*
The first are red with pride and wrath, the next are white with
*   pain,*
But the third are black with clinkered sin that cannot burn again.
("Tomlinson").

'But till we are built like angels—with hammer and chisel and pen,
'We will work for ourself and a woman, for ever and ever. Amen.
("An Imperial Rescript")

Ship me somewheres east of Suez, where the best is like the worst,
Where there aren't no Ten Commandments an' a man can raise a
thirst;

. . . .

An' I seed her first a-smokin' of a whackin' white cheroot,
An' a-wastin' Christian kisses on an 'eathen idol's foot.
("Mandalay"—Barrack-Room Ballads)

Upon the whole the book is rather disappointing. Much of it is
simply rubbish—like much of the author's prose.

1716 Cambridge St.
Cambridge, Mass.
October 19, 1892

I would have written before this, but I wanted to know what
you thought about the periodical business, so I waited. And now
I will say that I am not altogether satisfied with the arrangement
as it stands. The *Mahogany Tree* is a very neat little paper in its
way and in the course of a year would doubtless contain a good
deal of interesting matter, but when we pay four dollars for it
with such papers as *Harper's Weekly* and others at the same
price, the thing does not seem altogether satisfactory. I have ran-
sacked the shelves in the library and the counters of every book-
store in Cambridge, but cannot seem to find anything to suit my
taste. I never knew there was such a scarcity of literary papers.
If you prefer *Harper's Weekly* to the M. T. I am quite agreeable. Or, if you can suggest anything else, I shall be glad to hear
from you.

Just at present, however, I shall not be able to attend to it, for
two reasons: I am decidedly short, and my time bids fair to be

pretty well taken up for the next week. That ear operation has got to come and I have made arrangements to submit myself to the carver's hands on Saturday next at 3.00 P.M. You can think of me then stretched out for all the world like a corpse, filled with ether and letting Dr. Green and two assistants (probably Harvard Medics) do whatever they think will give them the highest satisfaction. Shall be obliged to keep dark in a private hospital in the City for four or five days, and then by the grace of God (if the ether does not kill me) I may be on my feet again. I have not much faith [in] the business, though; I have had an idea all along that the necrosis has got in beyond the small bones. If it has, I may hear a trumpet blow a little sooner than I would ordinarily— that's all. I am reading Blackmore's *Alice Lorraine*, it is very fine, like all of that author's books. Will write next Sunday if I can wiggle my fingers. Be sure and write yourself.

#38 Commonwealth Ave.
Boston, Mass.
October 23, 1892

Well, I have had my ear bored out, and cannot say that I feel much the worse for it. I took the ether yesterday afternoon about half past three, and was under it about an hour. Three hours after I "came to," I was hungry and about eight o'clock in the evening I ate some crackers and drank some tea—which kept me awake about all night.

This hospital life has few attractions for me. About the only pleasant thing about it is the expectation of getting out some time. I shall be mighty glad when tomorrow morning comes (I expect to be released tomorrow afternoon) but I suppose I ought not to complain when I think of those in the house who are so much worse off than I am. That does not help matters much, however. About all I can do is to pity them, and ache to get away myself. There is a big operation of some kind just about to be begun now in some room on the fourth floor.

When I awoke last night a nurse felt my pulse and took my

temperature, recording the same on a "Clinical Chart,"—all of which made me very tired. This red tape in such cases as mine only goes to make one feel needlessly uneasy. The doctor tells me that I may go out for an hour's walk this afternoon. Why I cannot keep on and walk (or ride) to Cambridge I cannot tell. Perhaps he would feel cheap to give the house such a poor job.

I am not altogether affecting my levity, for I really feel encouraged. Two bones were removed—hammer and anvil, I suppose,—and about half of the anvil was gone or eaten up. The fact that he left the third one is enough to make me feel as if I were not in quite so bad a condition as I supposed. I can't tell you much about it yet, however, as the doctor has not made any detailed statement regarding my condition, nor has he given me any particular directions. I shall learn that tomorrow.

I hope we shall get that paper business settled after a time. If the thing is agreeable to you as it stands now, then go ahead with it. The *Critic* is not all I looked for, but I guess it is as good as we can get. Write to Cambridge as usual.

1716 Cambridge St.
Cambridge, Mass.
November 21, 1892

The dungy Thanksgiving week has come again and the College yard is reeking with the strong but honest odor of New England ordure. There is also another kind of dung that is noticeable here, particularly by those more interested in athletics. I speak of that rubbed in at the Harvard-Yale foot-ball game at Hampden Park on Saturday. I was sorry that you could not be here, but perhaps it was better for your peace of mind that you were not. If you had seen that game your adoration of Yale's "manliness" would have received an unpleasant shock. I send with this a copy of the Sunday *Herald* and a copy of the *Crimson* for this morning. Yale's deliberate plan to physically disable Harvard's strongest end was so obvious that it was disgusting. The whole thing was much like the Colosseum of old—twenty thousand people and two men half-killed. A life time is not well lived without seeing this game once. I only got my ticket at the last minute and I am mighty glad that I got it. I don't think you need hesitate to pay ten or twelve dollars for the day if you ever get a chance to take the game in. The mere game is by no means the whole of it. All I hope is that you will never see such brutality and dirtiness displayed upon any field as that which characterized Yale's play on Saturday. Between half murdering two men and having the umpire cheat us out of a touch-down, the score does not reflect any great credit on the Yale men—though no one thinks that Harvard would have beaten. It would probably have been a tie. I do not think you will have any complaint to make with the *Crimson's* account of it. It may surprise you to see me enthusias- tic over foot-ball, but Saturday would have excited a corpse.

I sent you the books this morning. They are 45c each.

I ran across that *Critic* with Pres. Hyde's book-notice in it and will send it along. I bought a copy of Austin Dobson's *At the Sign of the Lyre* and was disappointed. I prefer Kipling's *Ballads*. At first I did not care much for them but now they are great.

> *"Yes, the old lost stars wheel back, dear lass,*
> *That blaze in the velvet blue.*
> *They're all old friends on the old trail,*
>   *our own trail, the out trail,*
> *They're God's own guides on the Long Trail—*
>   *the trail that is always new," etc., etc.*

1716 *Cambridge St.*
Cambridge, Mass.
November 29, 1892

Your letter came this noon, and I will answer it now without putting it off any longer. I should like to go home when you do but it is impossible. I shall get a week somewhere around Christ- mas and shall probably return the 2d or 3d of January—though perhaps before—I do not know just when the recess comes. We do not have "vacations" here—I suppose the word does not sound well to a Cambridge ear. But it makes little difference what they call it, as long as they let a fellow go home and see his friends. I have so many dear friends in Gardiner that it will probably take all my time to get around and see them all. How is it with you?

I bought Maspero's *Histoire Ancienne des Peuples de L'Orient* a week or so ago and blew myself on a binding for it. I wish you could see it. You can twist it around anyway you like but it makes no difference. I cannot well see how it can wear out. There is a peculiar satisfaction in having books bound to your own taste. I do not know of any more refined vice than buying imported books in a foreign language and taking them to McNamee's in the Square and looking over his samples of crushed morocco in all colors and grades. If you have any books you would like rebound it will be to your advantage to send them to me. You can get an elegant binding for $1.25 or so that will make your heart glad and improve your appetite.

I am up to my ears in German. It is harder than I expected but very interesting. I am now reading Hauff's 𝕾𝖆𝖎𝖉𝖘 𝕾𝖈𝖍𝖎𝖈𝖋𝖆𝖑𝖊 which is very good and tolerably easy—though it takes me two hours steady grinding to read a hundred lines. We have to do all our writing in the German script, which is rather attractive but thoroughly nonsensical. At least, that is my opinion.

The worst thing I have is French Comp. I wish you could hear one of Prof. Norton's lectures in "Fine Arts." They are simply magnificent. Today he said that there was not half as much buncombe in the Darius Inscription which May Rawlinson spent ten years in copying from a cliff in some god-forsaken region in Mesopotamia as there is in one of Chauncey Depew's after-dinner speeches. He likes to swipe the World's Fair and enjoys telling the anecdote of the Chicago man who said "they had not much culture out there yet, but when they got it, they were going to make it hum." You know John Ruskin calls Norton "his first tutor." I suppose there is no doubt that he is by all odds the greatest man in America, and I am beginning to realize what a privilege it is to sit within six feet of him three times a week and hear him talk.

Hope you will get up here sometime before June. Thanks for the dollar, it came in good time.

1716 Cambridge St.
Cambridge, Mass.
December 4, 1892

Here it is Monday again and now before the week goes on any farther I will write you something to let you know that I am still here and rather anxious to get back to Gardiner. I am not feeling very lively today, as I worked last night until about one o'clock and then lay awake until four. That kind of thing takes the ambition from a man about as quickly as anything I know. The principal things I have to trouble me just now are a midyear examination in Logic to come some time and a thesis on the British Periodical Essayists (which I think I have mentioned) to come just after Newyears'. Yesterday I took out John Dunton's *Life and Errors* and the supplement to his *Athenian Oracle* to consult for the groundwork of the thing I expect to write. John Dunton was the founder of the so-called "Athenian Society," which consisted chiefly of himself, and professed to answer all questions in its power through the agency of the *Mercury*. This seems to be the original form of that class of literature so well known in the *Spectator*, etc.—Some of the propositions and answers are, to say the least, curious. For example take the following:

Queſt:—"Why does a Bladder full of Wind, thrust by force under the Water, aſcend ſuddenly on the top thereof?"

Answer.—"Because the Air, or Wind, wherewith it is filled, returns to its natural place which is above the Water."

Question. "Why does a Dog, of all other Animals, remain attached to the Bitch after Copulation, being not eaſily to be ſeparated?"

Answer. "Alexander Aphroditius ſaith, Prob. 75, it is becauſe the Bitch has the Paſſages of Nature very ſtraight; and the Yard of the Dog ſwelling within by the ebullition of the ſpirits, it is difficult after Copulation to withdraw it."

This book was printed about 1700 and was presented to the library in 1837. I find by the slip on the inside back cover that it has been taken out by two persons besides myself since Dec. 13, 1881. You see there is not a great call for Mr. Dunton's work, though I will say that his *Life and Errors* is stamped with a few more dates. An incidental phrase in one of Mr. Gates's lectures put me onto them. I am not exactly discouraged over this thesis but somewhat uneasy. If I had a chance for a general "spew" like my last year's paper on *Pendennis*, I should not be troubled. But then I think I shall get through it in some way.—Don't know exactly when I shall go home but probably somewhere about the 23d. Shall be glad to see you once more and have a pipe with you. I am smoking "Catac" right along now—find that a light tobacco goes better in the long run.

1716 Cambridge St.
Cambridge, Mass.
December 11, 1892

This has been a lazy day with me and I doubt if I shall be able to say much that will entertain you, but I will try and you may take the will, etc. This forenoon I wrote out some German sentences, which I suppose is about the highest form of mental torture, and after lunch I read the greater part of Steele's "Lover" papers. They are easily "eighteenth century" but well meaning and interesting. There is something unique in the writer's apparent seriousness that places them in a class by themselves. To my mind they are the best things Steele ever wrote and I shall tell Gates so in my thesis, although he quite overlooked them in his lectures. The *Tatler* and *Spectator* are by no means the only 18th cent. essays worth reading.

I will now revive that periodical question and I think I can "hit" you. I cannot think of any more satisfactory choice than the *Critic* and the *Nation*. It is strange that neither of us could have thought of it. By taking those two papers we could not only keep posted upon literature but life in general. In the *Nation,* the literary departments are conducted more upon the plan of the English reviews—but then you probably know it well enough. Perhaps the best way to do will be for you to subscribe for whichever you like and that will save all difficulty. Let me know which one you want (if you have not soured on the project) and I will take the other.

Dr. Schuman dropped in for the first time yesterday afternoon, and I read him some Kipling. He had to confess that it was worth reading. I suppose you have seen the Christmas *Century* with his poem and Miss Wilkins' imitation of the French pastel. It is not as bad as the drool she had in the November *Harper's,* but I cannot say that I look forward to the day when the pastel will be a recognized form of American literature. The novelty has already worn off in what we know of the French. What I am waiting for is the influence of the French daily newspaper. Our dailies are a disgrace to civilization—that is, of course, with a few exceptions. I guess I am getting a little "grouchy"—so will stop.

[P.S.] Expect to leave for Gardiner about the 20th.

1716 Cambridge St.
Cambridge, Mass.
January 13, 1893

I suppose you have put me down for a "flat" (whatever that is) long before this but I trust you will not be too hard upon me. I will not say that I have not had time to write, as that excuse is too threadbare. I suppose the chief reason is that I thought I would wait until I subscribed for the *Nation.* For some reason I have failed to do it, but will see to it the first of the week. Your *Critic* came all right.—That thesis is due tomorrow and I have written after my own way. Have no idea what mark it will bring and shall not hear for five or six weeks.

The mid year examinations are only a little over a week ahead, and I do not know where they will land me. I have a difficulty in expressing myself at times which leads one to think I know less than I really do—which, God knows, is little enough. But then, I shall not worry about it. The only things that trouble me to any great extent are Logic, of which I am entirely ignorant, and German Composition, which I lack the logic, or something else, to put together in the right order. However, I shall steer through it in some way and will soon be beyond these small rocks, and out into the ocean of life, etc., where, I am told, the rocks are of much more portentous dimensions. This life is a curious mess, after all. Sometimes I sit here by my fire and wonder how it is all coming out. I look back upon the millions who lived and died a thousand years ago and wonder if it makes much difference how it comes out, after all. I do not look pessimistically upon the matter. I am inclined to regard it more in the light of a big joke—whose joke it is, or whether it is a good one, I cannot tell. Maarten Maartens has written a novel called *God's Fool*. Think I shall read it. Bought a copy of *Tom Jones* the other day and shall read it soon in my English course. Butler, who has the room next to mine, began it yesterday noon and finished it at four o'clock this morning. About a thousand good sized pages. I do not know whether to look for another letter from you tomorrow or not, but will be glad to get one.

1716 Cambridge St.
Cambridge, Mass.
January 23, 1893

It is Monday noon and I will write you something now while I have a good chance. I have several minutes before lunch and after that I must grind upon Psychology. The mid-year examinations will begin Wednesday, and my first (French) comes Thursday. College shuts down for about three weeks, in which time the students are supposed to be at work. I have made great resolutions but do not expect they will amount to much. They never do, as regards my studies. For instance, in French I am supposed to be thoroughly acquainted with the first book of La Fontaine's *Fables* and able to quote four of them from memory, *Les Trois Mousquetaires, Marianne* (Geo. Sand), *Les Frères Colombe* (G. le Peyrebrune) and some odd plays. But the bulk of the exam. will be the translation of English into French, and that is where I am generally at sea. The German does not worry me—though I shall probably make a botch of the composition. I can get through the translation in some way or other.—I am very happy to say that I am at last able to send you a copy of the *Nation.* My first number came Saturday, so you may hereafter look for it with my letter—that is, when I send it. I will try to be reasonably regular, however, and hope you will find no cause for complaint.—No, I don't quite understand the paragraph in the *Critic* about Blackmore and Hardy. I should think that was enough to damn a paper of its character as a reliable sheet for reference. There is no excuse for such a blunder. It may be a printer's error, but I can hardly understand what the proofreader was doing. I doubt if you find the copy of the *Nation* very entertaining; it is not a star number, and for that matter I am sure that I shall have to educate myself into reading it. Did you ever meet a fellow brought up on the New York *Tribune?* If you have you will understand what I mean.—I have not been doing much of any reading lately—except an occasional story in the magazines, which I am getting more and more disgusted with every day. I think *Harper's* is easily at the head now, and there is much in that that nobody but a scholar or a lunatic would care to read.—I am getting more and more soaked in Rudyard Kipling's poems, and I was glad to read of him in the *Athenaeum's* summary of English literature for the past year. In poetry they mention Tennyson first, William Watson, and then the *Barrack Room Ballads,* mentioning in particular, "Tommy" and "Mandalay"—"on the road to Mandalay, where the flying fishes play, etc."—"Come you back you British soldier, come you back to Mandalay." And, by the way, did you ever think what a figure Kipling and his kid must cut among the Vermont farmers? especially when he (Kipling) goes to get his mail. I have been hoping that the English club here would get him to lecture, but have not heard it mentioned. After writing the "Rhyme of the Three Captains," it seems a little inconsistent for him to live in America, but it must be confessed that he writes a good deal for effect—and he generally succeeds.

Well, the hands of my clock have come together and there was a time when I could tell when they will be in that situation again, but I could not now to save my life. I can see occasional hungry men drifting into Memorial from my window, and I will put on my galoshes and try to find something to be thankful for. Think I shall blow in five cents and have some fried hasty-pudding. That is about the only thing one can depend upon here. Hope to get a letter tomorrow morning.

1716 Cambridge St.
Cambridge, Mass.
January 31, 1893

You must excuse the light character of my correspondence this week, but I will try to do better next time. I say this almost every time I write, but this time I mean it. There will be no excuse for my not writing a half-decent letter, at least as far as length is concerned, on next Sunday. Until then my time will be pretty well taken up, as it has been all the week. This forenoon I took the mid-year in German, and read about 120 pages of Hauff in preparation for it. I killed the translation, but am not so sure about the composition. I always split there in languages. Next Thursday Fine Arts come and it will be nothing but read, read until then. Wish you were here to see *Lady Windermere's Fan.* I sent programmes with *Nation,* which may interest you. Friday night Saben holds a literary smoke (and drink for those who feel the need of it) and Schuman is to be there. Wish you could be present. There will also be a Mr. Mohun, an Englishman, and

Mr. Knight, a grey-haired Boston lawyer who quotes Homer and Horace in the original. Rather good company, I think, don't you? All I am afraid of is that Saben will get drunk and do all the talking.

[P.S.] These Columbus stamps remind me of the time I wore a porous plaster on my lungs for a cough. I think the country will be tired of them before Fall—though I must confess I rather like the look of them.

1716 Cambridge St.
Cambridge, Mass.
February 5, 1893

Now I will try to write you a letter, though I am feeling about as miserably as a mortal can, and be religious. I have had a tremendous pain in my left lung for the past two or three days and now I am "broken out" in big blotches both fore and aft. I have no idea what it is, but will consult an M. D. tomorrow. I always prided myself on my strong lungs, and if there is anything the matter with them I shall feel rather down in the mouth. I hate to kick, but it seems as if the Fates kept something in store for me all the time to keep me in hot water. After that long siege with my ear which no one can appreciate but myself, this thing comes on like a cannibal after a missionary. It may be a cancer or a lupus; if it is, I shall dodge the exams. in English VII and Philosophy (Logic and Psychology) on general principles, and so gain something. Last night the thing acted so that I went down to the square and got a porous plaster, which I fancy relieved it somewhat. In order to drive the pain away I read Emerson's essays on "Love," "Friendship," "Prudence," and "Heroism," but am afraid I did not get much out of them.

As you have already seen, I did not go to town last night, but stayed in Cambridge. Schuman failed to turn up at the gathering in Saben's room but the others were all there. Saben got drunk, as I expected, and made a learned ass of himself. He read Bob Ingersoll, Coppée, Omar Khayyam, and the "Elegy in a Country Church Yard" as only a drunken man can. The audience seemed well amused, but there is something rather degrading in it, after all. Perhaps I would have enjoyed it more if I had drunk something, but I have practically given it up, if I ever drank enough to say that. The pipe does me very well.

I will send you the *Nation* with this. It contains some rather hard remarks on Blaine, I think, but then the *Post* is a democratic paper as much as the Boston *Herald* and the party spirit must show itself in dealing with such a prominent character. There is something very pathetic to me in Blaine's hand-organ man. I suppose you read of it in the papers.—I have been reading more Thomson, and Perry's *Eighteenth Century Literature* in preparation for the English VII examination but have found it pretty hard work with the devil in my chest. He is digging away at my back now for a change, which is not altogether disagreeable. To-morrow at this time I hope to know what is the matter with me. I think I am inclined to look upon the bright side of things after all, and hope for favorable news. Since beginning this note I have thought of carbuncles, but hope I am wrong. They are the devil's own joy and [I] will "have none of them" if I can help myself—which I probably cannot.

Next Monday we begin a German farce entitled *Einer Muss Heiraten* (*One Must Marry*). If the opening speech is a sample of the whole, I think I shall have trouble with it. I wonder why it is that every new German book seems like another language?

Took the Fine Arts examination last Thursday and enclose a list of the questions. I think you would like the course—in fact, I know you would—for you have a fondness for the better things in life, which I sometimes think may be a misfortune rather than a blessing. Wholesome, healthy ignorance and indifference is a thing to be envied.

Well, I think I will stop now and smoke a pipe before going to bed. Hope to get a letter from you Tuesday.

It is now five o'clock in the afternoon and I have about three-quarters of an hour before dinner—though it will be a mighty small dinner I shall eat—and I will take this time to write you a few lines and tell you about my mysterious illness, which I suppose interests you somewhat.

When I wrote a week ago, I had no idea what ailed me and I was pretty well stirred up. Tuesday I went to an M. D. and was informed that I had the "shingles." Now there is nothing romantic or poetical about the shingles—and I am afraid that I was disappointed for a few minutes,—then I was glad that it was no worse. This may make you laugh, but I assure you it is no laughing matter when a man lies awake for nine hours suffering the tortures of the inquisition, and wondering what the devil he was put here for, anyway. But I fancy they are leaving me now, and though I am pretty "ragged" I hope for a better condition soon. I got excused from two examinations, and tomorrow shall go to U. 5 and [ask for a] week's furlough. Then I shall take a grand loaf, though I shall have to read *Tom Jones* and keep up my German after a fashion. Yesterday I took Wm. Black's *Magic Ink* from the library. It is pitiful drool and I was sorry for the author. In the evening I prowled down to the square and bought *Rudder Grange* (Stockton) and three cigars. Between the two (or the four) I passed the time quite pleasantly—though the twinges were pretty sharp at times.

I am beginning to be sorry that I was not "educated" to the *Nation* years ago. It comes harder than Logic to me now. There is something elegantly dry about the sheet that compels my admiration, but I must confess that I pass over many columns.

I am hesitating whether to go to chapel this evening and hear the Rev. Washington Gladden of Ohio. I don't think I shall, though I probably should were I in any kind of shape. I should be tremendously pleased if you could be with me tonight but there is no use in asking for the impossible. So good-bye, and write me another sheet of your reflections when you feel in the mood.

Cambridge
February 21, 1893

Here it is Tuesday evening, and I think it is high time I was writing to you. I have not received any letter from you yet, but I suppose the rail-roads have been so blocked that everything is delayed. Or possibly you have not written. Such a thing may happen and I can easily excuse you if that is the case. If I remember rightly, I have been guilty of such negligence myself—the present instance seems to be something very like it.

I began college work again yesterday and now it seems quite natural again. I read, or thought I did, a German farce during my sickness, but I find the second reading about as hard as the first. There seems to be a devil in the German language that refuses to be cast out. But I suppose that like everything else that is difficult, time, patience, etc. is the only successful treatment. I had hopes of being able to read German tolerably well by June, but I must confess that it looks a little doubtful now; but when I look back, I remember that after four months of French I knew practically nothing about the language. If I make the gain in G. that I did in French during the last half-year I shall be pleasantly surprised.

I got my thesis back in English 7 yesterday with a clean A. That made me feel a little better, though I do not think a mark here signifies much of anything, as a rule. In German I got a C on the midyears. Poll asked me if I was satisfied with it and I had three minds to tell him that I was not. I thought better of it, though, and said that it was all I expected. We are beginning to translate stories into German, which is hell for me. I can go the translation very well, but draw the line at composition.

I would give a hundred dollars (if I had them) to get over my nasty habit of microscopic writing. I cannot seem to cure it, try as hard as I may. Four or five years ago I wrote well enough, but I seem to have gone steadily down hill in that way (and perhaps in every other) during the later years of my life. There may be an explanation for it, but I cannot find it out.—I found a paper covered edition of Rudyard Kipling's poems today and it is the nearest to a complete edition that I have seen. There are some important ones omitted, but it is quite a pleasant volume. Will send it to you tomorrow.

Tomorrow is Washington's birthday, and I shall spend my time in reading French, committing a fable, and writing an essay on "Fielding and Thackeray."—I have lately finished *Tom Jones* (1084 big pages) and have no desire to repeat it. It is great, but there is a lack of human interest to me which makes it a little slow. The introductory chapter to the various books is the (are the?) best part of it.

Read Mrs. Browning yesterday all through one of Prof. Royce's lectures. This may startle you, but he is not at home in psychology, and I get absolutely nothing from what he says. Prof. James' book is quite enough. My eyes are a little lame this evening, so think I will stop here. Hope to get a letter from you tomorrow. Sent two *Nations* yesterday.

Cambridge
February 27, 1893

My time was pretty well taken up Sunday, and this is the first chance I have had today to write you a letter. It is now about 11 P.M. and I will admit that I am a trifle sleepy, so you must excuse me, if I fail to be interesting. After dinner I worked for an hour on a French composition and then went to Mr. Black's lecture on Daniel DeFoe. It was excellent, like all of his lectures, though as I have just been over the ground in English 7 I did not learn a great deal. When I came home I had a smoke and read some of Matthew Arnold's poetry. Now I am trying to write something to you. I know you will not object to the time spent with the pipe and the poetry, if I did indulge in them at the expense of your letter. I fancy it makes no great difference in the quality, as my mind has not been particularly brilliant at any time today.

Friday afternoon I cut Prof. Royce's lecture on Neural Activity and went to a symphony concert in town. I think I got more from the concert than I ever did from one of the lectures, and intend to repeat the deed next Friday. I wish you were here to go with me. Mendehlsson's "Fingal's Cave" overture is enough to render a man indifferent to all worldly woes and blasted hopes while it lasts, which is some twenty minutes, I should say. Today, however, I went to his lecture and found him rather more entertaining than usual. He must be great in his own field.

Saturday evening I went to the Museum with Schuman to see *Shore Acres*. It is a great piece of work, filled with human interest. The scene is at Frenchman's Bay, Maine, and the characters are Maine Yankees—by far the best stage Yankees that I have ever seen. There is a vein of pathos running through the whole thing, and the best of it is—it never gets ridiculous. There is, in reality, no "horse-play," and if you have ever seen Alvin Joslyn and like caricatures, you will realize what that means. Mr. Hearn [sic] is an artist, both as playwright and actor.

The other day I sent you the *Nation* (which I hope you have got more from than I did) and a book of Kipling's poems. I would have sent them before, but I didn't. That is about all the excuse I have to make, and I think it is a pretty good one.—In German we have begun Freytag's *Soll und Haben* (*Debit and Credit*) and I find it pretty stiff reading. It is a great novel, though, and there is some satisfaction in knowing it. When a man knows he is reading a masterpiece he can go to work with better courage. If you ever feel that you would like to amuse yourself with a French or German novel let me know and I will get you anything you want at a very low price. They are all bound in paper and range from thirty to ninety cents a volume —according to the edition.

Well, I think the best thing for me to do will be to stop and go to bed. Tomorrow morning I have Fine Arts and French.

The contrast between Norton and Brun is painful, but I have to stand it.

I did not get a chance to write to you Sunday, nor yesterday; but I sent the *Nation* together with some *Crimsons*, which you have probably received and digested by this time. The *Crimson* is probably more or less interesting to anyone who has ever been inside of a college, so if you care for them I will stuff in two or three with each *Nation*. I did not get your letter this morning, but considering the fact that I had not even written one to you, I did not feel much like "kicking." I think I shall have to be a little more regular in my correspondence; when I let it go over Sunday, it is a doubtful affair.

Julia Marlowe is here again, and I went last night to see her in *Twelfth Night*. ("Last evening" would be a little more elegant and euphonious, but we will let it go). I do not [know] what there is about her, but I should like to go every night of her engagement. There is something "unprofessional" in her acting that is refreshing. She is best as Rosalind, and will play that part next week, I think. Sir Toby and Sir Andrew had their midnight drunk over again and sang, together with Maria and the Fool, "Which is the properest day to drink, Saturday, Sunday, Monday? Each is the properest day, I think, Why do you mention one day? etc." Shakspere didn't write the song, but it is a good one for all that. Taber made a good Malvolio, but not as good as Hanford's last year. Shall go Saturday evening and see *Much Ado About Nothing*, if my money holds out.

I have some pleasant news to tell you, if you do not know it already. I saw in the London *Athenaeum* that R. Kipling has a new book of prose tales in [the] press entitled *Many Intentions*. [sic]. The title is not particularly attractive, but you can tell about as much from his names as from John Ruskin's. I am glad that the book of poems I sent pleased you, but there are some omissions, as I said, which detract a great deal from its value.

You have probably discovered before this [that] the best things in the book are in the department entitled "Barrack Room Ballads." "Tommy," "Danny Deever," "Gunga Din," and "Mandalay" could not be improved much, in their line. I think that "Mandalay," after about 47 readings, appeals to one's humanity as well as to one's ear. Surely, nothing could be more musical. There is also a twist in "Route Marchin'" that fetches me, about the "regiment acomin' down the Grand Trunk Road, etc." I am [afraid] that the "Envoi" is not in the collection I sent you. Neither is the "Ballad of East and West" or "Bolivar"—"Seven men from all the world, back to docks again."

I do not know where this German composition will bring me to. That is the devil of the language courses here. The translation is taken as a matter of course and no particular credit is given for it. I suppose this is what one may look for in high class instruction but I have not been used to that kind. French composition is not so bad, though God knows that is bad enough. Did you have much of this business at Bowdoin? If you did, you can sympathize with me. You have probably had enough of it in Latin and Greek, anyway. I had about four weeks of Latin composition with Theodate Smith and then it stopped. That was in Jones' reader and decidedly elementary, but the red ink was in abundance, just as it is today in my German. We are translating fairy tales into German. Have Comp. twice a week and translation four times, so you see that I am rather fortunate, if the work is a trifle hard. The only time I really kick is when we have four or six pages of *Soll und Haben* to read between 4.30 Thursday and 10.00 a. m. Friday. It makes my optics ache to read the stuff by lamplight and I breathe a long sigh of relief and smoke a big pipe when it is over.

As you will see, or have seen, I started in to do a particularly [good] job (for *me*) in the way of penmanship, but I soon slouched back into my own peculiar way. I do not know how much you read of what I write, but I trust you are able to make something of it—that is, when there is anything.

To quote from you, it is now the witching hour of eleven P.M. and I will try to write you a little something before going to bed. I have been hammering away at French and loafing all the evening, by turns. (Another one of my loose sentences, but please excuse it).

I sent you a *Nation* and some *Crimsons* this morning. I must confess that I am sorry that I ever subscribed for that paper. It is a kind of feeble imitation of the English reviews, and the pedantry of its book-reviews is amusing rather than entertaining. The *Athenaeum* would have been far better, and the Specker, or *Spectator*, better still. Of course the political part of the *Nation* is all well enough, but the party spirit runs too high—if possible, worse than the Boston *Journal*. The J. is getting to be a creditable rival to the *Globe*, and is rather a sad spectacle upon the whole. The Boston daily papers are decidedly second-class. I wonder why it is? Irishmen?

I am reading About's *La Mère de la Marquise* and find it rather dull. I am coming home on the 5th or 6th of April and during my stay shall read Balzac's *Eugénie Grandet*, which I suppose is one of the world's great novels. I am totally ignorant of Balzac, which is hardly a good thing for a man to say in these days. This summer I intend to fill up some gaps in my reading. By the way, it may interest you to know that I have bought a full set of Lowell's writings—prose and poetry, including the *Later Literary Essays* and the *Old English Dramatists*. If you have any leisure through the summer months we can have several symposii (?) and good ones too. Have you seen Thomas Hardy's *Pursuit of the Well-Beloved?* I am told it is quite a thing—rather fatalistic and decidedly human—perhaps too much so for the Harpers to publish. Blackmore's *Perlycross* and Black's *Wolfenberg* are also interesting to anticipate.

Well, you must excuse me this time. I am about ready to turn in, so will close. I hope you will come tomorrow.

I sent you the *Nation* and some *Crimsons* Saturday which you have by this time, no doubt. In the *Nation* you will find a rather interesting piece on Taine. There is a description of the new private dormitory in one of the *Crimsons,* and perhaps some other matter more or less interesting to you.—I am sorry to hear that you have given up the idea of taking your A.M. Are you sure you are not making the greatest mistake of your life? The work is of so definite a nature (I think you said it was translation) and the reward so large, that I hope you will reconsider the matter. I do not think you realize how easily you are getting, or have been on the way to get it.—It takes a year of mighty hard work here to do it—and more than that, one must get A's and B's.—But then, I do not wish to get you disgusted with me, and I am probably talking of matters that I know nothing about. As to your health, of course that is another matter, but if I [had] the thing two-thirds done I should hate like the devil to give it up. I should be tempted to throw up the school first—for the rest of · the year. But that might be inconvenient, so I will shut up, and simply hope that you get the degree in some way. I am glad that you have the new school, though of course wish it was of a different grade; but then, what difference does it make? The money is the main thing until we get where we want to be, if we ever do. I gave up that idea long ago; and upon the whole, I do not think I ever knew where I wanted to be.

This forenoon the morning was glorious, and I took a walk out by Longfellow's House to Elmwood. Now it is snowing and until a few minutes ago was dark and gray. Now it is sunny, but the snow keeps on falling. It looks most like a flight of ants in September or whenever they fly. Sometime about then—you've seen 'em.

Shall be home in two weeks. Will you be there then?

I was intending to stay in my room last evening and write letters, but I was cajoled into going to town to hear Lilian Russell in *Giroflé-Girofla*. I suppose it was a very good thing in the way of comic opera, but I have come to the conclusion that I do not care much for that kind of celebration—for it always seems to me to be celebration of some kind. This was a particularly spectacular affair and Lilian sang in the punch scene with great gusto. There is so much going on now in the way of entertainments that I am a little dizzy. I want to see Willard and the Daly's—the Hasty Pudding Burlesque and the Italian opera week after next. I also have a thesis to write which must be done in two weeks.

I have just done up two *Nations* for you, which, I trust, will make your heart glad. I cannot understand why it is that America cannot publish a decent review. I read the Specker yesterday morning and it made me feel sorry for my country.

Have you ever read Molière's *L'Avare?* If you haven't, I will send it to you. It is easy and it is magnificent. No one seems to be able to write anything nowadays in the way of a comedy that is worth reading—hardly worth acting.—I have heard considerable lately about a new English novel—two, in fact—*Ships that Pass in the Night,* by Beatrice Somebody, and *The Heavenly Twins.* The last named deals with sexual questions, and [is] called rather effective. Something after the manner of Zola, with a more direct moral purpose.

I haven't seen anything of Kipling's new book yet. Have you? I do not even know if it is on sale, though I presume that it is. It has always seemed to me that Kipling could do something much greater than anything he has yet done, if he set himself to work in good earnest. *The Light that Failed* was something above the ordinary novel, and I should like to see him try it again.

Prof. Henry Drummond preaches in the chapel this evening, and I shall try to hear him. Have you ever read his *Natural Law in the Spiritual World?* I never have, but mean to soon. Just as I mean to read a good many other things.

Cambridge
May 2, 1893

I hope you have not come to the conclusion that I have gone back on you, for that is hardly the case. I have at last shaken off that thesis and the French essay and as soon as I get some French and German composition copied—six or seven hours work —I shall begin to feel like a free man. We have finished *Soll und Haben* and are reading *Wilhelm Tell*. The novel of Freytag's is horribly hashed and practically spoiled in the abridgement, and it is quite evident that the man, or woman most likely, in the *Critic* did not take the trouble to look it over. I like Schiller first rate. Have been reading Victor Hugo's *Hernané*, or rather have been hearing Sumichrast read it—and it is a great thing in the way of romantic drama. These things are about all I have read excepting the books dealing with my thesis and Balzac's *Eugénie Grandet*. I believe that has the reputation of being the only novel he ever wrote that would not make a horse blush. I believe Zola used that expression once, at any rate, it is not original with me.

Oh, I forgot to mention Thomas Hardy's *Group of Noble Dames.* These stories are decidedly good. If you have never read them I will send you the book. I ask you this, for I know how disappointing it is to find a book in the office and open it to be disappointed. If you want it you may have it.—There is a book of some kind for graduate students to be published this summer by Harvard, Columbia, and Johns Hopkins. You may have seen something of it. I think it is mentioned in one of the *Nations* I send with this, but am not sure of it. Now I think of another book I have read—Alexander Kielland's *Tales of Two Countries*—translated from the Norwegian by W. Archer for the Odd Number Series. They are damned suggestive,—not vicious, but rather dark in their coloring. A good many plain truths are sent home, and it is hard to decide whether one is better or worse for reading things like "Withered Leaves," "A Good Conscience," "Romance and Reality," etc. For they are unquestionably the work of a great writer, and told in a masterly way. Excuse the slovenly rhetoric and, for all I know, grammar, in this, as I am in a great hurry. Took this time to make sure of it—but did not take quite enough. Yours came this morning.

1716 Cambridge St.
May 7, 1893

I am straightened out again at last and will try to write something that will be at least rational, though I have nothing of importance to say. I was going to put it "communicate," but I was afraid you might overlook a very mild joke and lose your good opinion of me.

I have spent the past day or two in reading George Meredith's *Diana of the Crossways.* There is a good deal of Meredith in it, but it is decidedly worth reading. Full of philosophy and sharp sayings, but rather heavy upon the whole for a novel. It might be called a "study" and come nearer to the truth. Here are a few sentences from it as I remember them:

"An empty house is colder than out of doors." "The debts we owe ourselves are the hardest to pay."—I have the ideas of dozens more, but find I cannot quote them. You had better read the book and see what you think of it.

Last evening I put my foot in it to a certain extent. Latham is always growling about novel-reading, and asks me why I don't read the "American Statesmen." I have been trying all winter to get him to read *Tess,* but have failed. At last I told him if he would read it I would read Lodge's *Life of Alexander Hamilton.* He agreed, and I am rather glad that I did. I have no doubt it will do me good, though I must confess that I do not anticipate any great pleasure from my part of the bargain. I may be agreeably disappointed, however, and am generous enough to hope that I shall. Last fall I bought a cheap copy of Chateaubriand's *Atala* and have neglected reading it until today. This forenoon

I took it up and read it at one sitting. It is very easy and more than interesting. I will send it to you after reading the other pieces printed with it. When the masterpieces of the world's literature only occupy a hundred small pages, there is no great excuse for letting them pass unread. It is hard to believe that such a bold subject can be handled with such delicacy. The girl dies for want of something she comes dangerously near getting. But then, you must know the story—and will see at once that the above sentence is brutal—not to say cruel.

I commenced this letter yesterday but was interrupted when half through so you will get it a day late. It is now Monday morning and I am feeling pretty rocky on account of the siege I went through last evening. Saben and Crapo struck an argument at 7.00 P.M. and kept it up until 12.00. I began to get crazy about that time and drove them both out. I do not know that I ever passed through the mental suffering in my life that I did during those five hours. I was a fool to stand it as long as I did, but one of the men was a comparative stranger to me and I felt a little delicate. But I have now come to the conclusion that courtesy does not demand any such a sacrifice and I shall not be so squeamish another time. I didn't sleep any to amount to anything and am about played out today. I cut *Wilhelm Tell* and must go to work now to make it up. After that I must read on Hume and in the evening go to a lecture on Wordsworth and write a German composition. The afternoon is taken up in college exercises, so you see it is a busy day for me—especially if I crowd in an hour or two of *Kenelm Chillingly* and write two more letters.

Well, I shall stop now and see what my tired and if I may say it, outraged brain can do with German blank verse. The morning is fine and there is a handorgan playing "The Irish Washerwoman" somewhere in the distance. I think I should like to have him grind under my window for about three quarters of an hour. I could let the German go to the devil willingly.

Shall look for your letter tomorrow. Send a bundle of paper and Mr. Bolle's pamphlet.

Cambridge
May 14, 1893

I am glad to hear that you think of coming this way. I shall be very glad to meet you next Saturday if you will kindly tell me what wharf or station I am to go find you. I think it would do me good in more ways than one to have you here for a time, and I have no doubt you could enjoy yourself. There are pretty fair attractions at the theatres now and we have our tongues. There is good tobacco in Boston and beverage, if you want it, of many kinds and colors. The last thing I drank was a pint of claret; it made me sick but I shall doubtless drink more of it before I go home. I do not care anything about the stuff, but there is a kind of pleasure in sitting at a table with a friend with something in front of you. I know we could pass a glorious afternoon or the latter part of one in some such place and finish up with *Shore Acres* or *The Ticket of Leave Man,* and not feel that we had broken any moral laws. I do not care to break any moral laws myself and see no necessity for it; but then, I won't try to speak for people at large. At any rate, you come up and I do not think you will have any cause to regret it. If it rains all the time, there will be nothing lost except the fact that the college yard will not look at its best. I should like you to see it on a sunny morning, but you can doubtless supply the sun to some extent if the weather proves bad. I mention this to let you feel perfectly safe in starting away in the rain, if rain comes at that time. Personally, I rather hope it will rain part of the time you are here—I want you to realize what our Cambridge sidewalks are in wet weather.

I have just finished Bulwer's *Kenelm Chillingly* and have found it rather entertaining. There is a good deal of "E.L.B.L." in it, but not as much as in some—*The Disowned,* for example. It is intended to be a perfectly wholesome book, and it is if the reader can forgive the occasional bursts of Bulweresque rant that characterizes all the author ever wrote. Unless circumstances force me to it, I do not think I shall ever read another one of his novels. It is not worth while. Every one ought to read *The Last Days of Pompeii* and *What Will He Do with It?* and one or two others, but beyond that, Bulwer is unnecessary—except for his plays.

Cambridge
May 20, 1893

I have not yet got over my grouch on account of your not being able to come. Saturday was a magnificent day and I am sure you would have enjoyed yourself. But there is no use growling, I suppose. I hope, though, that you will try to come up next Friday or at least sometime before I leave.

It is pretty hot this forenoon and I am feeling rather dull. If you were here I fancy we would both be smoking pipes or something else, and trying to keep cool and in peace with the world in general. I drank a pint of Ulumm last evening before going to the theatre and it knocked my stomach out. I find the less of anything I drink in that line, the better I feel. I had been making plans to go to the theatre with you Saturday evening, so I will send you a programme with another big bundle of *Crimsons* and *Nations*. The play did not amount to very much, though it was above the average.

It was enough to do a man's soul good to sit in the Common or Public Gardens yesterday afternoon. It would be hard to imagine anything more pleasant. I had an engagement at four, but went in early to have a smoke and watch the people. People are rather interesting after all, if you don't have to talk with them.

Did I tell you that I went into Schoenhof's not long ago and spent the afternoon there? It was a rainy day and I drifted in to look over the French and German books intending to buy one or two to take the "cuss" off. I met a congenial soul and also many volumes that took my eye, and ended up by ordering fourteen dollars worth of stuff of various sorts—including much of

Coppée, Beaumarchais, a copy of *Faust*, Voltaire's romances, and some stray novels and plays. I managed to curb myself and refrain from buying a magnificent two-volume edition of Freytag's *Lost Manuscript* and Heyse's *In Paradise*—in German. I suppose I shall have to get them before the year is over, but if my eyes keep on as they are now, I shall have [a] hard time reading them.

Now make it a plan to come up here sometime during the next month. If you once get yourself started I know you will always be glad. I do not mean this as an intimation that you might have come this week—you must have had some good reason which I trust will not occur again.

Cambridge
June 4, 1893

You have probably, for something like the twentieth time, come to the conclusion that I am a rather uncertain correspondent, and I have no good excuse to make this time, either. I could not write last Sunday, but I might have Monday or Tuesday. I did not, however, and then thought I might as well let it go until today. It is a pretty tough job writing now on account of the heat, but I will put it through as I know you will rather look for a letter on Tuesday. I like letter writing on general principles, but sometimes the performance is hard. You know that of course and will not lay up any hard feelings against me for my negligence.

The chief thing I have to say to you today is concerning your coming to Cambridge. The Yale Harvard Game comes off the 22'd. Can't you arrange it to come up somewhere on the 20th and go back with me? We could have a great time here together for a few days at a small expense. The "pop" concerts are in full blast with music and beer galore. Or anything else you like— light opera or a good cigar on the common. I would not urge [you] so much were I not sure that you would be glad you came. Just get started once, and you will see that I am right for once in my life.

Today is hot and rather muggy but the Lord thought to add

a good breeze. Were it not for that, the day would be unbearable. It is doubly unwelcome as I have an examination (final) in German tomorrow forenoon and I find it positively impossible to prepare for it today. All I can do is lie around and cuss. It is too hot to smoke. Cigarettes would go. I have become so disgusted with them that I can hardly tolerate them. The more of them I smoke, the less I like them. For which I am duly thankful.

About half an hour ago I drifted into Butler's room (next to mine) and he was counting over dining-hall checks. He had a bunch of twenty 5's, good for a nickel at the Hall, and I proposed matching coppers for them. By a curious run of luck I won them all in less than fifteen minutes. All of which was very wrong, but pardonable on account of the temperature of the day. Such mild viciousness must be overlooked by the powers that run the mercury up to 98° when a man wants to read German. And besides, I have the checks, which will come in handy at the Hall tonight.

I have not read much of anything lately except work bearing upon Fine Arts. I forget most of it—especially Greek History. I wish I could remember things of some account, but it seems to be impossible. Well, I have written four or five pages without saying much of anything—except the invitation (which I hope you will consider seriously) and will stop right here.

Will send another wad of papers tomorrow.

Cambridge
June 11, 1893

Here it is Sunday morning again, and hot enough to roast heretics. There is no such thing as comfort on such days, and as for writing letters—well, you know a man can do almost anything if he sets his mind upon it. I know that if I do not write today, the probabilities are that I shall let it go until Wednesday or Thursday; and as for waiting until this afternoon—I have done that before. This afternoon it will be so hot that I shall simply sit in the darkest place I can find and be miserable until a change comes, which will probably be somewhere about 3.00 A.M.

I have two more examinations yet to take, French and English, and then my Harvard career will be at an end. I have no particular desire to come another year, but I would hate to part with the experience of the past two. I have lived, upon the whole, a very quiet life, but for all that I have seen things that I could not possibly see at any other place, and have a different conception of what is good and bad in life. From the standpoint of marks, my course here has been a failure, as I knew well enough it would be; but that is the last thing in the world I came here for. Grinding for marks does not command my admiration except in case of pecuniary necessity. Under those conditions, it often borders on the heroic. You have no idea of what some men go through here, unless that little book on "Students' Expenses" worked upon your imagination to a considerable extent.

I shall look for a letter from you tomorrow or Tuesday telling me whether you intend to come this way or not. If you are sure that you are not, I may come home before Class-day, but would rather not.

Cambridge
June 21, 1893

Well, I have about come to the "end of things," as the old man says in the "Children of the Zodiac" (which is the best thing I have ever seen by Kipling). It is in his *Many Inventions*. I have read most of the stories but have a few left. You have doubtless read them all, provided you have the book. It has been floating around here for two or three weeks, I think, but I have hardly heard it mentioned, and have never read a review of it. It is a little more mature, perhaps, than *Life's Handicap,* but does not show up as well on the whole. "The Record of Badalia Herodsfoot" seems to me the best thing in it next to the "Children."

I went into Schoenhof's yesterday and bought some more books. The list may interest you:

Der Verlorene Handschrift—Freytag. 2 vols. (A gift).
Im Paradise—Heyse (2 vols.)

Contes Choisis—Daudet   bound
    "   "   —Mendes   "
Madame Bovary—Flaubert   paper
Manon Lescaut—Prévost   "
La Capitaine Fracasse—Gautier (2 vols.) paper

During the past three weeks I have spent over twenty-five dollars for foreign books and have about come to the conclusion that it is time to stop. The books themselves are bad enough, but when I go in for fancy bindings or at least respectable ones (not the kind you saw last summer) it makes culture too much of a good thing. A man is pardonable, however, for almost anything he does while in Schoenhof's. It is the most fascinating place I ever struck and you are used so well that you wonder [where] the difference comes in between foreign and American shop keepers. There is a difference, though I cannot tell just what it is.

I shall probably come home next Monday. It is so devilish hot up here now that I doubt if you would care much to come. You see I am very honest. Of course I should be marvelously glad to see you, but cannot speak with the surety of your enjoying yourself that I could before the hot weather set in in dead earnest. It simply "knocks me out" and I do not go out of my room unless compelled to. With the blinds closed and the windows open, one can live, and that is about all.

If you can come up and stay over Sunday and go back with me, then do so if you are willing to run the risk of a cool day. If it proves hot, all we can do is keep still and talk or swear. I shall be a good deal stirred up in packing but that will not take all the time. I want you to enjoy yourself if you come, but am not quite sure that you will if you come now. This accounts for any apparent coolness in this invitation. I haven't enough confidence in my abilities as a host, to feel sure of conquering hot weather. That's all.

I suppose this is the last letter I shall ever write you from Harvard. The thought seems a little queer, but it cannot be otherwise. Sometimes I try to imagine the state my mind would be in had I never come here, but I cannot. I feel that I have got comparatively little from my two years, but still, more than I could get in Gardiner if I lived a century. I am looking forward to some Sundays like those of last summer. If you are not at home through the hot weather I don't know what I shall do with myself. When a man sets himself down to it he can generally count the friends of his native town upon the fingers of one hand, and then have digits to spare. At least, I can.

∗
∗ ∗
∗ III ∗
∗ ∗

TOWN OF BANISHMENT
(October 1, 1893 ~ November 1, 1897)

You are probably getting a little impatient by this time, but I have made a "big brace" at last and am going to write you a letter, or something that will take the place of one. My room is too cold for a free flow of thought, and I may get discouraged at the end of the first page; but my inclinations are all right, and with a little effort of imagination you will be able to fill in as many more pages as you like.

I have nothing in particular to say except that it is rather lonesome here without you, and on dark, dull Sundays like this I find it [hard] to be cheerful and optimistic, and everything else that a useful man should be in order to fill his place in nature to the satisfaction of himself and his dear friends who feel so much for his welfare. I am half afraid that my "dear friends" here in Gardiner will be disappointed in me if I do not do something before long, but somehow I don't care half as much about the matter as I ought. One of my greatest misfortunes is the total inability to admire the so called successful men who are pointed out to poor devils like me as examples for me to follow and revere. If Merchant A and Barrister B are put here as "ensamples to mortals," I am afraid that I shall always stand in the shadow as one of Omar's broken pots. I suspect that I am pretty much what I am, and that I am pretty much a damned fool in many ways; but I further suspect that I am not altogether an ass, whatever my neighbors may say. I may live to see this egotistic idea exploded, but until that time comes I am to hug my own particular phantoms and think as I like. If I turn out a failure after all, and go hopelessly to the devil, I shall have Aldrich's lines to console myself with:

"Then if at last thine airy structure fall,
Dissolve, and vanish, take thyself no blame:
They fail, and they alone, who have not striven."

For I am going to strive, and strive hard this winter. My eyes
are a little better, and I am pretty well convinced that I shall be
able to work three or four hours a day without injuring them any.
I know from experience that five hours of the kind of work I
mean is all, if not more than I can stand. I can work ten hours
with my arms and legs if the occasion requires it, but not with
my fancy—I will not yet presume to give it the title of imagination. Fancy and imagination brings to my mind the "hell" sonnet
that you wanted me to copy. I will enclose it with this letter if
I do not forget it. My fancy gets a little lively in those fourteen
lines. I have never been quite able to know what to make of
them. They may be nothing but rot—they surely are if the reader
can make nothing of them—but I have always cherished the idea
that there is a thought mixed up in them that is worth the
trouble of the thinking. Saben's over-friendly statement that the
thing is a "great poem" doesn't affect my opinions much, as his
enthusiasm is liable to run away with him when it has a chance
—especially in matters where his friends are concerned. He is a
magnificent fellow with all his peculiarities, but not just the one
I should go to for an impartial criticism. I do not think it possible
for a friend to criticise another's work, without being influenced
in his favor to some extent. I hate self-praise, or much of it, but
it really seems to me that I have brought out the idea of the occasional realization of the questionable supremacy of ourselves
over those we most despise in a moderately new way. If there
is a little poetry in it, then all the better. There is poetry in all
types of humanity—even in lawyers and horse-jockeys—if we are
willing to search it out; and I have tried to find a little for the
poor fellows in my hell, which is an exceedingly worldly and
transitory one, before they soar above me in my ignorance of
what is, to sing in the sun—not in triumph over me, but in the

glad truth that destiny has worked out for them. I will state here that the verses in question must be taken as rather vague generalities: they will not bear, and I never intended them to bear, any definite analysis. To me they suggest a single and quite clear thought; if they do as much to you and to any other person who has seen them, I am satisfied.

Excuse this flourish of trumpets and let me have a smoke. I wish you were [here] to have it with me, but as you are not, I shall try to make the best of it as it is. You may smell the tobacco from where you are; it is bad, but it burns.

[P. S.] I called at your home some time ago—about a week. Your father and mother were hardly reconciled to your absence and the place seemed strange. When you come home again we will have sessions.

[Enclosed with the letter of October 1, 1893.]

SUPREMACY.

There is a drear and lonely tract of hell
From all the common gloom removed afar:
A flat sad land where only shadows are,
Whose lorn estate no word of mine can tell.
I walked among the shades, and knew them well—
Men I had scorned upon life's little star
For churls and sluggards,—and I knew the scar
Upon their brows of woe ineffable.

But, as I moved triumphant on my way,
Into the dark they vanished, one by one;
Then came an awful light—a blinding ray—
As if a new creation were begun:
And with a swift importunate dismay
I heard the dead men singing in the sun.

[Signed] E. A. Robinson

A Book of Verses underneath the Bough,
A roaring Blaze, an Ear of Corn, and thou
Beside me smoking in the Wilderness,
Oh, Wilderness were Paradise enow!

It is a warm and magnificent day after a long cold rain, and I naturally think of the spot where the ashes of our old fires, with a few shrivelled corn-husks, are all there is to tell of the many jolly symposiums we held there only a few weeks ago. It beats the devil how time creeps away with those skinny shanks of his. Before we know it, spring will be here again, and who knows but we shall spend the same sort of a summer together as the one just past? I know it is past, for the hornets have left the orchard and the big flies are come to take whatever of summer there may be left in the dried pears and apples. "The bee has quit the clover" long since, and we shall not see any more of him until another year. By the time five or six more of these years have left us, we ought to have some idea of what we are good for.

I am afraid that I had too much to say about myself in my last letter, and too much about that bogey sonnet of mine. At any rate, you know that it is not vanity on my part, so I am not so much concerned as I might be under different circumstances. There may be something to the thing, and there may not; I am sure I cannot tell. Schumann has written a "Ballade of the Law," with the refrain,

"He sells his soul for a paltry fee."

It is a very good thing, though perhaps a little strong in places. I will send you a copy of it next week. He has another on doctors, "This marvellous medical man," which I do not think anything like as good as the other, though he professes to prefer it. One cannot tell much by what the Doc says about things, however, so I have many doubts as to his opinions on anything. I know he likes Swinburne and Austin Dobson, and Schuman a little better than either—that is no more than human nature, I suppose. I am not saying anything against the doctor, for with all his faults, I like him, and know he has done me a great deal of good by the negative example his life and opinions have set for me, and by the direct influence of his almost finical precision in the use and pronunciation of words. He "stoops" occasionally, but he never forgets that he is speaking English. The thing has got to be almost a disease with him now, and if I by chance say "noozpaper" he goes for me with a figurative picked stick. I find it pretty hard to speak correctly in a town where man, woman, and child says "ain't" and "he don't," and sometimes I am more than half inclined to let the whole business go and become one of the multitude. Isn't it better after all to renounce the Muses (I mean the whole of them) for Mammon, and try to make a dollar? Sometimes I think it is, and have a great mind to do it. But there's the rub. I am perfectly helpless in what the world calls business, and you know just about what I think of the successful business man, as we call him. But I won't keep on drooling on this same old subject. It injures no one but myself, and that is a rather expensive amusement for a man in my position.

I suppose I shall have to write a "Ballade of Dead Mariners." The idea, with three or four others, has been chasing me for some time, and I know of but one way to get rid of them—write them out. Even that doesn't always do it, but one feels better after making a trial. Here is the "envoi" as it came to me of a sudden:

"Days follow days till years and years are fled;
Years follow years till hopes and cares are dead,
And life's hard billows boom their message home:
Love is the strongest where no words are said,
And women wait for ships that never come."

This is in the rough, and may be changed more or less. I never tried one in decasyllables before, but I think I shall like [it] as well as the popular eight-syllable form. The things may not be worth the trouble of the making, but there is a fascination about them that I cannot get over. Trusting I shall get a letter from you tomorrow, I am. . . .

Gardiner
October 22, 1893

It may please you to know that I am writing you this letter in the woods—to be more explicit, in "The Pines." Uncle Joe is here with me reading a book of Stockton's stories and everything is peaceful. I wish I were in your woods with you and a volume of verse or two, but I am pretty well fixed as it is, so ought not to growl, I suppose. You must excuse my writing if it is a trifle jerky as my desk is a "geography book" on my knee. My pen doesn't go very well, but I think you will be able to make out what I say with a little labor. It will be a good change from your regular routine work.

I didn't write you last week, for which I trust you have pardoned me. I had considerable to contend with, and hardly found time to do anything. Will explain more fully to you sometime. The fates have stirred me up considerably during the past fifteen years, and sometimes I fall to wondering how much I am to blame for my failure thus far in life. Perhaps I am wholly to blame, but I do not like to think so. If this is cowardice, then I am a born coward and shall never be anything else. I never posed for a hero, so I do not feel as many qualms as I might otherwise.—You may not like it, but it really seems to me that you are taking things a little too hard. I would not say this, but when you speak of other men reaping in the world's goods in a tone that implies that you are not, I wonder if you stop to consider your age and the salary you are getting and compare it with that of the majority of men of your years. Mind you, I am speaking wholly of worldly goods now, and do not include intellectual advancement. You are dissatisfied, as any man in your place would be provided he had a brain; but from the mere standpoint of money, I think you are far ahead of most fellows whose homes are not over-feathered. Mine is bared now to an extent that worries me, in spite of what you said to me one day by the fire.

I intend to get down to work as soon as the "chores" around the house are done and then I shall try to find what is in me. My work will go into the oven before long and as I think of it I repeat to myself the lines from the potter's song in Longfellow's "Kéramos"—

> "Tomorrow the hot furnace-flame
> Will search the heart and try the frame,
> And stamp with honor or with shame
> These vessels made of clay."

If mine are stamped with honor, generally speaking, I shall not be altogether surprised, nor shall I be if the opposite lot comes to them. It is all in the future, and it is best that it is so. I am thankful that I cannot see a life of failure before me. When I picture it to myself there is a dim vision of something else that renders it impossible for me to wholly give up the fight. I half feel that I have a Palladium somewhere that sends a "ruling effluence" upon my life, and though the waves of fight seem just now to be rolling against me I have not yet fallen—at least I tell myself so, and feel encouraged.

There are better things before you than you know. I say this as an observer. The tremendous change that has come over you during the past four years can only point in one direction, and that is—success in higher things. I am not say[ing] this to make you feel encouraged, but because I fully believe it. If I am wrong, I shall be glad to have known a man of whom I could think such things. You and Tryon are going to make something and I want you to meet each other. So do not let anything get between you and the proposed trip to Boston. We can make something like an epoch of it if we go to work in the right way.

I received a long letter from Saben yesterday in which he tells me that he has given up for good his idea of taking a course in divinity at Harvard. He thinks his past life and reputation there would render it impossible for such a course to be taken seriously by either the students or the faculty. The old man has changed his mind [and] is going to Oxford. I hope he will carry this idea out, as he is unquestionably gifted with a fine intellect. He is not very well balanced, but that is not to be laid at his door. He is as he was made, and sometimes I think a little more so.

Joe is making frequent interruptions and his cheerful profanity doesn't at all jar upon the stillness of the day or upon the distant sound of bells that are summoning poor devils like you and me to divine worship. He maintains that it is a hell of a day and that he is thinking of you every hour. He sends you his love, and asks certain questions that do not seem just fitted for a letter of this kind. I will not write them, but leave you to imagine them for yourself.

Did you know that Gledhill was married? Well, he is and is Professor of Mathematics in some New York institution. "Professor" sounds rather large, but as I do not know any more about the matter, I can make no comments. All I know is that Gledhill is a good fellow, and I wish him all success.—I intend to smoke a pipe now and then write two more letters before going home— one to Tryon and one to Gledhill. You may not be able to read this but at any rate, it will show you that I have written. I hope you will excuse my carelessness in punctuation and grammar, as it is next to impossible for me to write good English under the present circumstances. The forest is a fine place to write a thing in the rough, that is, anything that is to be copied; but when it comes to a letter, you must look for a style that is easily colloquial if not slipshod.—Good-bye, and come down next Sunday if possible.

Gardiner
November 5, 1893

Here it is Sunday again, and time for me to write you according to agreement. It doesn't seem a week ago that you were here, but the calendar says that it is. Before long we shall be walking the streets of Boston if nothing happens. I am looking forward to that dinner at Young's, or wherever we choose, with more enthusiasm than I have felt over anything for a long time. I want to see men that I can talk with once more. I want to get out of Gardiner for a time, and with God's help I am going to if I can. I see nothing now to prevent [it] and shall try not to borrow any uneasiness. Be sure and find out what time your train arrives and at what station. We will have a breakfast at Parker's and then a good stroll over the city. I intend to go up about the first of Thanksgiving week and stay about ten days. I may change my mind though and do nothing of the kind.

I suppose that you are back in your old rut again and are moderately contented with the present state of things—that is, as far as what we call the present itself is concerned. I cannot say as much. This eternal doubt as to how things are coming out, keeps me in a perpetual state of discontent. The worst of it is a certain guilty feeling that I am not producing anything. I am neither benefiting myself or anyone else. I am making no money wherewith to buy the world's goods and I have no settled occupation to keep my conscience clean. I am fixing up my room now and it will soon be ready to go into. The improvements are chiefly a radiator and a bookcase. When it is all settled it will not be the worst place to sit and work in. But there the old question comes up—what is my work going to amount to? I think I have a little originality, but have I the genius for selection that is the one requisite of a literary man next to an easy flow of language?—Not necessarily rapid, but easy in effect. I could never make a rapid writer; I am too fussy. I have fiddled too much over sonnets and ballades. I demand a certain something in the arrangement of words, and more in their selection, that I find in very few of our writers today. The question is—will it be found in what I write? and if it is, will the public care anything about it? I do not wholly believe in art for art's sake, but I do not think that anything is good literature when art is wholly sacrificed to the subject matter. Well, Atwood has just called and I'll draw this to a close. Shall look for a letter tomorrow.

Gardiner
November 11, 1893

Don't write so damned coarse. Do me this kindness, and humor me. It takes away about half the interest from one of your letters to have it spread over six times the paper it calls for. I do not mean to give offense, but I am truly in earnest. It is pleasant to know that you are good natured, but can't you make a footnote of the fact, when you do not feel sure that the letter itself shows the state of your mind?

I sent you the "Ballades" after some delay, and you doubtless have them before this. I must ask you to be as careful as possible of the book, for I think a great deal of it. It has followed me for three years, and has become one of those things without any particular price—of no value except to the owner. It cost me thirty-five cents, but it would take dollars to buy it. You may think I am a fool, and if so, I shall not attempt to deny it. You have no idea how much associations are to me. Some little thing, almost ridiculous in itself, acquires a value in my eyes that sometimes makes me ashamed of myself. But then, we all have our peculiarities and that is one of mine. I rather think you can appreciate it enough not to write me down an ass.

This would be a fine day for a session at your place, but you do not seem to be at hand. So I live in the expectations of Thanksgiving and our dinner. Throwing out leaving Harvard, this trip, if we make it, will be the event of this year for me. I am like a child in some respects, and am glad of it. I only wish that I could be more like one sometimes. Victor Cherbuliez, in that remarkable novel of his, *Jean Têterol's Idea,* says "the first duty of youth is to be young." Crawford says the same thing in *Sant'-Ilario,* some years after. If you have never read any of Cherbuliez you have a great time before you. He is altogether [apart] from any writer I know and yet he is so true to life that he startles one at times. If I ever get able to read again, I shall make up for lost time, but do not think I shall ever do anything more with German. I hate to drop it, but there are other things in the world; and it is better to have those without the German than not to have either, as would probably be the case if I put much time upon it.

Tryon sent me two theses last week on the "Journalism of Events" and "A Journalism of Life." They are part of his Philosophy V work last year—Prof. Peabody's course in Ethics. He sends them to me for criticism, and places me in a rather delicate position. The matter is first class and he is continually saying good things; but his style smacks of the newspaper, as I knew it would. I shall give him my candid opinion on it, and it is a pleasure to know that it will be taken kindly. I fear I can criticise better than I can write, but I am going to wait and hear what the years say. I may end up as a clerk in a dry-goods store and acquire "ease of manner." That would be more of a transformation than I ever dreamed of. If I should turn out to be a society man, via a dry-goods establishment, how the Gardiner public would congratulate me on my coming out! They might think there was some hope for me then, and a prospect of a still better "job." Life is my job just at present, but it will be more interesting when I get settled down for the winter. I have done great work in forestry this fall and have now arrived at the last stage—"blowing up" the butts. When they are sawed and split I shall consider myself free from a long but upon the whole rather pleasant piece of work. I have no doubt that I have made three times the work of it that was necessary, but I have done it sympathetically—with a poet's eye, fine frenzy and all. There is poetry in reducing a sprawling apple limb but Joe cannot see it. I doubt some if you could, though you might.

Gledhill sent me a picture of his wife the other day. She is not pretty—I cannot call her handsome; but G. writes that I cannot see her mind, and so cannot form much of an opinion. There is a case of your "mixing up of souls," I expect, that is worth considering. If she is all he thinks she is, they will be tremendously happy. But when the kid comes I am half afraid that Art will feel so hopelessly jubilant that he will have to get drunk. I hope not, though, as a wife sometimes fails to appreciate such emphasis. I am pretty sure that it would go hard with me, were I a woman—that is, if it got to be anything like a periodical affair.

I think I have written enough to bother you for a good half hour, so will stop. If my letters are hard to read, they at least afford a change of occupation. Don't send me any more of that big, bellying chirography of yours, but write as you used to before the devil put this last crotchet into your head. Believe me, it takes all the character out of a letter, no matter what you say. More than that, it leads you into the self-deceit that you are writing a letter of respectable length, when you are not. Find out about your train and get your stomach in order for the 30th.

Gardiner
November 19, 1893

If there is one thing in the world that I intend to do more than another, that is to mind my own business; but I must ask you to reconsider your scheme of making the coming trip to Boston by boat. By so doing you will not only lose the whole of Thanksgiving Day and probably the evening, but run a good chance of spoiling yourself for Friday. I can only judge by myself, of course, but if you have never taken an all-night trip in a steamboat, I wish for your sake and mine that you would not try it now. The loss of a day in town is what troubles me. With only Friday and Saturday I do not think you would call it economy in the end. Sunday will be dull at the best, far duller than Gardiner without the woods or the apple-tree, and then would be the best time to economize, provided a boat leaves Boston Saturday night. But no, we want the Saturday night in town. Well, do as you think best, only remember that it may be a long time before we get together there again, and you may find ample opportunity to draw in the strings a little this winter to make up for the four or five dollars sacrificed to the M.C.R.R. I myself could save $3.50 by taking the boat, but would about as soon think of walking. I would suffer the whole trip and be used up the next day. I have done it three or four times and shall never do it again as long as there is a man or woman in the state of Maine that will lend me a dollar and seventy five cents.—I am making this trip in far more straightened circumstances than you realize, but still I expect to enjoy myself if my stomach holds out. When that goes back on me I am totally done up. About all the money I can see is spoken for in gifts that I owe. I suppose I shall end up by borrowing some of Butler or Barnard, with great hopes of paying it sometime.

George and Joe tell me that they had an advantageous sitting with you in Rockland last week. It probably seemed good to see some Gardiner faces once more, notwithstanding your indifference to the place. Speaking of that, I do not think I ever before realized what a hermit I am getting to be. Were it not for the B. brothers I should be absolutely with[out] intimate friends of my own age. This is considerable to say, but it is practically true. And the worst of it all is that the truth does not trouble me half as much as it ought. I know there are fellows somewhere who are congenial—that is a great deal. It is much more to me to be able to write a letter to you and know that it will be read with a friendly eye than to converse an hour with someone who is no more to me than are the majority of good fellows who make the world. The people who interest me are my close associates and the creatures of my own fancy. I have a dozen or so of the latter who have kept me company for a long time. Now I want to see them on paper, and if the fates are will[ing] I propose to before spring. Perhaps no one will see them save myself, but there will even then be the satisfaction of knowing that I have done something. But, woe is me! where are the shekels? This feeling of dependence is hell. You cannot imagine it if you try. I do not mind so much what other people think, but I cannot help wondering if I am not making an ass of myself. Two or three years at the most ought to tell something. If I then find that I have [been] laboring under a delusion for the past fifteen or sixteen years, it will not be too late to start out for an occupation and a living. It will be another case of a disappointed life, blasted hopes, and the usual accompaniments. Whatever I do outside of literature will be done as a task, pure and simple. Some of my friends seem to have confidence in me with nothing in the world to base it upon—that is, nothing in the line of writings. Where they get their opinions is a mystery to me and I am weak enough to let their words encourage me a little. I expect a grand collapse some day and then I wonder if they will all (!) stand by me?

It is time to have a smoke now, so will descend to the cellar and send strange odors up through the floors into the parlors. Mother objects and I shall probably quit soon and do my smoking in my den. If that stinks up the house I may stop the whole business.

Trusting you have decided by this time regarding the Boston affair, I await what you have to say with much interest.

[*Gardiner*
December, 1893]

Another week has gone somewhere and it is my turn to write you another letter. The house is so stirred up now that I find it difficult to do much writing in anything like an imaginative vein, though I peg away simply out of principle, doing perhaps from five hundred to twelve hundred words (first draft) every day. This does not mean much, for I have only written two of my sketches since reading "Marshall." They are each a trifle longer than that now, but after the revision (perhaps I had better say rewriting) they need, I fancy they will average about 4000 words —enough for a short story and too much for more than half [those] that are printed in our popular magazines.

I have been reading the *Biglow Papers* this forenoon and find myself coming to be more and more an admirer of the book. I have had an almost bitter prejudice against it all my life—on account of the dialect, I suppose, but the thing is so inordinately clever that one is compelled to praise it before he reads many pages. I do not know of anything more ridiculously satirical than the letters of "Birdofreedom Sawin." What could be more specific than this:

—"*Anglo Saxondom's idee's abreakin' 'em to pieces,*
An thet idee's thet every man doos jest wut he damn pleases."

"*How dreffle slick he reeled it uff.* . . .
About the Anglo-Saxon race (and saxons would be handy
To du the buryin' down here upon the Rio Grandy),
About our patriotic pa's an' our Star-spangled Banner,
Our country's bird alookin' on an' singin' out hosanner," etc.

"*It ain't disgraceful bein' beat, when a hull nation does it,*
But chance is like an amberill,—it don't take twice to lose it."

I suppose you will say this is a weak dodge to fill up paper, but that is not my intention.

I think I am suffering from "ennui" or something else. To live week after week without a soul to speak to on any congenial topic is hell for a man of my nature. But I won't pull this old string today. I am not feeling particularly "elegant," and want to [go] either to Rockland or to Boston—anywhere out of Gardiner. But then it would be all the worse when I got back so I'd better stay where I am and not growl too much. When the kids have left the house I may feel better, but I shall never be good for much until a part of this damned uncertainty is lifted. Work will either do one thing or the other, so work it is. I have taken much pleasure from the *Lyre Francaise* I borrowed of you some time ago. I am not quite ready for it, but for all that it is a welcome guest in my den.

I am glad to find myself deceived regarding my suspicion of "martyrdom" on your part, and shall look forward to the coming summer with renewed pleasure—that is if your geological frenzy does not crowd out everything else. I regret that I cannot join you in your pilgrimages but I told you how it is in my last letter. My will is good, and I hope you may acquire no end of knowledge of the boulders and brick-bats that sprinkle the iron-mine and its adjacent territory. I admire and envy your thirst for natural science but alas, my mind is constructed upon a plan that will not admit of such interests.

Yesterday I finished my sketch—the revision—called "Three Merry Gentlemen and their Wives." It is not a particularly cheerful thing but I cannot help having some faith in it. Tomorrow I shall commence a sketch which I have some fear of never bringing out to anything like satisfaction on my part. It deals with the selfishness of self-denial—a peculiar but by no means rare flaw of human nature, but perhaps a little beyond my poor abilities. I shall have the thing done by next Sunday, and can tell you more about it then. I am beginning to realize my artistic deficiencies, and can look ahead without many qualms to a hard apprenticeship. As it is, it takes me about a week to get out the first draft of a four thousand word sketch—so you see I do some work. Four hours a day is my limit at present, after that my head spins.

Yesterday afternoon I began to read Coppée's *Toute une Jeunesse*—a personal narrative modeled after *David Copperfield*. It begins magnificently and I look forward to much enjoyment from its pages—a little over 300. The book is published in English under the title of *Disillusions*. I am already much interested in the schoolmaster with the geographical cranium, and the artist with the Abd-el-Kadir pipe.

I have just smoked a long pipe myself, by the way, and my hand trembles a little on that account. Hence this more than usually bad chirography. I shall have my type-writer going pretty soon and then you may rejoice. I suppose my letters are pretty hard to decipher, and I thank you for your patience. Your handwriting is a miracle to me and quite beyond my comprehension. There is a firmness in it that will carry you through a good many tight places, if fate demands it.

I have a new employment now, which may interest you a little. Next week I shall begin to tutor a young lady in French preparatory to her entering Wellesley College. She has everything else, with a little brushing up, and hopes with what she knows of elementary French to take the maximum requirements and so get rid of the Freshman course in that language. Perhaps I have undertaken more than I can carry out, but I can make a giant bluff and trust in Providence. It will involve a review of Chardenal and the reading of five or six hundred pages of French prose before the middle of September, together with the reviewing on her part of Latin, Greek, Algebra, Arithmetic, Physical Geography, Ancient and American History and steady work on German and English. If she succeeds I shall be glad and at the same time feel rather small. Of course, the programme sounds larger than it really is but it represents a good deal of work for all that. The realization that I am going to be, at least going to try to be, of a little use in this world, makes me rejoice.

The foregoing statement may cause you to smile a little, and possibly feed your fancy a little too much. But you cannot wonder at my admiration of a girl who has the courage to enter the Freshman class of a college five years after graduating from the high school (Instinct prompts me to spell "high school" with small letters).

I am afraid I shall impose upon your good nature if I keep on writing much longer. I do not know that I have anything in particular to say except that I have been re-reading Matthew Arnold's *Culture and Anarchy*. The book is full of good things, but a little too much drawn out. That is Arnold's great fault in writing prose. His "mission" stopped his poetry and I have always regretted it.—A day or two ago I looked over Sir Thomas Browne's *Urn-burial,* and found that I must read it. It is magnificent. The book is edited by Symonds in the "Camelot" series with the *Religio Medici* and a few other papers.

P.S. Had a 20 page letter from Saben last week—nearly as long as "Marshall."

Gardiner
February 4, 1894

I find that I misjudged things in telling you that I should have my study of "the selfishness of self-denial" finished by today. The fact is it is only a little over half done, but I think I see my way out of it. I have to put a good deal in a few words and there is a great danger of a general effect of "roughness." When the thing is smoothed out and copied it will be the best piece of work I have done yet, which, I suppose, is not saying a great deal. It is "No. 4" in my recent ambitious series, and, as I said in my last, a little too complex for a short sketch in the hands of a novice. I am anxious to read it to you and get your candid opinion of its merits or faults, as the case may be. My next work will be in a lighter vein—the sketch of a philosophical tramp ("Anxious Hendricks," probably) looking for rest. Merely an experiment in a new field.—Forgive me for saying so much about myself in this and my past letters, but you see what a hold the scheme has upon me. If it fails totally, I think I shall get drunk and then hunt for a "job." "Let the dream go!" says the poet. Good advice, perhaps, but like all good advice, hard to follow.

I have only worked five or six hours during the past week. I had an itch for reading and tired my eyes in consequence. I finished *Toute une Jeunesse* by Coppée and did a lot of browsing through various books of poems and essays. Tomorrow I hope to settle down in earnest and bring something to pass before next Sunday. When the five sketches are all finished up to the best of my ability, I intend to copy them on the machine, and start them somewhere. The expectation of a returned manuscript is better than no excitement at all.

I have [been] thinking up a little scheme for this summer, but shall make no promises, even if it is agreeable to you. I think you first suggested something of the kind. My scheme is to make a metrical translation of the *Antigone*. You might find pleasure and profit in writing out a correct prose version of the play, keeping the Greek spirit as much as possible, and in guiding me in the choice of words and suggestions as to the classical effect of my verses. My choice would be to make it in the main unrhymed, depending upon sonority and picturesqueness for the effect. If the thing should prove anything like a success we might have a small edition printed at the cost of an ordinary indulgence in the world's pleasures. A title page something like this would not be bad:

"The Antigone of Sophocles: A translation by Harry de Forest Smith and Edwin Arlington Robinson.— An edition of fifty copies printed for private circulation. Gardiner, Maine. REPORTER-JOURNAL JOB PRESS (!) MDCCCXCIV."

This will probably end up like the stone house on the hill, but we have a right to build castles in Spain or where we please. This is a kind of a Spanish castle in Greece. I wonder if the shade of Sophocles is grinning over my shoulder as I write this? If he is, I suppose he knows how the thing is coming out. The one great objection to this performance is the time it would take. The question is, would the time be well spent? Somehow all my schemes involve the spending of money instead of the making of it. If time is money, I make way with a fortune every week. I suppose I shall keep on doing this and live from hand to mouth all the days of my life. Sometimes the realization of my non-success thus far in my life make me totally discouraged for days at a time.

Then it clears away and I am full of hope again. The things that I enjoy the most—no matter how much labor they may require are the things that keep me from getting on in the world, as the practical men say. You, who are making a living, cannot imagine how cutting it is for a man of twenty-four to depend upon his mother for every cent he has and every mouthful he swallows. But I won't dwell longer upon this,—I begin to hear the dog in the manger.

I began my French lessons with Labiche and Martin's comedy, *La Poudre aux Yeux*. This business will give me considerable pleasure, and be a good thing from an educational point of view. A thorough review of the elements of the language will be a great thing for me.

Well, my fingers are getting stiff, and my writing correspondingly illegible; so I will stop here and await your opinion of the *Antigone* business. I shall probably be the one to throw up the sponge, but still it is worth thinking over. Hoping for a letter tomorrow, I remain . . .

Gardiner
February 11, 1894

I received a very fine letter from my friend Hubbell (you may have seen his name in connection with your reading of Harvard athletics) in which he spoke of many things—among them, in a gentle way, of my handwriting. So much has been said to me of late on this subject that I have become somewhat alarmed, and am beginning to wonder if it would not be better for me to give up writing with a pen altogether. I know what the boy in the book would say, but I assure [you] that the thing is almost an impossibility for me. The more I try to improve, the worse success I seem to have; for the criticisms often come after what I consider a praiseworthy effort. I suppose the real fact in the case is that I don't care enough about the matter. Good penmanship is to me, in most cases, a fortunate accident. I may be too apt to consider all the virtues and accomplishments in this light—I have always confessed fatalistic tendencies in things both great and small.

I think I can appreciate, perhaps to a greater extent than you think, your uncertainty as to keeping on in the dead (?) languages. It would be unpleasant and useless meddling on my part to offer any advice, so I will hold my peace after offering one suggestion that may tire you a little, but, I trust, will not awaken any lasting animosity.—I would say that if you think yourself sufficiently imbued with the Greek spirit—the "sophrosyne" of the Periclean age—to temper yourself in the smash of American life, and feel that your place is where conquests are being made, you cannot be too soon in realizing the absolute necessity on your part of a practical familiarity—I won't say mastery—of the French and German languages. I would not seem egotistic, but I honestly think I have had a little better opportunity than you to know the truth of what I am now saying. The knowledge of these languages is no longer looked on as [an] accomplishment, but as a working tool—intellectual and social. In other words, it is taken for granted; and you are probably doomed sooner or later to work them up—provided you continue to aspire as you have during the past five years. You will find the work pleasant after your conscientious and moderately satisfactory work in Greek; you will feel that you are working nearer today, and at the same time hear the accents of the past sounding in your ears with a comforting familiarity.—I am right, old man, and I know it, but of course you have the born right to "Anglo-Saxondom's idee."

It does me good to "chin" in this way all by myself, and as long as you feel that it does you no particular harm, I trust you will pardon me my familiarity. I have great faith in you, but I wish you were not quite so damned energetic and exemplary in some directions: you make me feel uncomfortable and a little out of place. It is only when you smoke a pipe and build houses "founded on the rock" that I feel wholly your equal. And yet, I have been doing some pretty good work of late. The study of selfishness that I spoke of in my last two letters is, I am happy to say, written and revised. The thing gave me far more trouble than I anticipated and I am much in doubt as to what I have brought to pass. I am convinced that it is either pretty good or pretty bad. In writing, I have a pestering tendency to repeat small expressions, and my experience with "Marshall" showed me that nothing will reveal this fault so well as reading aloud. When you come to Gardiner again I hope for your kindness to listen to perhaps half a dozen sketches written in aching earnest in the cause of art and strength: these are the things I am after, from the mechanical point of view.

I have been reading this forenoon a long-short story by Coppée. The title is "Une Faute de Jeunesse," and the story an old theme in the hands of a master. *Toute une Jeunesse,* which I have lately read, is very fine work, but too thoroughly French to be read sympathetically by the General American reader. The tone is wholesome, still I doubt if it is much to my credit to say that I thoroughly enjoyed it; but I did, as I do everything written by the author of *Les Vices du Capitaine.* One of the most human things ever written.

My machine keeps getting away from me today, and I think I had better stop now and go over what I have done, with an eye for corrections. It is easier for me to do my correspondence in this way, but it seems to take half the character from a friendly letter —to kill the sentiment, so to speak. Do you ever think of that?

Gardiner
February 18, 1894

Boreas has been on the rampage during the past week, and the weather has been damnable. This morning began with a mild rain storm, and the present outlook is that we are going to have what our ancestors called a "soft spell." With almost four feet of snow in many places, it will be a little too soft for man's convenience, but the powers seldom stop to consider that. I have shovelled snow until my heart aches to think of such business, but I suppose there is more coming.

I was seized with another reading fit last week and took up Cherbuliez's *Meta Holdenis,* a queer kind of novel filled with a quiet humor and glittering with sharp sayings—characteristics of *L'Idée de Jean Têterol* and *Samuel Brohl & Cie,* by the same author. Have you ever read any of his books? *Jean Têterol,* one of the best novels in recent literature, is published in English by the Appletons. If you care to amuse yourself by reading books of that class, you cannot do better than to buy it. I feel quite safe in recommending it, as I have read it twice, and have felt a broadening of my humanity after each reading. The French text of the book is reasonably difficult, the author being gifted, like Daudet, with an extensive vocabulary of common words for describing common things.

I see by the *Journal* that the Symphony Orchestra played another symphony by Brahms last evening—No. 2. Sometimes I get so discontented here in Gardiner that I feel almost desperate in my desire to see and hear something; but when I pause to think the matter over I realize that [I am] best off where I am in my present straightened circumstances. "To stay at home is best." I live in hope that a time may come when I shall have all those things near at hand, and at the same time sufficient capital in my pocket to take the benefits they offer. It is a shadowy hope, but for all that my courage is wonderfully good, as I have said before. Were it not for that persistent presentiment to which I have referred once or twice in our conversations, I should have little concern for the future. But such things are in other hands than mine, and I have no better direction than that of my own reason when it tells [me] to do the best I can and wait the issue. It is but a matter of a few years anyway, and then we may all laugh that we ever took life so seriously,—for I think we all take it a little more seriously than we like to confess.

I have been rewriting my sketch of "Lévy Condillac." The thing has given me a deal of trouble and even now I am far from seeing my way out of it. It is not an easy task to kill a woman in childbirth with nervous prostration brought on by excessive clarinet playing on the part of an over-enthusiastic young husband, without bordering on the ridiculous. This is what I have been trying to do, and I have had the satisfaction of proving to myself that the thing can be done provided sufficient skill is exerted. Whether I can do it or not remains to be seen. Sometimes I fear that I am trying to straddle to the stars in this scheme of mine and may be obliged to come down a little before I realize anything. That will be hard, but not impossible when I set my reason to work.

I received a letter from my friend Ford in which he tells me that Rudyard Kipling is doing some fine work for *St. Nicholas.* I have heard of it before, but have never seen any of the sketches. Do you know what they are like? I wonder where that new novel, *The Stone Bridge,* is and if it will be as long making its appearance as was *Many Inventions.* Somehow I hope it will be a little more satisfactory when it does come; the other book was in many ways a disappointment to me. There was too much journalistic stuffing in it. Remarks like these show how easy it is to find fault, but I am sometimes half inclined to think that fault-finding, in its various forms, is one of the great pleasures of life. Sir John Lubbock does not find a place for it in his book, but even the great are apt to occasionally overlook things. And by the way, has it ever occurred to you that that book reveals an almost superhuman familiarity with the world's literature? I do not refer so much to his list of "the hundred best books" as to his quotations and general remarks scattered throughout the book. When I try to conceive of that man's brain power, I shudder at my own littleness. Then I stop shuddering and try to make myself believe that I am as great as anybody, or rather that I shall be when the final examination comes. I cannot believe that these tremendous worldly differences are to be carried on through the second life. I cannot conceive of eternity as an endless panorama of "busted ambitions." That would be hell with a vengeance. I cannot believe that we poor devils deserve any such punishment. Life itself is no joke to a great percentage of us, and all things seem to point to an improvement of our condition when they are explained. I am not preaching, but I believe in immortality—I can't help it.

I am glad that you are taking lessons in music because I can come to you for points. My knowledge is merely the natural outgrowth of an enthusiasm, and includes practically nothing of the real science. My fondness for music is wholly of an emotional kind—I care nothing for it unless it suggests something more than mental gymnastics on the part of the composer. Piano concertos are my worst enemies at a concert.

I understand that "The Old Folks at Home" is one of the themes in Dvorak's latest (American) symphony. You know it is built from Negro and Indian airs. Does it occur to you that it is a trifle galling to have no native composer to do this kind of thing? The chief use of America in the aesthetic world seems to be to furnish material and suggestions for others to take advantage of. I hope that a time may come when we shall have a romantic spirit of our own, but perhaps we are too young. This may be the reason that there are no spirits in our ruins. All our romance is cen[tered] in the traditions of the red men, and there is a sad lack of human interest. This truth is best illustrated when we try to put ourselves in sympathy with an Indian love story. They are different creatures from ourselves.

Perhaps I have said enough for today. I feel the need of a pipe and wish you were [here] to keep me company.

Gardiner
February 25, 1894

There is a kid asleep in the next room so today I shall use a pen instead of the machine, trusting you may be able to make out what I write after a little struggle.—In the first place, what are you having for weather down in Rockland? This morning at seven o'clock our thermometer stood —20° in the sun. I like cold weather but this is a little too much even for me. I think, though, we feel better at such a time.

The past week has been a rather dull one for me and pretty much wasted. I have not been able to do much of any work, for some reason I cannot explain. I have felt well enough bodily but I have been in a bad mood. Yesterday I partially drove it off by making a rondeau and a villanelle. The latter is a little mystical perhaps and is an attempt to show the poetry of the commonplace. Here it is,—you may judge for yourself. Tell me what you think of it and do not be afraid of hurting my feelings.

The House on the Hill.
(Villanelle of Departure.)

They are all gone away,
The house is shut and still:
There is nothing more to say.

Malign them as we may,
We cannot do them ill:
They are all gone away.

Are we more fit than they
To meet the Master's will?—
There is nothing more to say.

What matters it who stray
Around the sunken sill?—
They are all gone away,

And our poor fancy-play
For them is wasted skill:
There is nothing more to say.

There is ruin and decay
In the House on the Hill:
They are all gone away,
There is nothing more to say. . . .

This kind of thing may not interest you much, and please do not hesitate to say so if that be the case. These old French forms always had a fascination for me which I never expect to outgrow. I don't know that I care to outgrow it, but still it interferes with my more serious work to an unpleasant extent. When one of the things begin to run in my mind there is little rest for me until it is out. Fortunately this one was made very quickly (in about twenty minutes) so did not steal much of my time.

I have been thinking a good deal lately about the *Antigone* scheme. I like it and would like to carry it out; but I am half afraid that the double load of that and my prose work will [be] a little too much. On the other hand, the time and trouble might be a good investment for the practice it would give me in the choice and arrangement of words. Perhaps we had better try it and see how fast we progress. I could hardly hope to arrange more than ten lines a day. At that rate the thing would be done in about a year if I have a correct idea of the length of the drama. Isn't it something like three thousand lines? I should want a good translation to thoroughly familiarize myself with the work and then you could send me your version—a little at a time. At this rate we ought to do a thousand lines during your vacation, which would be a good start. I am inclined to think, upon the whole, that the time would be well spent, though as I am now situated it is a question of conscience rather than labor. When I have one definite idea to work out, have I a moral right to let such a laborious amusement interfere with it? That is the trouble. It is a little different with you, as you are making a living and have the summer to improve as best you may. I know something about the labor involved in a task of this kind from my past experience in translating Virgil and an ode from Horace. In the "days of my youth," about eight years ago, I put the whole of Cicero's first oration against Catiline into blank verse. I began it for fun and carried it through to save myself the chagrin of giving the thing [up]. Sometimes I am afraid it would be the same with *Antigone*, though of course I should go into this work with much more earnestness. I have a presentiment that the thing will be done, and that we shall be vastly glad that we have done it. It is no small undertaking, and must reflect some credit upon the men who carry it through—even though it be a questionable success. In years to come we could look back upon the business and feel that we had left the common ways of men and at least striven for higher things. When the thing is completed (if it ever is) it would be a good plan for you to submit it to some Brunswick man whom you think well qualified to test its merits from all points of view—that is, if you are upon sufficiently familiar terms with any of them to warrant your asking so much. If it were good for anything it would be folly not to preserve it in print. I should prefer to do the metrical work without having seen any poetical translations whatever. Then I could feel that I was not imitating. I should want a Greek text to follow the form of the lines (a knowledge of the alphabet would be enough for that) and I think it would be a good plan for you to bring the books you mentioned in your letter. I do not mean that I intend to attempt anything like a reproduction of the Greek metres—my idea is merely to suggest a little of the original form to the American eye—thus preserving an ocular resemblance between the translation and the Greek text.

I trust your belated letter of last Monday will not interfere with your writing today.

Gardiner
March 4, 1894

Your good letter came last Thursday and I was somewhat amused at your remarks on my perceptive powers. I do not think I get a very clear view of the wrinkles on the cerebrum of the men and women I meet, though I generally form some idea of their characters before a very long acquaintance. There is more in every person's soul than we think. Even the happy mortals we term ordinary or commonplace act their own mental tragedies and live a far deeper and wider life than we are inclined to believe possible in the light of our prejudices. I might name one or two as examples but it is not always best to be too specific upon paper. I think that I am somewhat inclined, with all my abstract sympathy, to take an unjustly narrow view of many of my acquaintances; but some unseen force (much the same force, I presume, that led Frederic Harrison to call Matthew Arnold an "elegant Jeremiah") often leads me to say disagreeable if not cruel things to my neighbors. I do not always mean all that I say, but I must acknowledge the dismal truth that the majority of mankind interest me only as studies. They are to me "a little queer," like the Quaker's wife. I often wonder whether I should be happier if I had the power, or gift, of making friends with everybody. I suppose it stands to reason that I should, but if I were given the opportunity of so changing my nature I am afraid my vanity would keep me as I am. I tread a narrow path, in one sense, but I do a considerable amount of observing. In fact, I observe so much that my feet often slip and I am forever stumbling over little things that other men never notice. This is one of my drawbacks, but it is not without its benefits; it opens one's eyes to the question of happiness and leads him to analyse that mysterious element of human nature from many points of view. I have discovered by this means that most of my own happiness is of a negative quality—a kind of sublimed selfishness, so to speak. As you know, I seldom laugh. The smoothest part of my face is around my mouth, where the only wrinkles of youth rightfully belong. My wrinkles are in my forehead and I have been more than once reminded of the fact. That, I fancy, is because I think more than some people, and do my laughing in my gray matter instead of upon my face. Real solid laughter is almost a physical impossibility with me. When it occurs it almost frightens me. I grin upon the slightest provocation, however, but my grins are not of the sort that makes friends. Somehow I feel that they are all for myself—there is nothing contagious about them.—At a theatre, for example, I may be highly amused, but I cannot give way to my feelings in the ordinary manner. The fact of appreciation seems to monopolize everything else, and I have no doubt that my lack of a reflex expression at such times takes a certain hold upon my vitality. One might find a comparison to this intense mental receptiveness in the bursting of a barrel of beer.—Now I am down upon the earth again and shall endeavor to stay there. Excuse my big words, but they came quite of their own accord. If they convey any meaning to you I shall be glad and I have little doubt that you may interpret them after a fashion. The fact is, I am in a somewhat finical mood today and consequently I write finical sentences.

This morning I read two acts of *Measure for Measure* and was thunderstruck. It is one of the few plays of Shakspere with which I am not familiar to some extent and for that reason was particularly fascinating. The theme, as you know, is not pleasant. It is a comedy of the flesh and a tragedy of the soul. The flesh is paramount, however, and the carnal proclivities of Angelo are wonderfully contrasted with the purity of Isabella. I shall know before night what is needed in the last three acts. Dark as the subject is, there is a rich vein of a rather broad humor running through the play which lends to the whole thing that wonderfully human effect which is a synonym for Shakspere. It seemed like meeting an old friend when I came across the familiar quotation, "Our doubts are traitors, etc."—I won't ask you to read the play, as it would do no good; but I am well enough convinced that the time is coming when you will find the gold in these plays and wonder at your past indifference to their greatness. Were I the stranger to Shakspere that you pretend to be I should begin with *Troilus and Cressida.* I don't know that I agree with Richard Grant White in calling [it] the wisest play of them all, but I think it is the widest (which is perhaps after all the same thing) in that it gives us a chance to admire the author from so many points of view. It is in that play that we find:

"The end crowns all;
And that old common arbitrator, Time,
Will one day end it."

From this I should turn to the narrowest of the plays, *Timon of Athens*—which is perhaps the most entertaining of them all—in a restricted sense. Forgive this patronizing air of mine, but I am anxious to have you take back your remarks. It is hard for me to conceive of a man who revels in almost everything that is great and good in literature, to overlook the great William as you do.

Did I tell you in my last letter that I had lately read Daudet's *Jack?* It is a strange thing—as Henry James says, "a brilliant photography of pain." James goes on to say that "it is all told with a laugh" but I only half understand what he means. There is humor in the book but the general tone is one of grim inevitableness mixed with a kind of cynicism. Daudet is strangely irreverent, and perhaps this is where the laugh comes in. It is a great book anyway, and ought to do its work in the world in the way of opening people's eyes and widening their sympathies. I suppose you are tired of hearing me talk about sympathies, but withal my coldness I am at least charitable in my feelings. I am slow to blame people for their misdeeds and (I may as well confess it) equally slow to praise them for their good works.—Well, I have given you an evening's occupation in deciphering this and will stop when my conscience tells me it is time.

[P.S.] Do you know of any small book which might have for its title The History (literary and mechanical) of the Greek Drama? I know of books in which the subject is treated more or less, but I am on the watch for the one little volume which must, of necessity, exist. If you do not, will you kindly make inquiries at the Bowdoin library?

Gardiner
March 11, 1894

Your third belated letter came Saturday, and I was glad to hear that you are coming home in a fortnight. You say that your time will be pretty well taken up, but you may be willing to take one or two brief vacations and listen to my five wild sketches—not including "Marshall." I have another in my mind on the philosophical enmity of two brothers who were not born for the same purpose. I think I see a chance for a good thing, but I am beginning to ask myself if these complex affairs are not a little too heavy for my experimental work: it is a pity to waste good material in practice, if the same end can be attained—and I have little doubt but that it can—by careful and conscientious work on more meagre and less valuable matter. A light sketch, written with no thought of publication, but still written with all possible care and earnestness, ought to bring its reward; and I think seriously of giving the coming summer to that kind of work—together (I trust) with *Antigone*. But for the present I shall tinker over what I have written and wait your candid opinions, trusting much to your choice for the selection of three to be sent to my uncle, who thinks he may get them read—and probably damned—in the *Atlantic* office.

I wonder why it is that we poor devils are so cursed with high ambitions? Do I ask this question in every letter I write you?— If I do, it is because the matter is forever in my mind. This and my fatalism have interfered to an alarming extent with my pleasure in life: the belief that we have done well does not amount to much if we cannot bring ourselves to feel that we deserve the credit. For example, I gave a kid some old postage-stamps yesterday: his eyes snapped at each one I gave him, and I think that I enjoyed the business fully as much as he. That youngster went away with a glad heart, and I felt a quiet satisfaction myself— until some devil or other made me ask myself why I did it. Most men would have followed the natural bent of their natures and the kid would have been dismissed and not thought of again. I followed the natural bent of my nature and spent an hour overhauling an old cigar-box full of stamps. I did it because I enjoyed it—because I was prompted to do it by some inner selfishness over which it seems that I had no control. This same characteristic leads me to give a beggar a nickel sometimes, while another mood at another time often compels me—can I call it anything else?—to pass him by without a care or a thought. This all goes to show you how finical I am, and what a bundle of crotchets goes to make up my ego. When we feel in a mood like this, it is good to quote Hartley Coleridge's sonnet, beginning:

> Let me not deem that I was made in vain,
> Or that my being was an accident
> Which Fate, in working its sublime intent,
> Not wished to be, to hinder would not deign.

For the past day or two I have been reading Daudet's *Tartarin de Tarascon*. At first I did not understand how a man is able to write such a book, but now I think he did it by hard work. The book is very small and the chapters so marvelously short that it seems incredible that such a satisfactory effect can be attained. The reader forgets that he is reading a microscopic narrative, and all because the author makes every sentence count. The thing is tremendously funny in places—particularly the chapter describing the hat-shooting tournaments. There is no game in Tarascon, so its inhabitants become "chasseurs de casquettes"—of whom the greatest is—of course—Tartarin. Eventually he goes to Africa to shoot lions, and falls in with the wily Prince Gregory of Montenegro. Through the kindness of this prince, Tartarin lives like a small sultan for a time with an Arab girl, Baia, forgetting all about the lions. The whole thing is a mild satire on the French people, and is magnificently done. It seems incredible that the book should be written by the author of *Jack*.

I am afraid that my brain is too nearly empty today for me to write much of a letter. There is very little weather outside—one of these dull dirty days when everything stagnates. I fancy it is much the same in Rockland; in fact, I rather hope that it is,—for in that case you may feel something as I do at present. I cannot describe the feeling: I can only say that I have a half active desire to eat, drink, read, write, and smoke. Do you know what kind of a feeling that is? If you do, you will excuse me for breaking off here and descending to the cellar for a whiff of Virginia. And by the way, speaking of smoking makes me think of the coming summer, and indirectly, of the Greek Drama. I shall go over the hills before long for your books, and shall be very much obliged if you bring Mr. Moulton's book from Bowdoin. The more I think of (is this a warning?) the *Antigone* scheme, the better I like it. Only I foresee the necessity of a great deal of preparation in order to make the work anything like adequate.

Before many weeks I shall surprise you with a specimen of my reformed penmanship.

Gardiner
March 18, 1894

I worked my way over the hills to your house the other day, and brought back a satchel full of books on the Greek drama. I think I have managed to get a fairly good idea of the general scheme of *Antigone,* though I cannot help thinking that there is a book in existence that would tell me many things I do not know. I have about concluded to write the body of the play in regular English heroic verse, making up a kind of irregular ode for the chorus—I mean irregular in meter but to correspond in the antistrophes, thus making the thing balance and showing up a definite plan on my part. I have this in mind for an opening:

$$\acute{-} \mid \smile \acute{-} \mid \smile \acute{-} \mid\mid \acute{-} \mid \smile \acute{-} \mid \smile \acute{-} \mid \smile \acute{-}$$
$$\acute{-} \mid \smile \acute{-} \mid \smile \acute{-} \mid \smile \mid\mid \acute{-} \mid \smile \acute{-} \mid \smile \acute{-}$$

This, as you see, is very simple, but not too much so, if I can keep up a sufficient sonority. I cannot recall anything just like it in English poetry, but it must have been used before now. If I remember rightly, the envoi in *Many Inventions* is very near to it, though I think it is slightly different.

I am afraid I have undertaken a task beyond my abilities, but there will be some satisfaction in an honest attempt. If I fail, the trial must be worth something for the experience it will give me. I have been thinking the matter over during the past week and wondering whether the project is asinine or not. To be sure, Bryant translated the *Iliad* and *Odyssey* without being a Greek scholar, but regular hexameter verse is marvelously different from the split metres of the drama. I am just mutton-headed enough to carry this thing out, if I can, without looking into any English poetical translation. If I make the ghost of Sophocles shudder, I cannot help it. Sometimes I am foolish enough to believe that my ignorance of Greek (I think I have said this before) may be a benefit rather than a hindrance. I know that I have something of the Hellenic spirit in me, and have a pretty good conception of what the word means. I may lack some of the "serene and childlike joy of life" but I have the spirit of wise moderation and love of classical completeness which, I suppose, is more marked in the later poets of Pericles' time than in the Homeric period. This will help me amazingly in *Antigone*. You have much of this appreciation and I shall depend to a large extent upon your judgment as to the choice of words.—Do not think by this everlasting talk of my own part of the business that I overlook your own part of the work; for you know you must give me something more than an ordinary slipshod class-room rendering. You must weigh your words and keep the original spirit in the prose version which I must try to intensify in my verses. In short, you must do your best to make your prose version a work of art. The result will probably be that your rendering will prove more satisfying than mine—provided you do your work as conscientiously as you do almost everything you enter upon.

Today I shall finish the revision of my "Parable of the Pines." The scheme is pretty good and I really think that the thing might be of some benefit to the world, on account of its subject matter alone, if it once got circulated. This is my seventh and last sketch for the time being. My work for the next two or three weeks will be the general polishing up and final copying of what I have done—preparatory to sending it away. I want your opinions very much, and shall probably tire you a little with my questions. But you know that I would be willing to do the same for you if the chance was offered, so you may be able to wake a little enthusiasm in the matter. All of my last six pieces are entirely different from "Marshall," but I am beginning to doubt if they are any better.—Yesterday the idea of a very simple and appropriate book-plate came into my mind and I proceeded to draw the rough sketch I enclose. It hardly seems possible that it can be original, but I do not think I have ever seen it.

Gardiner
April 15, 1894

This is a magnificent Sunday for the forest, but alas, we are not there—at least, I am not. I suppose I might be if I took the trouble, but there would be a painful absence of you and your shining visage—to say nothing of your pipe and your conversation. A book would be good—*Views and Reviews* if we had it, or better still, a volume of Browning. I think I have found your poet in Browning (leaving out Arnold, of course) and I am anxious for you to read him. Houghton Mifflin and Co. sell him for something like ten dollars (six volumes, and pretty big ones, too) and I mean to acquire them at the earliest opportunity. I found Volume II at Barstow's and have held great sessions over it. It contains "A Blot in the 'Scutcheon," "Luria," "Colombe's Birthday"—and many other things, of which none interested me more than "Waring." Most of Browning's more familiar short poems seem to be in this volume, but of course not "Agamemnon," the thing I want most of all, just at present.

I cannot join you in your depreciation of Mr. Mosher's bookmaking. *Old World Lyrics* is a jewel of workmanship in my eyes, and puts the Riverside Press to shame. I fancy half my enthusiasm over the book is the unexpected discovery of the title printed horizontally (shall I say perpendicularly?) on the back. The contents are pleasing, though it is rather startling to find John Payne's version of Banville's "Ballade des Pendus" preferred to Lang's, which is infinitely better. But how Rossetti does beat them in his "Ballade of Dead Ladies." He seems to keep up the old French spirit without Payne's archaisms. Payne can write sonnets and he had better stick to them. Do you know "Hesperia" and the others in Sharp's collection? If you do not, look them up and judge for yourself.

I have copied "The Pines" on my machine, but have concluded to rewrite the last part of it. That is the part that demands the best work and which seems to have received the worst. It is too careless and does not give the sketch the "send-off" which the reader might naturally expect. I say "reader" with vague feelings of guilt and presumption, but my conscience may be clear as long as I confine myself to the singular,—which means—you!

I wish you would read the second book of the *The Task*, and then tell me you don't like Cowper. I am getting infinite pleasure from that poem now and I am glad that I am only half way through it. This is saying considerable of a poem containing two hundred pages. It is more than I can say of *Paradise Lost*—though I would not place the two in comparison. One is majestic, the other is merely great. In reading Cowper you feel yourself in the country, with London, which you do not somehow care much for, not far away. I won't ask you to read the whole of *The Task*, as it would do no good—only I hope you may fall in with it some-day. That will be enough. You won't find anything in it like "When the liquor is out, why clink the Canakin?" as you do in Browning, but you do find, as you well know, "God made the country and man made the town," which, I think, is quite as good as the former—perhaps a little better.

Today I have been reading *Une Idylle Pendant La Siège* by my old friend Coppée. This is the last (I mean in the order of my reading) of his prose and it makes me feel badly to think of it. I suppose he will write more some-day, however, and give me a chance to draw good lessons from his healthy naturalism. He always leaves a good taste in one's mouth, which is hardly true of most of his confrères. The *Idylle* [is] largely descriptive of Paris during the siege and on that account would be more entertaining if I knew more about the time. Love and war are wonderfully mixed—so mixed that I am quite willing to forgive the hero—if I may call him one—for not being a better soldier. He is in love with a young married woman whose husband is a cad; and the reader never once thinks of there being anything like moral crime in the affair. And there isn't, for that matter—at least, not yet. He has kissed her twice—after the most approved methods —but that is all. He is a moral young man and does not like the idea of finding "Cousin Robert" in her friend's room at nine o'clock in the morning.

I have had two pipes this forenoon and am in a fair way to have another before long. Tomorrow morning I go to work in earnest and hope to finish the other two sketches in time to pack them off by a week from today. When they come back, I shall feel queer, but it won't last long. You see, I have had experience. —And, by the way, I am sadly in need of those shoes. Why doesn't the *Dial* respond? I think I must write and tell the editor of my condition. Try not to be so irregular in your correspondence this term, and excuse my gall in asking so much of a man with an occupation.

Gardiner
April 22, 1894

I have just read your letter, and must confess that I envy you for the books you have been reading. I neglected Lang's *Old Friends* for two years, thinking it to be a volume of compilations. If I had [known] what it really was we should both have had the benefit of it long before this. Well, that is my way—continually missing good things when they are right under my nose. If I keep on doing this, and I probably shall, I shall feel pretty thoroughly dissatisfied with myself by the time I am eighty. It positively frightens me when I think of the opportunities, small and great, which I lost while in Cambridge; but then, I am thankful for what little I got, and feel that my life is infinitely larger for my going there. I have said all this a dozen times before, but [you] will excuse me, as you must know what those two years were to me, who had lived like a snail for twenty years before. It was not in the nature of things that I should reap all the good things offered me; I was not educated for it; I could only pick here and there, and, of course, miss much of the very best. I could appreciate those things now, but—woe is me!—I am not there, and cannot get there—not even for a week in June to see Ford and Tryon take their exits. This is the one minor thing that galls me now above all others. If I could take that week with anything like a clean conscience, I think I could jump for joy, though God knows what a figure I should cut in such a performance. Can you imagine me jumping for joy—or for anything else, unless it be a hornets' nest?

Excepting *The Task,* I have read little during the past week. I wonder why it is that I like Cowper as I do? Something tells me that he is not, and never will be, one of the really great poets, although in occasional passages he is well nigh unsurpassable. There is much of the sandy desert in his work, but still it is comfortable travelling. The green and glorious places that come every little while are all the brighter for the comparative barrenness around them. His religion is akin to mawkish to a man of my doubts, but I readily overlook that in the consideration of his temperament and his surroundings. He is popularly and justly, I suppose, called feminine; but human nature has a word to say regarding such matters, and a little sympathy is not likely to be wasted upon this poet. His timidity was a disease, and the making of verse and rabbit-hutches, together with gardening, was his occupation. He was a strange man; and this strangeness, with his almost pathetic sincerity, go to make up the reason for my fondness for his poetry. He stands between Thomson and Wordsworth, and for some reason, he seems to stand on pretty firm ground. I do not think another half-century will disturb him to any great extent. His description of the wood-cutter and his dog cannot die while men and women care for true art in homely things.

I have written a queer poem, but I haven't the nerve to send it to you yet. It needs a little revision before [being] subjected to even the most friendly criticism, and it is in this little revision that my difficulty lies. The whole thing—forty lines—was written between twelve and one o'clock while I was waiting for my dinner, and has an air of unsatisfactory completeness about it which I am at a loss to overcome. When I fix it, I shall send you a copy —yes I will send you two stanzas now while I am talking about it:

> *Yes, this is the end of life, I suppose—*
> *To do what we can for ourselves and others;*
> *But men who find tragedy writ in a rose*
> *May forget sometimes there are sons and mothers—*
>
> *Fathers and daughters of love and hate,*
> *Scattered like hell-spawn down from Heaven,*
> *To teach mankind to struggle and wait*
> *Till life be over and death forgiven.*

I call the thing "Doubts." The stanzas quoted are the fifth and sixth out of ten. I think that there is at least a straightforwardness—what a devil of a word that is!—about the poem, which you will like. There is nothing artificial, and, I fear, little intelligible; but for all that I rather think you will like it better than the "House on the Hill." As for myself, I think I prefer the villanelle. I have a weakness for the suggestiveness of those artificial forms—that is, when they treat of something besides bride-roses and ball-rooms. *Vers de société* pure and simple, has little charm for me. Austin Dobson might be twice the man he is if he were —somebody else, I suppose; but it does seem that he might have used his talents to a little better advantage. "Don Quixote" shows what is in him; if it could be let out, England would be the richer by another poet.

I wrote a long letter to Saben yesterday, but it was hard work. I am not in the mood for much letter-writing this week, but I felt that common courtesy demanded that I should not neglect him any longer, so I made the effort, and so, to a small extent, conquered myself; and the man who does that, you know, is greater "than he who taketh a city." I trust that you will pardon me for not writing before this, considering my explanation. When we do not feel like doing anything at all, we often do the thing we least expect to do.

I had a good letter from Butler last week, accompanied by Thomas Hardy's *Life's Little Ironies*. The book is very good, and, as far as I have read, written in a more pleasant vein than *A Group of Noble Dames*, which is the model of the second part, entitled "A Few Crusted Characters." Butler's gift was very opportune, as I have wanted the book ever since I saw it advertised. You will enjoy it next summer, or before that if you wish it. Two of the stories, "To Please his Wife" and "The Fiddler of the Reels," are already familiar to me; the others are all new. The opening one, "The Son's Veto" is particularly good.—I am getting to think more and more of Butler every day—not because he sends me books, though of course that is pleasant—but because I am beginning to realize that he is an exceptionally fine fellow. He has been spoiled a little, and that leads him to say unpleasant things; but that is a small matter in the long run. I have often thought that you must have been a little surprised at meeting him in the Parker House when you went to Boston last winter. Well, he is a pretty good man to meet in a strange land, and you doubtless welcomed his broad smile. I think a great deal of that smile, and wish that I had even the ghost of it to lighten my semicadaverous countenance. Perhaps I shall learn to grin again some day—when that leaky ship of mine comes in.

I shall go to your house sometime this week and get my beans and Matthew Arnold. When I send you the poems you request,

I shall also send a little copy of *The Task* which you may browse over at your leisure. Never read it when you are in a hurry, depend upon finding much that is commonplace, and do not let Book I count for too much in your opinions. You must read with an eye ever open for detached good things rather than for a continuous procession of splendid poetry. I fancy that Books II and V will please you the most of all. And while I think of it, you must be prepared to treat Cowper kindly for his intense Calvinism. His religious reflections are not always pleasant to a modern reader, especially if he is inclined, like you and me, to be liberal in such matters.

This is a gray sticky day that makes me think of everything but the sun. I am not wholly in a grouch, but I think it is just as well for you that I am not with you. I fear that my company would not be much better than my handwriting. Perhaps you will understand my feelings a [little] better, and perhaps not, when I tell you that my French lessons are over. You may interpret this as you like, but I fancy you will not get far out of the way in your conclusions. Anticipation and realization are two different things. Take this for the text of this letter, and remember it. It may do you good someday, and lead you to be more careful in your actions than I have been. This business, with two funerals and the receipt of Butler's suggestive book on top of it all, have made the past ten days a little strong for me. Coincidences are strange sometimes—perhaps a little cruel. Life's Little Ironies are not wholly fancies. Kindly tear this into seventy pieces after reading it, and when you write next Sunday tell me what you think of *Views and Reviews.*

Gardiner
May 6, 1894

This is a model day to read *Life's Little Ironies* and Molière's *Le Misanthrope,* as I shall probably do when I finish this letter.— Let me say, to begin with, that I have been so stirred up with spring work and other things during the past week that I have had no chance to go out to your house; and I doubt if I go today, unless it stops raining. I must go soon, however, and shall send you Matthew Arnold sometime this week,—probably Monday or Tuesday.

I see nothing ahead of me for the next three or four weeks but hard work—not with my fancy but with my hands; which, I suppose, is vastly better for my general economy. I think I need something of that kind in my present loneliness. When you get back, everything will seem different; but until then I must live it out as best I can. The only thing to do is to keep busy at something, it does not matter much what. Class Day week I shall take a poverty trip to Cambridge, per steamer, and thus shake the dust of "this my town of banishment" from my feet for a few days. I cannot afford the trip, but I must do something. A week with Tryon, Ford, and Butler would put new life into me, although the feeling that the last of my friends leave Harvard this spring is not pleasant. That is the way of this life: we meet and get acquainted, and then we are scattered over the country— hundreds of miles apart. As long as you are in Maine and Butler in Boston and the others in Cambridge, I feel that I have some- one near me; but when the time comes for you all to change your locations, God only knows how I shall feel. There is no prospect of my getting out of Maine for a long time to come, and I some- times find myself almost wishing that you will not find any better position than you now occupy, to lead you into new fields. Of course these are not genuine feelings, and you will understand me well enough not to lay anything up against me for what I say. I have had a horrible dose of the blues during the past fort- night and my feelings must be to some extent reflected in my words. So take them for what they are worth, and don't call me a jackass.

Yesterday morning I sent off my three sketches, but have hardly thought of them since. I am getting more and more con- vinced that they do not amount to anything, and that they will soon come back with perhaps a little faint praise, leaving me just where I was before I sent them. I am afraid I have made a giant blunder in this literary business. Here I am in my twenty-fifth year, with absolutely no prospects, no money, and not much hope. Still, I lack the courage to upset the whole scheme of my life and face the world with buried ideals. If I must do this some-day, I can foresee the result—a hand to mouth existence picked up by odd jobs during the rest of my days. However, when this cleaning up work is over, I shall settle down to hard work once more—harder work than I have ever yet done—and wait the issue. I am one of those unfortunate devils who must have a little en-couragement before they can put their heart into what they do. In my business, this encouragement is necessarily slow to come, and, even then, damnably uncertain.

Yesterday I received a long farewell letter from Saben, who in-tends to sail for England on the nineteenth of this month. It makes me feel queer to think he is going away, but that is the way of things. Good letters from you, Ford, and Butler also made the last week marked with something pleasant, so I have not been so badly off, after all. A letter from a friend is an event in my life (did you say something like this, once on a time?) and without them I should be where Saben once told half the first balcony of the Hollis St. Theatre he would be without his books —in hell. S. has a way of yelling in public which is characteristic, and at times embarrassing to the man who asks him questions.

The *Dial* has not yet taken the trouble to send back my sonnet. It seems to me a little lack of courtesy, but I suppose editors have the right to do as they please. I have my shoes, though Heaven only knows when they will be paid for.

As I look out of the window now, it seems to me that all the world needs the washing it is getting. Everything looks dirty, the sky most of all. I fancy I am dirty myself, and a good bath will make up a part of the day's programme. I can be clean if I can-not be contented.

Forgive me for thus wreaking my bile on you, and hope for something in a more cheerful vein next week. Just at present, I do not see much to make me laugh—so shall not try to.

Were it not for a trifle too much wind, and a howling dog across the way, this would be one of God's days, as Tryon used to say in Cambridge. As it is, it is marvelously pleasant, and were you here to reap the benefit of it with me, life, for a time, would be great. But you are not here, and that is the end of it. My loneliness nowadays is complete, and I seem to be slowly getting used to it at the expense, I fancy, of mental prosperity—if you know what that is.

It is a little strange that I have never said anything to you about *Ships that Pass in the Night*. Butler sent me the book about a fortnight before he sent *Life's Little Ironies*. I think the man must be a mind-reader. At any rate, the book came at a queer time, and was consequently doubly suggestive to me. If you wish for my opinion of it, I will say that it is, to my mind, well worth reading. At first I tried to think it great, but was compelled to let greatness give way to cleverness. I do not particularly like the word "clever," but it seems, in its best sense, to be the word for this novel. It is not necessary for me to add that it made a great impression on me—an impression which I shall never wholly get over. There is a strain of sincerity in it, or apparent sincerity, which appeals to anyone who has ever had any great trouble—especially trouble of a particular sort that comes to us mortals now and then. The "jewel" of the book to me is a little sentence uttered by the poor neglected devil who called Bernadine "Little Brick":—"Those who ask for little get nothing" —or something like that. It is not wholly true, but true enough to be a proverb: something like Oscar Wilde's "We are all in the gutter, but some of us are looking at the stars."

This is one of the days when my machine does not work to suit me, but I cannot lay everything to that. I do not think I have written a decent letter for a month. In fact, I have not done much of anything but peg away in my garden, trying to fancy that I am enjoying life. My literary scheme looks darker and darker, although my fat uncle tells me that my sketches are marked with a "real maturity" and some other things which an uncle would be likely to say. Like you, he is inclined to think "Marshall" a little better than the others. I hoped he would have a word to say about "The Pines," but he says nothing. Perhaps the subject is not one to particularly interest a man nearly seventy years old. He goes on to say that he will put the things in a way to be examined as soon as possible. I may be surprised, but I do not now anticipate any such thing.

Excepting a little Molière, I have not read anything lately. My farm work takes almost all of my time, and I am gradually getting to be a horny-handed son of toil. My face and neck are burned to the color of leather, and I think I feel a little proud of the fact. But what a figure I shall cut on Class Day! I have become so thoroughly fossilized during the past winter and spring that I am half afraid to go; but then, I was always a fossil, and I suppose I always shall be one. It makes no great difference, as far as I can see. I was born awkward and I cannot help it. I do not say this for effect: it is the truth, and experience is continually reminding me of it. I am fortunate, however, in having a few real friends who do not make much of such trifles, and I feel sure of a cordial welcome when I go to Harvard this coming June. I shall have at least two college rooms to smoke and sprawl in, and men to talk with whose goddess is not engraved on a silver dollar—men whose literature is not newspapers. If I could have these men—including you, of course,—with me all the time, I should be infinitely better off. But they are not here.

I shall attend to the books you mention at the earliest opportunity, and am glad for the chance of doing you a favor, however slight it may be. It is a pleasure to work for others if they don't work you too hard. As Mulvaney says, "This is an epigram. I made ut."

I suppose, to use a worldly expression, this is one of the lousiest letters I have ever written; and upon the strength of this supposition I must ask you to destroy it. I know I show my weakness in making this request, and I fear I have made it too often in the past, but there are times when it seems to me that my letters are positively disgraceful. And yet, this may be a masterpiece. If it is, keep it.

I read a review of *Ships that Pass* etc. more than a year ago in the London *Athenaeum*. The review struck me as peculiar and something seemed to tell me that I should hear more of the book. The author has written another called *In Varying Moods*—as you have seen in the *Dial*. What do you think of William Morton Payne's wholesale reviewing of poetry and fiction? It seems to me that he does it a little too easily.

Gardiner

May 20, 1894

I knew that things were going well with you as soon as I opened your last letter. The big sprawling lines, which I so dislike, told me that. I hate to disappoint you, but I was not in the least startled by the fact that you are engaged to be married. I knew well enough that you were in love with somebody and have known it for a long time: your actions have told me that and I was glad, upon the whole, as my suspicions became more and more firmly fixed in my mind. It seemed to me that you were trying to tell me of the fact without saying as much in words. I don't suppose you will believe me when I tell you that you have been slowly putting me away from you for the past six months but such is the truth. I honestly think that you did not realize that such a thing was going on; but I, who had every chance to observe and feel every little difference, could not shut my eyes to the truth. Do not misunderstand me in this; do not think that I mean to hint that you really think less of my friendship than you did two years ago, for I know that is not the truth. It is merely a case of "not that I loved long Robinson less, but—oh, yes, Adela—more." In short, I have lost you, and, for your sake, I am heartily glad of it. All this will displease you at first, but you will gradually come to understand me. Of course we shall sit and read and smoke together next summer, but there will be another person there besides myself. I say this, my dear fellow, because I know only too well what I am talking about.

Ever since the great change for higher things came over you —it began three or four years ago—I have felt your worth and have had a corresponding admiration for you. I have felt the countless weaknesses of my own flickering nature and wondered that a man of your strength should find so much in me to like. All this was well grounded before I went to Harvard. Then I found that there were other people besides yourself who could find something in me worthy of their friendly attention. The only thing that saves me from total discouragement is the knowledge, or at least the belief, that such men as you, Tryon, Saben, Butler, and Ford, look upon me as a person worth knowing. This leads me to think that I am not wholly an ass. These I have named, with one or two others, are my friends; and where are they? You alone are where I can still feel that you are near me. Tryon and Butler are hopelessly out of my way—except through correspondence; Latham, that mysterious man you have never seen, I may never see again; Ford is just now in Harvard, where I expect to see him for a day or two in June,—after that, perhaps never; Saben sailed yesterday for Europe, and I have seen the last of him—at least, for many years. So you see I am pretty much alone, and perhaps you will not think it so strange after all that I am not so jolly as some fellows you know. More than this, all my life at home has been a kind of hell from which there seemed to be no release until I broke from my harness and went to college. I have queer feelings of cowardice as I write this, but I depend upon you to take it in the right spirit.

You are engaged to be married, you are happy, and the world and the future look bright in your eyes; I am not (now) engaged to be married, I am not happy, and the world and the future look so dark and gloomy that I look mostly into the past. Here is the difference.—But the Fates have been kind to me in one respect,— they have given me the ability to rejoice in the happiness and good-fortune of others. So I am happy on your account and am glad for what seems to be in store for you. Did I ever tell you of a kind of intuitive sense of prophecy I sometimes feel in the presence of my friends? Of course it does not amount to anything, but still you may be glad to know that I have never once had the trace of a doubt as to your ultimate welfare. I do not think that you will ever be rich, or publicly great (in the bow-wow sense of the word) but you will, if you live, fill an eminently respectable place as an intellectual American citizen; as a married man you will be happy and make your partner the same; and whenever long Robinson comes to see you for a day or so, you will treat him like a brother. So speaks my prophetic spirit.

Yes, I am glad you are going to be married. I have always looked upon a bachelor as only half of a man, though this is of course too violent language to use. I have always believed in love, and always shall believe in it. The fact that so many thousands go astray sometimes shakes my faith a little, but it always rights itself after a time. There are natures that positively cannot be faithful to a single companion, and sometimes the people who have them seem to be the happiest in the world; but I think if we knew them as well as they know themselves (I use "know" in its everyday sense) we should find there is something in their souls that is never satisfied,—their lives are not complete, they live without a mission. Their life is a fevered irregularity, and, when they are past their forties—and oftentimes long before that —the original nature stamps itself in the face, and those lines of hardness, which we have all seen, tell us that something is wrong. S— [sic] is an extreme example of this class of men. In my opinion, the true happiness requires no such stimulation as that which these people demand.

"L'Amour" is pitifully abused in spoken and written literature. The word is used without a particle of consideration as to its better meaning. Love and lust have become so mixed by our poets and novelists that we poor puritans are half inclined to wonder, as we read, whether there is such a thing after all, as a better nature in man or woman. The modern French school is doing its best to kill these higher sensibilities, and their work is not wholly a failure in that direction. It may sound foolish, but I know it to be a fact that many fellows who ought to know better are mentally and morally debilitated by the matchless trash produced by such writers as Maupassant, Mendès and Gautier. I can stand a good deal in the way of freedom of expression, but I am disgusted with many of our modern tendencies. I make these few remarks on love because I am glad to know that there are still men in these progressive days of ours who can value it for its true worth. When you get to read Shakspere (you are bound to do so someday) you will find in all his later plays an undertone of manly melancholy which you will naturally trace to a love of the higher kind, which, for some unknown reason, was never satisfied.

This is a good time for you to read "The Queen's Gardens" aloud. Whether Ruskin was the man to write that essay or not, I cannot say, but it stands for what it is, and the author is loved and respected. So I think it is safe to take it as a work of sincerity. Of course you have read it, but sometimes we read things for a second or a twenty-second time.

It seems to me that I have written almost enough of this sort of thing, but have I written enough for you to fully understand me? Do you fully understand that I am glad that this change has come to you—that your life is beginning, in the true sense of the expression, to mean something to you? When the time comes to put away childish things, the individual stands in a new light. The lost days of boyhood and youth begin to put on the appearance of broken toys in a dusty garret. The man has come and has taken the boy away. The child has grown to maturity without knowing what has been going on. Youth is over. This is something the way of it with most people, I fancy, but somehow I, with my crotchets and my childish sensibilities, cannot put away the old things. The world frightens me; my "one talent" is forever laughing at me. When I look far into the future, I see myself—sometimes in the light of a partial success—living alone in some city—Boston, most likely—with a friend or two to drop in upon me once in a while, and a few faithful correspondents.

When you are married you must not ask me to come to your wedding. I can fancy now the effect it would have upon me, and the sorry figure I should cut. When I began this letter I intended it to be good-natured rather than melancholy, but I fear I have only half succeeded in my purpose. Do not read too much vinegar into it, however, and consider, as one of its lessons, the inevitable truth that a man cannot be a good husband and still be one of the boys. Then comes the time when Memory must take the place of Reality, when the new life must draw its curtain over the old. All I ask or hope is that there may have been some one little act or word on my part that you will feel and remember as a part, however small, of your life. You have my heartiest congratulations and best wishes. In the meantime, I await a long pipe under the pines, and remain,

Always sincerely . . .

[P.S.] I shall see your mother today and arrange the books you mentioned a week ago.

Gardiner
May 27, 1894

I have just been setting out, or rather getting the ground ready for Dean to set out, thirty-six tomato-plants, as a kind of Sunday thanksgiving for the past rain. Now I have had a good smoke and washed my hands, and shall go on with my good work and write my letter to you.

I think I shall be a happy man when I see your genial face once more, and feel that you are here for all summer. It would be about my luck to have some industrial or educational scheme turn up that would take you out of Gardiner and leave me to continue in my present solitary discontent, but I shall not worry myself with the prospect of such a thing. I look forward to many pipes and fires and books under the pines for the next three months with great pleasure. When you get married, of course there will be an end to all that; but until then let us make the

most of things and not forget *Antigone*. The more I think of
that scheme, the better I like it; and I am beginning to believe it
possible that we may do something that will repay us in more
ways than one for the time and labor we must spend in bringing
the work to pass. We must not look for money, but we may perhaps look for some good words from men whose words are worth
something. I dream of all this as a possibility—nothing more.—
And, while I think of it, let me say that I have a curiosity to
know how Phipter (is that right?) manages the "kindred form"
business. Will you kindly send me his version of the opening
line, in your next letter?

During the past week I have read Anatole France's *Crime de
Sylvestre Bonnard* in French. It is a queer thing, immensely entertaining and full of wise sayings. The book is supposed to be
the *journal intime* of an old savant and is written with a beautiful disregard for all sense of form. What little story there is is
lost again and again in the old man's eccentric digressions and it
is hardly necessary to say that the reader does not miss it. I hope
you may take a notion to read it some day. You will be glad
when you find that two pages of it are devoted, in a quaint way,
to the same Antigone in whom we are both so much interested
just now. Thomas Hardy also seems to know her well. In fact,
I am continually finding references to her lately. Have you ever
noticed how often that is the case when we are interested in a
certain name? We find it where we least expect it, and when
we do, it seems somehow like a reference to an old friend.

I have been too much occupied of late to do any writing except two sonnets and some ninety lines of a queer poem called
"The Night Before." I hope to have it done (there will be some
four hundred lines of it) by the time you return and I think you
may like it. It is a tragic monologue written in unrhymed tetram-
eters—that is, like *Evangeline*, with two feet left out. For example, here is the opening line:

"Look you, Domine; look you, and listen."

Yesterday I did fifty-five lines, but was pretty tired after it was over. You see the thing demands work—wasted work, most likely, but still work that I cannot seem to help doing. You will be glad, or sorry, to know that I have three prose tales well in my head and shall have them out as soon as I can settle myself down to such labor once more. The one I like best of all cannot fail to attract you, even when done in my poor way; but the title, "Theodore," you won't like. It seems to me, however, the only title for the story, which, by the way, is not just like most stories, and I could not think of changing it.

June 20 is a date that means considerable to me just now. Then I am going to Cambridge to see my two or three old friends before they shake the dust of Harvard from their feet and go out into this world [which] manages to kill, in many cases, all that is interesting in a man. I am glad to say that this observation does not, in any way, apply to you. On the contrary, the world has used you so well that I would not for anything deprive you of your Rockland experience. But it was a little discouraging to have you expect me to be startled upon hearing of your engagement. But that is all right. You did not know much of what you were talking about. "Her name is Adela—and we are engaged. That's all"—I shall keep that for a novel.

Gardiner
June 3, 1894

I naturally expected something of a remonstrance against what I said concerning your "drawing away" and I have nothing particular to say in my defense except to tell you that my words were true to my feelings. I fancy I said six months instead of three years because I have lately been in a mood to notice and magnify things that would not occur to me when I was in a different frame of mind. My failure thus far to accomplish anything or to be anybody in the world, rather than my separation from the one who is and always will be a part of my daily life, is the cause of all this. Until I feel that I am independent—"a man among men"—I shall not have much peace. My pride is almost unnatural and sometimes I wonder if it is not killing me by inches. This is enough, and now let us make an end of this lugubrious confidence which, undoubtedly, has long since tired you and compromised my worth in your estimation. When you come home you will not find me a broken down wreck or anything of the kind. On the contrary, I think you will find me surprisingly good-natured. There is but one thing that can make me disagreeable and gloomy. What that thing is, I shall tell you in person.

I have lately been reading Herbert Spencer's *Education.* I suppose you know it thoroughly so you will not need any of my comment. However, I must say that the idea of throwing aside the languages in favor of the sciences would make elementary education a terribly dry [word illegible] for me. I suppose, upon the whole, it would be a boon to humanity, but God help the poor devils who are constructed like me. His general theory of instruction is all right, though in no wise original. His English is rather hard and his affected use of big words is not always pleasing. But then, the book is one we all should read, as it is crammed with good things and filled with an obviously honest enthusiasm. If such a thing should be that you have not read [it], you will do well to do so this summer.

Yesterday I got my *McClure's* and read Kipling's animal story, "Kaa's Hunting." It is a queer thing, well done, of course, but I do not think I care for another like it. The author tried to do something new and succeeded; but I infinitely prefer Mulvaney and his comrades to snakes and monkeys. I tried to find an allegory in the stuff, but the effort was unsatisfactory. Perhaps you will have better luck. There are two or three fine touches in the piece such as "he (the python) seemed to *pour* himself along the ground." My taste in this direction corresponds with my indifference to the doings of trained animals. I prefer men and women who live, breathe, talk, fight, make love, or go to the devil after the manner of human beings. Art is only valuable to me when it reflects humanity or at least human emotions.

I do not think you will be surprised or offended at my preference for Cambridge to Brunswick during Class Day week. If I went to Brunswick it would be to meet strangers, while by going to Cambridge I shall meet old friends. I should have just about as much interest in attending the Bowdoin festivities at that time as you would have in going to Harvard when your own college was holding general "high-jinks" in your absence. So it does not look now as if we should meet until the first of July. Well, we must make the most of the time we have, and try to feel that we have accomplished something when the time comes for you to go away again.

If you wish me to get anything for you while I am in Boston it would be a pleasure for me to do so. Of course there is no need of my saying this, but it may be the means of your thinking of something that you would not otherwise. I am always happy when I feel that I am doing something for somebody else besides myself, so I rather hope you will think of something—even if it be rum.

I have written 225 lines of "The Night Before," and am getting rather enthusiastic over the thing. The story is pretty good and the writing of it is the most difficult thing that I have ever undertaken. These two facts serve as incentives. Fifteen lines an hour is good work and I feel much better after I have done them. The story is unpleasant, founded upon my system of "opposites" that is, creating a fictitious life in direct opposition to a real life which I know. My recent mental disturbances have rendered some kind of more or less literary expression an absolute necessity; and this story, which by the way, comes dangerously near to being what the world calls "hot stuff" is doing me a good service in working off my general discontent. It reflects, in a measure, my present mood in the narration of things of which I know nothing except by instinctive fancy. There is battle (of the worst kind), murder and sudden death in it, together with other things equally interesting were they put in the hands of a competent writer. As it is, I think you may enjoy it, but I must ask you not to expect too much, and to make a strong effort not to laugh at the attempted intensity of my murderer's confession. The success of the poem will depend wholly upon the success of this intensity, which ought to increase from the start and end with a grand smash. At any rate, you will think well of me for trying to do something a little above the ordinary, whether I succeed or not. Here is a little observation that will come in towards the end:

"I tell you, Domine,
There are times in the lives of us poor devils
When heaven and hell get mixed."

The main purpose of the thing is to show that men and women are individuals; and there is a minor injunction running through it not to thump a man too hard when he is down. This, however, is hidden, and would probably not be noticed by one reader in a hundred. If the poem is a little fatalistic, you must excuse me. I write it because I cannot help it, and this is also true of the way in which I do it.—I have just finished reading your *God's Fool* aloud to Mother. I liked it immensely. Butler tells me that he is disappointed in *Marcella* and has gone back to *On the Heights* (Auerbach) of which he never tires. This [is] another of my disconnected letters. Shall try to do better next time.

Gardiner
June 10, 1894

The three sketches which I sent to Cambridge some time ago have been through the *Atlantic* office with far from discouraging results. Of course they were not accepted—I never dreamed of such a thing—but they were damned rather pleasantly by Mr. Scudder, and pitilessly praised by Mr. Whittier, the ancient proof-reader of the magazine. By the way of salve, he tells me that Howells's *Venetian Life* was refused by Mr. Lowell, and goes on to say that your humble servant is "a coming writer," that his style "reminds him of Deming," that "Mr. Scudder is not infallible," and other kindred rot, which I take with many allowances for the old friendship between him and my uncle. Mr. Scudder himself writes: "These sketches seem to me not without some claim to notice. They show restraint and an effort at telling something worthwhile; but, etc." *"But"* is the biggest word in the English language.

If there is a corner in Hell for those who waste their time in this life, what may I expect for writing a poem of three-hundred and eighty lines during the past three weeks,—to say nothing of the coming revision, which must take place before the thing can be presentable? The first writing is all done now, with the exception of eight or ten lines, which I hope to do today. Then I shall go for "Theodore," treating him rather differently from any other of my other poor creations. The story is rather "bizarre," but not half so much so as real life. Theodore is not a typical man. The Italian stone-cutter, who whistles the barcarolle from "Sicilian Vespers," and comes at last to carve Theodore's monument, must make or spoil the story. I doubt if I get fairly into it until I return from my Boston trip, but we shall have it in the Pines before long.

In reading Tennyson the other day, I came across a little poem in blank verse dedicated to the Princess Beatrice, in which he speaks of her marriage as "that white funeral of the single life." A Poet Laureate is worthwhile when he says things like that. And, speaking of Tennyson, how would it do to read him some this summer? His greatest charm lies in the fact that one can read him over and over again without tiring of him. I have read *Maud* aloud three times, and am quite ready to do so again—or listen to you. Perhaps the best way to read a long poem like that is alternately. The metre, like the poem, is hard (in a certain sense) and strange. And there are always the *Idyls*. There is also another poet I should like very much to read in our bower: I speak now of Kingsley, whose *Andromeda* I have only read in short snatches. I think, if [we] have a mind to do it, we can make considerable of the coming three months, having say two sittings a week. *Antigone* need not take all our time—if we let it, I am afraid that we should get hopelessly sick of the thing—and I am sure that I shall not let my own efforts interfere to any great extent with things of more importance. *Antigone* makes me think of Latham, who writes that he is going to take a non-resident course—Syracuse University—in the Greek drama, and that he is intensely interested in our translating scheme. It is one of the regrets of my life that you cannot meet that man. It would take you some time to get accustomed to his strangeness, but after that you would soon discover his real worth. He would talk American history and read Matthew Arnold's poems with you from morning till night if you wanted him to. But such a meeting is probably one of the things that is not to be.

I have been reading Lowell's essays again. There is a mine of good stuff of which we know practically nothing, and I ask you, is it right that it should be so? Essays and poems are the two kinds of literature best adapted for reading aloud, and as we have between us an unusually good stock of both, we ought to make the most of them. Have you bought Barrett Wendell's book yet? If so, what do you think of it? And have you seen a copy of the *Chap-Book,* which seems to be making such a stir just now? The scheme of the magazine interests me and I am anxious to get to Cambridge and find out more about it. My chief fear is that it is too good a thing to succeed. I take Bliss Carman to be the guiding spirit of the undertaking.

"Ismene, mine own sister," is dangerously like the rendering I decided upon, but I do not think I have any reason to change it on that account. Of course there must be many little repetitions in the translation of a long work like *Antigone,* but they are not what count. The general effect of the play, as a whole, is the point to be considered; and it is to that end that I shall do my work. And, now I think of it, will you kindly refrain, as far as possible, from introducing poetical lines into your version?—that is, lines of ten properly accented syllables, which are so common in the Oxford translation. The more of them you make, the harder my work will be. You would understand this better if you were pulling my end of the string. I shall send you some *Chap-Books* from Cambridge.

Gardiner

June 17, 1894

The time is creeping on apace, and this is a devilish hot day—too hot to write letters or to do much of anything else. But when letters are expected at a certain time there is always a little disappointment when they fail to come, so I shall write enough to let you know that I am still in Gardiner and that "Theodore" is playing strange antics with me. He is giving me a hard tussle, but with the assistance of time, patience, perseverance, and a few other things I hope to do something with him before long. His story will be longer than the others you have heard—something like 7000 words, I should think, of which I have about 3500 written. The story is purposely artificial and my only chance of success lies in my possible ability of doing well enough, from an artistic point of view, to keep the artificiality in the background. It is good practice, at any rate, and must help me to a certain extent. I am now reconciled to the fact that my work last winter is of no value except for the practice it gave me, and I now anticipate another winter's work to the same end.—You may be interested to know that "Theodore" is a little study in anti-climax —not much like anything I have ever seen.

Yesterday I read 70 pages of Daudet's *Tartarin sur les Alpes* but the French was wofully hard, and [the] subject not fitted to my mood. I could not see the fun of it, so threw it down for *Oedipus Coloneus*, which I shall finish today if nothing happens to prevent [it].—When we get together once more, I want you to criticize my "great poem." The thing cost me much weariness as to my gray matter and I am anxious to fix it up as well as I can. You can doubtless make a few suggestions that will be of much value to me.

The *Critic* has seen fit to accept one of my sonnets, but it positively refuses to pay for my shoes. I have the consolation of a year's subscription, however, which is quite as good. I have heard nothing from the *Dial*, nor do I expect to. Upon the whole, I am rather glad to have my first publication of any significance (for I confess myself vain enough to think that there are damned fools in the world who cannot even get into the *Critic*) in the eastern review instead of its western brother. I have no great love for the west, and should not have, even if the *Dial* had published my "Poe." This is not "sour grapes," I am really better satisfied as things are. Of course the printing of a sonnet does not amount to much, but it may be a little help toward a beginning.

Excuse the personal note in this brief letter and send yours of June 24 to #404 Putnam Avenue, Cambridgeport. Poverty compels me to go by boat, so I cannot see you in Brunswick.

Gardiner
September 29, 1894

I have my choice this afternoon between working at my "profession," gathering apples, reading the *Yellow Book,* going to a foot-ball game and writing to you. I have decided upon the last.

No, I have not forgotten you. I have only been busy with my thoughts. Thinking seriously, but, I am glad to say, not morbidly, of the things to come. I think I have got almost through my morbid period. I am beginning to see that it is all a waste of time and of vitality and that if things are bound to go to the devil anyway the best thing for me to do is to let them go with a feeling that I have done as well as I can.

I have finished that little study in darkness, "The Black Path" and after reading two or three stories in the *Yellow Book* do not feel that my time is wholly wasted. It seems to me to be something of a gain on "Theodore," but I doubt if you will like it so well as you liked the longer sketch. There are no Sicilian Vespers in it, nor any educational uneasiness—except from a purely mental (I might say moral) point of view. I am afraid that there is a little of my old fault of over condensation, but I hope to overcome that someday. If I ever do, I shall reap big benefits from my present punctiliousness in writing.

If things go on as well as they have started (in my head) I shall have a good-sized volume by next May to correct and copy during the summer. My next thing to tackle is a marionette story touching lightly on divorce. I am afraid I shall make a botch of it, but there is always that chance to try. After that I think I shall take the opportunity to recast Theodore. He needs it.—With what I have written and am sure of writing, in my own way, I can now count on at least six sketches toward a volume of twelve or fifteen. The winter ought to finish it.

My interest in *Antigone* is increasing every day and my anxiety to see the thing in print amounts almost to childishness. So please give it to me as fast as you can with anything like convenience and then go to work on your notes. I have done all that you gave me that day in the woods but am a little in doubt as to two passages. One is the very first words of the Chorus after Creon's speech. I found it absolutely impossible to make anything like satisfactory poetry of your version so turned to your particular "black beast," the Oxford version, and found what I wanted. You must have left out something by accident, as you say "Your pleasure is this, O Creon—" The Oxford says something like "Your pleasure is this and my pleasure is yours." My version runs:

> "Your pleasure—of the friend as of the foe—
> Is one with mine, O Creon."

The Greek must say something of this kind or the passage is without any point at all. The other place that troubles me occurs somewhere about line 308. "For death alone shall not suffice before, hung up alive, you shall make clear this outrage, in order that etc." I suppose "death" means a natural death or the poor guard would have no chance to improve his ways. Kindly tell me what Plumptre does with this place, and give me your own ideas on it. Send me the next chorus as soon as you can and let me get at it—I want it over with.

I carried a handful of *Chap-Books* down to the Doctor the other day and he read, among other things, Sharp's second "Vista," "The Birth of a Soul." He says "It doesn't amount to a cuss" and I am inclined to agree with him. There isn't much satisfaction in showing anything like the *Chap-Book* to the "doc." He seems to be down on all the younger writers and I am afraid the cause is partly envy. It is not wholly strange if it is, as he has written poetry for the past twenty-five years which is better than the average magazine stuff—but, on the other hand, he has not made the slightest effort to dispose of it. He seems to lack all action. I have [been] trying for a year to get him to write a story in verse, but have failed thus far. I hope, for his own sake, he will start something this winter. The doc has reached that stage now when he is likely to do something great without in the least expecting it.

I stopped writing yesterday afternoon because I found that I was not in the mood. Today I am not much better—in fact I do not feel like doing much of anything. The weather is cold and raw and I am damnably lonesome. Sunday is a bad day with me now—can't do anything but chew tobacco and try to make up my mind to read something. Have read the *Yellow Book*—all I care for—and find it pretty thin. Henry James' story and Arthur Waugh's essay are the only things I care for. The *Yellow Book,* in my humble [opinion], is an elegantly got up fake and has no excuse for being that I can see. I have not read the second number—that is called an improvement over the first.

If possible, this letter is more disconnected and rambling than yours, but if it proves half as welcome I shall be satisfied. I can appreciate your remarks on the pathos of boyish ambitions. I feel it every day.—There was a foot-ball game yesterday between Gardiner and Augusta but I have not heard how it came out. Don't think I care.

Write and tell me what you think of *Trilby* compared with *The Greater Glory*—if there is any comparison.

Gardiner
October 7, 1894

The past week has been a dull season with me—nothing but ruminating and wheeling wood, and the worst kind of wood at that. Somehow I fancy that you do not know much about it—do you?— Split slab-wood of every shape and length imaginable—full of splinters and conducive to all sorts of swear words. But it is almost all in now, thank the Lord, and I could shout *jubilate* were it not for the apples. I never could find any poetry in gathering apples. It is the worst work I know of except washing dishes and listening to a debate.

I do not think I have read anything that will interest you— in fact I have read nothing but an occasional snatch of French and two or three magazine stories. The last *McClure's* is an unusually good number, containing among other things short stories by Conan Doyle, Robert Barr, and Bret Harte. Doyle's story is well nigh perfect in his way—I should say "its" way, for it is hardly characteristic of its author—and Barr's little satire is surprising and good. The difference between the two is that the second named is clever and temporary while the other is just simple and for all time—if time happens to look at it in that way. "Young Robin Grey" by Bret Harte does not impress me more than most of his recent work—that is, not at all. The scene is laid in Scotland and the atmosphere is supposed to be Caledonian; but there is a failure somewhere. Whether it is in the story, which is not much, or in its treatment, which is too strongly suggestive of so much per thousand words, I can hardly say. Buy the magazine and read Doyle's little three-page piece and tell me if you do not like it better than all the Sherlock Holmes you have ever read. I have never read any myself, but I have my opinions. —There is also a long sketch of Dana, the *Sun* man, and an article of Niagara turned into a mill-dam—which may be good if one cares to read it.

* 169 *

To return to *Antigone,* I am sorry to say that your quotation from Plumptre stopped just where I wanted it to begin. What puzzles me is to know how the fellow could have any chance to improve his ways by being advised to mend them just before he was hanged. If you will kindly finish out the speech in your next letter and send me some copy (if possible) I shall be accordingly obliged and grateful. I think I can patch up the other place, though I doubt if I can make as good a verse as I had before. There was something in the ring of the words, "one with mine, O Creon," that I liked. But I must write Sophocles and not Robinson (as far as euphony permits) I suppose, and so shall rehash the passage as best I can.

I am going to write some "Tavern Songs" this winter—down by the furnace with a chew of tobacco "in." This chorus will give you some idea of what they will be like:

> *"There's a town down the river*
> *Down the river, down the river,*
> *There's a town down the river,*
> *By the sea."*

I shall endeavor to put a little mysticism in them, and make them worth while as literature; at the same time trying to make them musical enough in themselves to be songs first and poems after. Of course I may not write them at all but I hope to do a few, at least.

The "long awaited," that is *The Globe* has come—two copies— one of which I shall send with this letter. The proof reader evidently has his own ideas of punctuation, but aside from that they (the poems) are printed quite to my satisfaction. The matter that troubles me most is the question whether they are worth printing or not. Sometimes I rather think they are, then I think they are not. I can only tell by looking at them five years from now. That generally settles such matters. I am beginning to think that Horace's advice to "keep your piece nine years" was not so far out of the way after all, though I think that it is now generally believed that the *Ars* was addressed to a poetaster whose work could be of no value if seasoned for a century. Am I right?

Do not hold me responsible for Thorne's nonsense at the close of the "Wreck of the Mayflower."

Gardiner
October 21, 1894

I have just read *Marjorie Fleming* and feel well paid for my time. I do not know when I have read anything that has struck me more forcibly than that little sketch. I think I like best of all the turkey mother who was "more than usual calm" and the young buck "whose only lack was in his hair." All this is genius, if a child did do it.

At last I have the worst of my "scrubbing" done, and shall soon be able to sit down to work with some feeling of freedom—that is, unless something new unforeseen turns up to hinder. Things are continually turning up—wrong side up—with me, so I do not dare to look ahead with too much certainty of peace. Still, I think I shall do something in my way this winter and hope to sink some hundreds of dollars sometime next year in getting something printed. That is, I hope for a chance to run the risk of sinking them in a good place—which is not always so easy to do nowadays.

I had a letter from Ford the other day in which there are some remarks on *Trilby* which may interest you. You are in a better way than I am to appreciate them, so I copy out a few lines: ". . . the writer plainly shows lack of experience and has done some things of which a school boy would be ashamed . . . In short the work is that of an artist" (used in the narrow sense, I suppose) "careless, but intensely individual and original. I have read nothing since the days of Thackeray which pleased me so much, and this in spite of the fact that the author has handled a subject which he had no right to undertake, which very few writers outside of the French circle could handle. The character of Trilby is as impossible as can be, and I suppose it is the great heart of the writer, and the happy careless life which he describes, with the little bits of French song thrown in, which makes the whole attractive."

I do not think you will wholly like this, but then, all men have a right to their own opinions. You know Ford was the man who criticised my chorus for its "Miltonic" slowness. I cannot help feeling that he is partly right, but for all that I shall not try to build it over. I am getting more and more convinced every day that blank verse is the form to put it in and shall keep on with it to the end.

And this makes me think of the chorus you have just sent me. I thank you for it and appreciate your little red-lettered sarcasm on the back. I have been trying for two days to put the first line of the chorus into metre but have not yet succeeded. The nearest I have come to it is this:

"Of all the many marvellous things that are,
There is not one more marvellous than man."

The trouble is, there is too much of the original for one English line and not enough for two—a case of sadly frequent occurrence. I shall get over this snag sometime, though, and then, I hope, go on with a little more ease. There is some satisfaction in knowing that when I have finished what I now have on hand, the work will be (in the rough) a third part done. The thing ought to be printed in the winter of '95-6 at the latest, and there seems to be no particular reason why it will not, if we both keep our strength and faculties. I don't anticipate very much enthusiastic labor on your part until your tongue is clean again, so kindly "work" Humphrey for all he is possibly worth and try to solace yourself with the fact that Edwin Booth's tongue was as black as the ace of spades nearly all his life. There is something in the company of a dead man—when he is Booth.

Yesterday I read my big *Chap-Book* and have come to the conclusion that "The Passion Flower" is above the ordinary. It is refreshingly clean, the italicized interludes helping the author and the reader to an incalculable extent. The story is long enough as it is. If I were one of the "rotten rich," as John Walsh calls certain of Gardiner's eminent people, I should buy Stone and Kimball's Poe, and the life of Villiers de l'Isle-Adam, together with twenty or thirty more volumes which I particularly want just now. But I can't do it, and I somehow feel that it is all for the best that I cannot.

The last *Dial* has a rather good article on Alexander Smith and some pleasing facts from the life of Wainwright the poisoner. Block, the "Globe Review" man, has a very commonplace review of Thoreau letters and Edith M. Thomas one of her little poetic icicles which do not please me. Edith is too cold for me.

George is reading *Treasure Island* aloud to me and I am getting deeply interested in the seafaring man with a wooden leg who has been shipped as cook. There is going to be the devil to pay. Read the book if you have not already. I can vouch for the first eight chapters and at the same time congratulate myself that my love for the romantic is not wholly dead. But I cannot read the *Man in Black*.

Gardiner
October 28, 1894

It gives me a comfortable feeling to have so much *Antigone* on hand, and, unless [something] unpleasant happens, I shall feel still more comfortable before long, when I have turned it into metre. I send you today the result of something over ten hours of diabolically hard labor. You will not like it at first because it is not literal, but if you will take the trouble to examine it a little more closely you will find that it is not so far from a translation as it seems on a first sight. I had to throw out "Many are the marvelous things" and that very uncomfortable expression "offspring of horses." The Greek language could say things which the English language cannot, and that is one of them. The Oxford Edition has "offspring of the steed," which is a little better, but still bad enough to spoil the whole strophe for me.

There is no need of worrying so much, however, over an occasional omission, as all translations are full of them. The first principles of poetical translation demand them, and I could do infinitely better work if I could bring myself to make my version a little more flexible. Over-fidelity to the original is the great fault of Longfellow's Dante and Taylor's *Faust* (I am not making comparisons) and if you will read a page of Longfellow's translation and then one of Carey's you will appreciate the truth of what I say. I have never seen Plumptre's version of this second chorus but I am willing to wager that he is farther from the original text than I, withal his advantage of writing from the original. I do not know how much more tinkering this of mine will require, but if you will kindly point out any parts that you think won't do, I will do my best to fix them.—While I think of it, let me copy this note by the editor of the Oxford version: "I cannot resist giving my readers this sentence from the translation of Adams: 'He traverses the hoary main in stormy winds, by the rattling tremors of swollen sails, and pierces the supreme incorruptible land of the immortal gods, year after year returning to plow it with horse-kind.'"

I received a letter from Butler not long ago containing the rather surprising statement that *Pembroke* is infinitely greater than *Trilby*. Perhaps that letter had something to do with my causing J. J. Ward to carry it (the book) back to the store when I got it and took it home. The book is strange in its very simplicity. Everything is drawn against a tragic background of subdued passion and some of the scenes are almost magnificent in their treatment. To the careless modern reader the plot—or rather the plots—will seem impossible and contrary to human nature; but to one who knows anything about Puritanism the book will be interesting and impressive. Narrow minded and unsympathetic readers had better keep away from it. It is a rather significant fact that it finds more appreciation in England than America, which is perhaps due to the fact of England's undeniable ability to tell a good thing and not be deceived by outward show, which I cannot help thinking that Time will prove to be a certain percentage of *Trilby*.

I was surprised to find some things treated so openly in *Pembroke*, and I rather admire Miss Wilkins' frankness and nerve, if the word is required. There are a few animal touches that are hardly like anything else that I have ever seen in novels. I hope you will see fit to read it before long, as I am anxious for your opinion. It is eminently qualified for reading aloud. It never drags for a page and is always either bright or gloomy. Although it "ends well" in a way, *Pembroke* life is not a summer vacation. It is pretty much like any other life—that is, relatively.

I was on the point of investing a couple of dollars in the first three *Chap-Books* but my scanty purse compelled me to do something else. I could have bought them then for ten cents a copy. Something told me that they would be valuable some day, and I think I told you as much. As it is, I am glad that I have one set.

George goes away tomorrow, so I must finish *Treasure Island* by myself. I like it immensely. There are no pseudo-historical caricatures in it with their long stilts and "I love thee's." It is all blood and thunder and rum and such like and I shall be sorry when I come to the end.

[Typed on an undated half sheet of paper]

Nothing is there more marvelous than man!
Driven by southern storms he sails amidst
The wild white water of the wintry sea,
And through the thunder of engulfing waves;
And Earth—unceasing monarch of the gods—
He furrows, and the plows go back and forth,
And turn the broken mold year after year.

He traps and captures—all inventive man!—
The light birds and the creatures of the wild,
And in his nets the fishes of the sea;

He trains the tenants of the fields and hills,
And brings beneath the neck-encircling yoke
The rough-maned horse and the wild mountain bull.

I have been compelled to mix up clauses a little, but it has been done with always one end in view—to get the *effect* of the original. That is my theory of translation. If you like it better, say *"while* the plows go etc." *And* is more poetical to me. "Light birds" overcomes the difficulty and will do whether the word means light-hearted or light in everything. Which seems to be a question.

OX.

Gardiner
November 4, 1894

I feel myself growing thin (!) under this second chorus. I have been working away at it all the week but have not brought anything to pass—that is, anything that satisfies me. I send you what I have done, however, to let you judge for yourself. I shall not do any more with it just now, but shall go on with the dialogue and return to the chorus when the rest of the play is translated, so giving the more difficult parts the benefit of whatever maturity of thought and expression I may acquire between now and the day when I write a preliminary "finis" to the business. You cannot imagine what a damnable job it is to make anything of these choruses. Plumptre's total failure, to say nothing of Franklin, will give you some idea of it. I am also having a hard wrestle with the two bits of dialogue following the epode (I suppose that is an epode where "Amazement!" comes in, isn't it?). But I can probably get over it in some way, and the messenger's speech is comparatively easy. At least I think it is from the quick translation I made yesterday.

Tomorrow I shall start on my prose work again and for the present give the translation one hour every afternoon. In that way I can average, I think, eight or ten lines a day, which will do very well. Then will come the re-translating of the whole play; and then, if the fates are willing, the printing and distributing of it. I still feel that it is going to amount to something. I have not yet seen anything (unless perhaps this second chorus) to discourage me, nor do I intend to let myself see anything that will. The more I think of what I have read of Plumptre's version the more I think that his great fault is his absence of dramatic force, of which there is plenty in the original; and the absence of that means the absence of dramatic poetry. The few scraps of Donaldson's translation given in the notes of the "Ox" are strong but not always pleasant; for example take line 387: "What hap holds sortance with my coming forth?" That is too archaic for my taste. The editor of the Ox says that D makes low comedy of the messenger's first scene with Creon and condemns him for doing so. That passage gave me some trouble, as I was in doubt whether to make it "funny" or not. In the end I did not. What does Jebb say and how does Plumptre translate the line, "Are you pained in your mind or in your ears?" Please remember this in your next letter. How do you like this:

"——money is the most accursed thing
That man has ever made; it strikes down cities
And scatters families; it leads away
Good souls of men to foul accomplishments
And teaches them the practice of all guile
And all iniquity."

Perhaps I have quoted this before; if I have, do not think too hard of me for it, for the merit is all in Sophocles; the translation is literal, or so nearly so that I do not pride myself much upon it. I must say, however, that I like the lines and cordially hope that Plumptre's are no better.

To return once more to *Trilby*, I am compelled to say that my best judgment of a book that I have never read leads me to think that Ford's criticism is the best I have yet seen. The Lounger in the *Critic* has some words that you will like and the last *Dial* is very pleasant with the book. Payne's criticism of *Lord Ormont* in the same seems to me almost an insult—not so much for what he says as for what he doesn't say.—I shall try to be a little more prompt in sending you my *Critics* hereafter. I find them worth looking over and fancy I see an improvement over the past numbers you gave me. I am doing my best to admire the *Dial* and partly succeed; but I cannot always admire their taste in selecting books for long reviews.

In the last *McClure's* there is a conversation between Dr. Doyle and Robert Barr; also a story by both men. Doyle's is a little uncanny but very fascinating for its way of showing a wholesome writer's way of handling a morbid subject. The last *Chap-Book* is pretty much a fizzle, only saved by P. B. Goetz's two quatrains. Goetz is a Harvard man, '93, and has done even better work in the college papers. The notes are entertaining, and I suppose you were glad to see that the Bowdoin Art Museum is a better piece of work than the stone shed I saw going up in the Harvard yard. Harvard architecture is so notoriously hideous that it would be a shame to start any innovations at this late day. I am glad for Bowdoin and sorry for Professor Norton.

I have not read anything during the week, putting most of my spare time (including six hours yesterday) on that infernal chorus. As to my variations in the number of lines in the strophe and antistrophe, I do [not] make any attempt at regularity. In the first chorus there was a still larger difference. I am simply making a poem of a play and do not bind myself in any way to form.

I should like very much to see that article you spoke of in the *Outlook*. I do not even know where it is published and am not positively sure that I ever heard of it before, though it seems to me that I have. If you do not treasure the copy too highly, perhaps you will send [it] to me and trust your chance of getting it again.

[And language has he learned and wind-
swift thought]
And speech and soaring wisdom has he
learned,
With human measures and a way to shun
The sharp and painful arrows of the frost.
Full of resource, of all the future brings,
Resourceless meets he nothing; Death alone — This is the part
He never shall escape; but he has found — that sticks me
[A cure] for life's unyielding maladies. [a — more than all the
cure]. — rest.

Antistrophe II

Thus gifted with a shrewd inventive skill
Beyond belief, now makes he for the right,
Now for the wrong. And first of all the state
Is he who honors most the nation's law
And the sworn justice of the gods; but he
Becomes an outcast whom rash folly binds
In evil fellowship, nor shall he dwell
With me, nor think with me, whose action
thus . . .

Unsatisfactory

I marvel at this portent of the gods! — The Ox breaks
Knowing her as I do can I deny — this line—you do
The maid Antigone?—O wretched girl— — not. I like it bet-
Child of a wretched father, Œdipus, — ter broken, but
Tell me!—they surely cannot lead you here — can easily change
Captured in this wild work against the king! — it. How do the
— anchorites agree
— upon it? Perhaps
— this will go.

Gardiner
November 11, 1894

This has been a clearing up week with me—not only outside
but here in my den. At last I have finished that infernal bug-

* 179 *

bear of mine, "The Black Path" and have it stowed away, after a third writing, for future reference. I have tinkered over *Antigone* a good deal, besides, and shall send with this a first draft (which means practically a seventeenth) of the girl's speech to Creon. That speech is strong stuff, and I must confess that I felt a little guilty when I undertook it. It is not done now by any means but what I send you may give you some idea as to whether I can make anything of it or not. You will find my version almost literal—too near it, I am afraid.

Yesterday I read a while in Longfellow's Dante and wondered if I were not an ass for attempting this thing. I cannot call his translation anything but a dismal failure; if that is the case, what will this *Antigone* be? But then, Sophocles and Dante are two different things, and I won't worry because Longfellow doesn't suit me. And there is another thing to encourage me: this play "is mine oyster" which according to my judgment, has never yet been opened. If I succeed in opening it to any great extent, I shall be highly pleased but do not think I shall ever try to open another until I am more at ease as regards my time. For some reason I work much more slowly than when I began—probably because I am getting more finical. Perhaps that second chorus stunted my imagination.

Your copy of the *Outlook* came all right, and I read the article on the poets with much interest but not much sympathy. Whenever I hear of, or read of, the Bodley Head I think of the *Yellow Book* and Mr. LeGallienne's adulterous nightingales and some other things that do not impress me much. They are all on the wrong track, excepting Mr. Gale, and he is almost sickening sometimes in artlessness, or whatever he calls it. If I rejoiced in cricket and football as he does I should not write some of the stuff that he has written. I say "stuff," but do not quite mean it. Whatever Gale does—at least, what I have seen—he does well; but his country maidens grow a little tiresome. Mr. W. B. Yeats looks as if he might have the afflatus, and pretty badly, too. His picture is not just what one has a right to look for in this nineteenth century, and I am too conservative to admire the taste that leads a man to make such a "holy show" of himself. That makes me think that I am getting very tired of having Conan Doyle's rather unexpressive mug thrust into my face from all sides, as it has been for the past three months. He has written some good things for *McClure's*—or they have printed them—and I have no doubt that I should like Sherlock Holmes if I once took him up. George has just read *Micah Clarke* but does not think over much of it. Joe has read *Trilby*—or "Tribly," as he calls it—and says it is queer. That is his only criticism. Everything that Joe reads is queer, or else it doesn't amount to a damn.

I have been trying for a long time to work up courage to read *The Greater Glory* and think I shall succeed before long. I know that I shall like it, but still I keep away from it—just as I do from *Madame Bovary*, which has been on my shelf for a year and a half. Yesterday I took up *Le Maître de Forges* (*The Ironmaster*) and found it very fine. It is a fairly stocky volume and probably [will] require eight or ten sittings. After that I think I shall be ready for Maartens. I looked into the *Prisoner of Zenda* the other day and found it decidedly attractive. It is prettily got up and finely printed on rather small paper—which I always like. Schuman has written some very warm blooded sonnets lately and takes infinite delight in reading them to me. They are refreshing to one who has heard again and again some two hundred and fifty of the things written in the same style and the same vein. This monotony, more than anything else, I think, will stand in the way of their publication. They are too suggestive of papers "of no particular value except to the owner," but I cannot make the doctor see it in my light. So I let him alone now, and hope that Thorne's prophecy, or statement, may prove true. I am afraid, however, that it won't, although the doc has done great work—chiefly in single lines such as:

"The desolate dim peaks loom vast and higher."

He runs Love a little too hard, it seems to me, but that is his business, not mine. I wish that he could realize a little better than he does that a love poem, to be good, must be very good.

I send a bunch of *Critics* with this letter and trust that you may find something in them to interest you. I am slowly but surely "souring" on the *Dial*. I think of what it ought to be, and then of what it is. And then of John Burroughs.

GUARD

Here is the guilty one that buried him—
We seized her in the work.—But where is Creon?

CHORUS

Returning from the palace—in good time
To meet your opportunity.

CREON

                      What is this?
I come to meet whose opportunity?

GUARD

O King, 'tis not for any man to say
What things he will not do; for second thoughts
Belie the first resolve. I could have sworn
That I should never come this way again
But slowly, for your threats; yet am I here
(For joy without our expectation
Has none to match it) spite of my past vow,
Leading this maiden whom we found at work
Over the dead man's grave. No shaken lot
Is this, but still my own good fortune—mine,
And only mine.—And now, O King, I pray you,
Take her and question her, and do with her
According to your will. But I am free,
And justly clear of this unhappy crime.

CREON

'Tis she you bring! and how? Whence do you bring her!

GUARD

She buried Polynices; you know all
There is to know.

CREON

Is this the truth you tell me?

GUARD

I saw this maiden burying the corpse
Against your order. Do I speak straight words?

CREON

And how was she discovered? and how taken?

GUARD

'Twas thus: In terror of your fearful threat,
As soon as we were there we swept away
The dust that hid the corpse; and having stripped
The body, damp with death, we placed ourselves
High on a windward hill to shun the stench;
And there we waited, busily alert
With hard reproach for any man of us
Who made a sign to shirk. So the time passed
Until the noonday sun stood overhead,
Burning us with his heat—when suddenly
There came an awful whirlwind out of heaven
That filled the plain and all the mighty air
And vexed the woodland with unwholesome dust.
This god-sent plague we suffered with closed eyes;
And when it ceased, after a weary time,
We saw this maiden coming; and she cried
With a quick bitter wailing, like a bird

Over an empty nest. So grieved she then,
When she beheld the body lying bare,
And called down imprecations upon those
Who wrought the deed; and straightway did she bring
Dry dust in her own hands, and from an urn,
Well shaped of brass and lifted high in air,
Thrice did she crown him with poured offerings.
   When we saw this we rushed at once upon her
And seized her, unappalled at our approach;
And when we there accused her of this crime
And of the first as well, she made no sign,
Nor uttered any word in her defense.
At once a pleasure and a pain to me
Was this: for, though it be a pleasant thing
To make one's own way out of jeopardy,
Painful it is to send another there.
But then all this was naturally less
To me than my own safety.

CREON *(To Antigone)*

Tell me, you
With your head bowed to earth, if you confess
Or you deny that you have done this thing.

ANTIGONE

Yes, I confess. [Mss. note:] It would hardly be kindness to Sophocles to reproduce an Attic redundancy in a
language that won't stand it.

CREON *(to Guard)*

You may go where you will,
Acquitted of this heavy charge.—(To Antigone) But you
Will tell me, and that briefly, did you know
The proclamation that made this forbidden?

* 184 *

ANTIGONE

I knew it, and why not?—'Twas very plain.

CREON

And you have dared then to transgress the laws!

ANTIGONE

Yes, for the word was not of Jove at all;
Nor was it Justice, dwelling with the gods
Below the earth, that framed your government;
Nor did I think this edict you proclaimed
So strong that I could break the laws of heaven,
Unwritten and unchanging. For, O King,
They are not of today, nor yesterday,
But for all time they are, and no man knows
Of their beginning. It was not for fear
Of any human will that I would pay
The gods my penalty—for I must die.
Well did I know that ere I ever heard
Your proclamation; and if I die now,
Before my time, so much I count my gain:
For whosoever lives as I have lived,
In many sorrows, will by dying reap
His best reward. Therefore to meet my fate
The pain is nothing; but if I had left
The child of my own mother to lie dead
Without a mound above him—that indeed
Were sorrow; but there is no sorrow now.
And if by chance you still declare
What I have done to be a foolish thing,
Then I am charged with folly by a fool.

Bring this with you, with what more I may send, when you
come home this winter.

I could not get a chance to write you a letter Sunday and am afraid that I am not in the mood for it today. Since the middle of last week I have been hopelessly "out of sorts" on account of the kids, who keep running by my door and shake the house generally. Sometimes I get desperate and go down street or anywhere I can cool off. If they stay here all winter God only knows what will become of me.

And yet I did something Friday. I did four pages, about 1600 words, of "Christmas Eve," a somewhat queer sketch which might easily become great in the hands of Kipling or Stevenson, but in the hands of "me"—well, I may do something with it and I may not. I was a fool to undertake it, as it is quite beyond me; but it kept bothering me until I took it up, and now I am letting it sizzle awhile before going ahead. I wrote too much Friday and shall have to write it over again. This sketch must be longer than the others—say 12,000 words. It reflects the wasted part of a brilliant but "unruddered" man in the company of a poor devil he has taken as a companion for the simple reason that he can master him. There is nothing that is improbable, but there is much that is impossible—for me to bring out.

Did you see what Bok had to say about *Trilby* and *The Manxman* in the Sunday *Journal?* It was a little stronger than anything I have yet read, but it has the savor of truth in it. The difference between Du Maurier and Harding Davis is ridiculously large, I suppose, but I cannot help thinking that America's preference for *Trilby* to *The Manxman* is due to the same reason that the average reader of *Harper's* seems now to be looking forward with far more eagerness to the appearance of the *Princess Aline* than to that of *The Simpletons*—or *Hearts Insurgent*. This comparison is mine, not Bok's. He simply says that the book of the year is not *Trilby*, but *The Manxman*.

Did I tell you that I was reading *Le Maître de Forges?* I think I did. There is something in it that makes one willing to forgive the author his unnecessary pages.—The other day I received a very acceptable little gift from Ford in the shape of a Clarendon Press edition of De Musset's *On ne badine pas avec L'Amour and Fantasio.* He apologized for the edition but assured me that the contents would more than make up for it; and from what I have read, here and there, I think he is right. There is something decidedly Shaksperian in Musset's best work—quite different from *On ne saurait pas,* etc. which you have read with *Il faut qu'une porte* and *Pierre and Camille.*

Hall Caine praises Sharp's *Vistas,* and thinks that if the book had appeared three years ago, we should have heard nothing of Macterlinck. All of which seems to me to be a slip of genius. You will see this in the last *Critic*—which, by the way, is exceptionally good. And I will say here that you need not return the *Critics* I have sent you. I have given up the scrap book scheme. Shall send the last number in a day or two.

[P.S.] I am on the last "bunch" of *Antigone.* Please send me another lot as soon as possible, and oblige, etc.

Gardiner
November 26, 1894

I had such a grouch Sunday that I could not write to you or anybody else. I do not know just what was the matter with me, but I looked at everything through blue glasses—everything but literature. My confidence in that sometimes almost discourages me, as it makes me think once in a while of what a collapse there will be some day if it all goes to the devil. I have a confidence in myself regarding that that is hardly natural to me and for that reason I am often wondering how it all will look to [me] five years from now. "Christmas Eve" goes on at the rate of from 1000 to 1600 words in a forenoon, which is faster than I ought to permit myself to write. It makes re-writing all the harder.

Last Saturday I ate beans with your father and mother and enjoyed myself immensely. After the beans I took a small chew of tobacco at your mother's invitation and heard your father tell shark stories. I am likely to write something about sharks almost any day now. That would be a little out of my usual line, but I think I shall have to do it.

I did my first book-buying for many weeks the other day, sending to Schoenhof's for *Mon Franc-Parler* by Coppée, *Le Violon de Faïence* by Champfleury and *Le Sécret de l'Echafaud* by Villiers de l'Isle-Adam. Not a very expensive lot, but quite an event for me.—And Schoenhof jewed me out of ten cents, which is not like him. Haven't I heard something about a successor to that establishment?

My thoughts this afternoon are pretty much like my handwriting. I grind hard all the morning at my vagabonds and do not seem to have much left for you. That is not just the way to do, and I shall try hereafter to write Sundays as I intend to do, and so treat you like a gentleman. I am trying to decide whether to tackle the third Chorus now or to let it go until I finish the dialogue. Somehow I dislike to leave anything undone, and shall probably go back on what I said in a recent letter to you and strike into it tomorrow. I was caught up now and then in that long scene where everybody talks in single lines, but upon the whole it was easy work. The Ox differs some from your rendering in the assignment of lines to the characters but is obviously wrong.

I have seen a good deal of pleasant criticism of *Songs from Vagabondia*—one in particular in *Town Topics,* which I will send you with some *Critics* and that copy of the *Outlook.*

I purpose to have my hair cut this afternoon—the first time for many long months. I suppose it is a moral duty, but it will seem queer not to have anything to run my fingers through when I am at loss for a word. That makes me think that I have written a "Ballade of Dead Friends," which will not strike you, probably, as you do not care for that kind of thing. I have also half written two Sonnets which I shall try to finish up before you come home. Life will seem a little more like something when you are here again and I look forward to some profitable sessions. When you come will you be good enough to bring the *Yellow Book* and if quite convenient, *The Manxman?* I hesitate in asking for the last, and would not have you feel at all obliged to bring it unless you can do so without interfering with anybody.

Town Topics will show you Doyle as a "swell." He carries his long coat and keg hat as well as one could expect but I am tired of him in any form. Everett Peacock is quite excited over *Ships that Pass in the Night* and has just heard of *Trilby.* Happy the man who has never heard of it.

My eyes have been so unsteady of late that I have not got into *The Greater Glory,* but hope to before long. I have not read anything since *The Iron-Master.* It will be worth your while to read that in translation, which may be found for a quarter at any newsstand. The book is a trifle long in the first half, but more than makes up in the second.

Gardiner
December 2, 1894

While fighting with the third chorus yesterday I became disgusted with everything under God's heaven and wrote a few remarks under the last antistrophe which you will kindly take goodnaturedly. I do not just understand that part nor the last lines of the strophe before it, beginning "Nothing of offense creeps etc." The Ox has that, "nothing comes to the tens of mortals far removed at least from calamity." To that there is a note by the editor stating that "This is very corrupt. Donaldson would have it 'In all the life of mortals mischief in every state her franchise claims.'" Which is like yours. Will you kindly translate these two passages again and be sure that you have the best authority behind you? I am doing this chorus more easily than any of the others, and but for this difficulty in interpreting it, should have had it done days ago.

The only fault I have to find with your translation is an occasional ambiguous sentence, like line 549, "Ask Creon, for you are mindful of him." Does that mean that Ismene is afraid of him or in love with him? I made it "Let Creon say; his words are your concern"—which, fortunately, will do in either case. There is an over frequent occurrence of "Hades" lately which I do not like, and so avoid it the best way I can. It is all right in Greek, I suppose, but it knocks all the poetry [out] of any line I can make. With every ten lines I feel that I am doing something and if you ever care to compare my version with yours you will see how much I am indebted to you for striking words and phrases.—Line 551 can also be read in two ways—with "if" or "although."

My eyes have been so weak lately that I have done very little reading—nothing definite except De Musset's *On ne badine pas avec L'Amour* and *Fantasio*. They are really great and in many respects the nearest to Shakespeare of anything I have ever seen. Think I shall have to make you a present of them in English— if you persist in refusing to read French. They are not very simple, so perhaps you could enjoy the English better just now. I have *The Prisoner of Zenda* and *A Study in Scarlet* to read but do not know when I shall get at them. I cannot seem to enthuse over Conan Doyle, but perhaps I shall be able to some day when I know him better—if that day ever comes. *Micah Clarke* repels me, so does *The Refugees*. Joe is reading almost everything now —the four just mentioned—*Marcella*—which seems to him in no wise remarkable but for a "hell of a lot of agony in it"—the Dashers [?], Capt. Marryat, etc. Joe is stranded and is waiting for the river to freeze over and give him a job. He had a good time in Fairfield but "didn't save a damned cent."

I am on the last quarter of "Christmas Eve" and am wondering if I shall tear it up when it is done. There is a pathos in striking such a happy subject (to my mind) and making a failure of it. I am too young in the business to do such things, I am afraid, but shall keep on with it and then write a little story about a girl called Antigone who disappointed a certain professor of Greek who found her on his doorstep when returning from his third lecture on The Children of Aeschylus—or something else. It ought to be easy work after what I am doing now, and will not in any way appeal to the classical public—nor any other, probably. It will simply show, or try to show, the obstinacy of human nature in an uncongenial atmosphere. I can foresee a danger of making the professor unreal and must try to avoid it. I write about my stuff as if every publisher in the land were clamoring for it; but you are the only man who knows anything about what I am doing—the only man in Maine, I mean—so you will forgive me and keep it to yourself. When the revelation of the damned fool comes, as it may, then there will be time enough to amuse ourselves over our fatuity.

You will be glad to hear that I was positively depressed over Harvard's double failure at foot-ball, but I see no chance for any excuses. There must have been howling in Pennsylvania Thursday night. It is not pleasant for me to look at the big H in my room and think of Harvard ranks—even in athletics. So you see I am not callous to such things after all.

This is not one of my days for letter-writing, and I fancy this will sound a little "forced."

[P.S.] This is not economy—I took it [his stationery] from a pile of half-sheets, supposing I should write three or four of them. But I can't do it today.

Gardiner
December 9, 1894

I am beginning to dread Sunday as I might dread doomsday. Everything is all right until it begins to grow dark, and then comes the trouble. If it doesn't snow too much today I think I shall take a walk out to your old homestead this evening and try to get your father to tell me some more shark stories.

The last time I saw your mother she told me that you were coming home for three weeks. Is that what you mean by your "short stay" or [are] you going to rebound after you have been with us for a day or two? Can't you martyrize yourself for a short time and forget all about it? If you keep on as you have begun, there will be the devil to pay sometime in the future, or I am no prognosticator. Better come back and be a child again and forget all about the cares of life and all. Come back and read books and eat apples and praise the Lord, and then when you go to Rockland you will be all the better satisfied with whatever you find there. This is as good advice as you can find anywhere in the big book—so I pray you not to pass it over too lightly.

Returning to *Antigone,* I think there must be something wrong in your rendering of Haenor's speech (683—). About three fourths of the way through it you say "the trees that bend are the trees that save their young branches, while those that yield (not?) perish root and all." There is also a place in the first part of this same speech which does not seem right to me. You say, "For your eye is terrible to a man of the people when such words as you would not enjoy hearing are spoken." Of course this is all straight but the Ox is so much better and so much deeper that I hope it may find some authority in its favor: "For your eye terrifies a common citizen from using those words you would not care to hear." This is infinitely better poetry but if it is not Sophocles, of course there is an end of it. I rather like my rendering of Creon's harangue on obedience—in fact, I think I surprised myself a little. The chorus, thank God, is done and is I think as good as any of them—excepting the first strophe of the second: "Nothing is there more wonderful etc."

The *Critic* saw fit to print my Sonnet in the Holiday Number and I expected to have one for you long before this. I shall send it to you (tomorrow probably) with a lot of other stuff. Mr. Saltus, the father of Francis Saltus Saltus, (the true-dictione poet) has asked permission to send me four volumes of the memorial edition of the poems, or rather three,—*Songs after Sunset, Flasks and Flagons,* and *Shadows and Ideals,* together with *The Bayadere and other Sonnets,* (Putnam's). I have given him my "permission" and the books will undoubtedly be here in time for your consideration. *Flasks and Flagons* is made up of sonnets to about seventy kinds of drinks—everything from Gin to Lachrymae Christi, including your much admired Benedictine, Chartreuse, and Anisette. I looked the volume over while at Harvard and admired it—particularly for its binding and printing, sm. quarto in half morocco and the portrait of a man who looks as if he were quite familiar with his subject. Saltus is not really a great poet, but he is a master of suggestive description. *The Bayadere* (which you must have seen somewhere before this) will tell you that.—Another constant reader from New York sent me two unpublished poems by the late Edward Rowland Sill, saying something about the vibrant note in my sonnet having awakened soul response in his heart and that he sent the two poems to show his gratitude. And Thomas B. Mosher has sent me his catalogue.

It all strikes me as a little humorous, but I suppose I am more or less pleased for all that. Schuman professes to take it far more seriously than I can possibly take it—but he professes a good many things.—I am now reading or trying to read *The Prisoner of Zenda*. It is exceptionally good of its kind but does not make any of my New York friend's soul response in my heart. To me its only value is conversation which is very bright.—Don't forget the *Yellow Book*, or *The Manxman*, if you are sure that it is not in use or likely to be for some time to come. Tell me when you are coming and how long you are going to stay.

[P.S.] Here is a little experimental quatrain in the "grand style which I think you have not seen. If you have, remember that I have a way of forgetting things:

> *As long as Fame's imperial music rings*
> *Will poets mock it with crowned words august;*
> *And haggard men will clamber to be kings*
> *As long as Glory weighs itself in dust.*

If I were going to buy any of Hawthorne, I should get what separate volumes I wanted and as often as I wanted them from the Little Classic Edition of Houghton Mifflin Co. They are very fine. Their Thackeray is also as good as a man needs. At least, that was the impression I got from Saben's set. I think you can get them for $1.12 per volume. The Hawthorne the same, or less.

Gardiner
January 12, 1895

This is a very "soft" day, and perhaps that is the reason that I am feeling rather slouchy. I have just played pitch with J.C. and beaten by a small margin, but that doesn't seem to invigorate me to any great extent. He has now taken up *The Phantom Ship* so I will take this time to let you know, among other things, that I have just seen an announcement in the back part of Burke's Speeches that may possibly interest you. It reads, "Essayes of Michael, Lord of Montaigne, parchment back (which you do not want) in cardboard box 5s.—Also 3s. 6d. in cloth." If this is Cotton's translation, it is probably as good an edition as you will care for. (George Routledge and Sons, N. Y.). In the Chandos Classics I notice Pope's Homer with Flaxman's designs, and Grimm's *Fairy Tales*. I did not know that either of them were in that collection. B. Franklin's *Autobiography* and Kinglake's *Eothen* are in the Knickerbocker Nuggets.

I have not been feeling particularly fine during the past week but have managed to do some work. Have almost finished the professor's story and have done the first chorus in "Aegeus"— about fifty lines, which seem to me to have a little swing to them. I shall have no trouble whatever in getting my book ready as far as quantity is concerned, but I am in much doubt as to the quality. However, I shall not permit myself to get discouraged, but shall hack away at it and hope for the best. The sonnet came back all right from the *Century* and the *Chap-Book* people have sent me a little notice saying that "Aaron Stark" will receive their consideration. Which means, I suppose, a little delay in its return. I am beginning a collection of declination blanks and hope to have one worth showing by the time you come to Gardiner again.

The other day I took up *McClure's* and tried to read Kipling's Jungle Story. Couldn't do it. Then I tried Doyle's "Green Flag" and met with no better success. Threw up the sponge over both. Is the fault with me or with them? I see by *Munsey's* that Sherlock Holmes is the bane of Doyle's existence—that he is ashamed of creating him. I hope it is true, and still I have no right to, as I have never read one of the S.H. stories. This morning I fell to thinking how it was possible for the American people to take *Munsey's* seriously. The article on the Novel in the last number is a fair sample of its literature. There is a pretty good thing, however, by Frank Chaffee (who was in the last *Chap-Book*), though it does not consent to anything beyond its brightness [sic]. If I ever publish anything I shall pray that I may never be called bright or clever. One might as well damn a man and be done with it.

With this I send you a *Critic* which I have marked in a way that I shall not mark another. It is a very good number—as good as I ever saw. I also send the comedies by De Musset which you cannot but like.—And while I think of it you can get the *Ingoldsby Legends* (with Cruikshank's pictures) in one volume of the Chandos. I have been chewing too much tobacco today and my hand trembles a little. I am going to stop the business soon and renounce the weed in every form.

Saltus writes me that his son's life of Donizetti will be published some time during the next two years and will be placed on sale. The next issue of F.S.S.'s poetry will be a volume of humorous verse. He has sent me the *Witch of Endor*, but I have not yet received it. I suppose it is in the office now.

Please excuse the rambling nature of this letter—and the more rambling nature of my chirography and let me know what you are doing for yourself in the way of editing, book-buying etc.

[P.S.] J. sends you his love and hopes you are leading a correct life.

Here is another week gone by, and I wonder what I have to show for it. A lot of thinking—music for one of Riley's poems—a little reading and 3000 words (two writings) of my reincarnation story which is giving me some trouble that I did not apprehend—that of keeping the idea of destiny ever present without saying much about it. The story is pretty stiff and ends with bullets and smoke—mostly smoke, I fancy, but, for all that, I refuse to call it sensational. I hope you will like it better than you did the one I read you during your vacation, but I rather think you will call it strained. It is funny that you and I have such different ideas of human logic. Without intending to defend myself at all, I must say that the two separations in *Pembroke* give my imagination something of a stretch while the disappearance of my strong man is quite natural. Do not mistake me in this and think that I would compare my stuff with Miss Wilkins's—that is not the idea.

Yesterday I fell again to reckoning up how much stuff I shall put into my book (?). After culling out all my conscience [rejects], I find that there will be anywhere from 350 to 400 pages, about 300 words to the page. This seems to me a little too large however, and I shall probably work it down.

I am now reading *The Manxman* again and am beginning to feel its prolixity. All those chapters about the wedding are a waste of time and paper, though it is easy enough to see the author's plan. Book IV ("Man and Wife") ought (from the point of view of pages) to have been over by this time and pretty much everything else with it. Caine is a great writer but not great enough to know his own weakness, and who is? Hardy surely isn't, but then Hardy will be great after Caine is totally forgotten. His work has something in it that cannot be found in *The Manxman*—something that I cannot define. If you are not quite willing to agree with me, read *Far from the Madding Crowd* or *The Woodlanders*—particularly the first named. There you will find something that you have never seen before and, I am afraid, you will never see again—modernized Shaksperian comedy. The bulk of the book, however, is something very different from that—mental tragedy. There it is like *The Manxman* but *The Manxman*, unfortunately, is not like that.

It is only when compared with the very few novels of late years that excel it, that this book is sent up in the balance and that fact shows how good a thing it is. I am glad for the chance of reading it but I cannot think of it as the much talked of "book of the year"—even after *The Ebb Tide*. Its size and elaboration are likely to dazzle one at first but one is conscious of a vast number of forgotten and unnecessary chapters by the time he is half through it. The same can hardly be said of paragraphs in Stevenson's book.

Stevenson makes me think of the *Chap-Book*. At last that disappointing little affair has printed something worth reading. I refer now to a little sketch by Kenneth Grahame, called "The Secret Drawer." I do not know when I have seen a little sketch that has interested me so much as that, or satisfied me half so much. It took an artist to even think of writing it. Mr. Bradley's book-plate is, according to my notion, well drawn, but I do not think I should care to paste [it] in my copy of Jeffrey's essays. People are going to weary some day of this black and white business and demand something more tangible. Here is a book-plate which may please you:

```
H. DeForest Smith,

      His
     Book

  Number 327.
```

I merely suggest this as an antidote for the modern craze. My only intention is to make you think a little of the strength that sometimes lies in simplicity.

On page xxii (advertising) of the Holiday *Critic* you will find an advertisement of books published by the Opus Club Co. If you have not already noticed it you may like to look it over. Have not yet heard from the *Chap-Book* or from *Lippincott's*, so there is a pause in the growth of my collection of blanks. W. C. Palmer seems to have forgotten my request for posters and I have spoken to Bissell. I cannot wake much excitement over the business or anything else but the one subject I am wrapped up in. When I emerge, I may collect birds eggs.

> Gardiner
>
> January 28, 1895

There is nothing to be seen today but snow and I rather like to see it. I cannot tell just why the sight of it pleases me but still it does and I sincerely hope that we shall get a foot of it. In the meantime, I shall read, write, and think—oh, yes, and chaw tobacco (until Feb. 1—then I stop) and try not to be disgruntled. I am getting along well enough with my work but am tormented with fits of wondering what it is all to amount to ("To amount to" doesn't sound well, so don't ever say it). Bad language may be a good school sometimes and I fancy I have profited a little by reading *Trilby,* which I finished about an hour ago.

I suppose you want to know what I think of the book, but I am not at all sure that I can tell you, as my ideas are rather mixed. When I had finished part first I was ready to swear by it; part second left me a little in doubt, and part third gave me a feeling that the bottom had dropped out and that it would be as well for me not to read any farther. The thing fascinated me, however, and I kept on; but the only part of the story that I shall ever remember with any enthusiasm is that dealing with the old days in the Latin Quarter when Trilby smoked cigarettes and wore an army coat; when *les trois Angliches* had their room in the Place St. Anatole; when they sat around the stove of a rainy day and smoked and talked of Thackeray and Dickens and Edgar Allan Poe and the glory that was Greece and the grandeur that was Rome. That is the kind of thing that sends the crinkles through a man even when the writer's English is almost as pathetic as his story—if not quite. I think *Trilby* would be a far better book if Du Maurier had kept them all there in that garret, permitted Little Billee's mother and brother-in-law to stay in England where they belonged, and little Billee himself to marry Trilby at the end of the book—closing the whole thing with a good wholesome melancholy booze between the Laird and Taffy—two of the best men in all literature. The "story" seems to me to spoil itself. Svengali and la Svengali made no impression upon me, and the only thing in Billee's loveless English life that sticks in my memory is that little game of cup and ball for shillings between him and Fred Walker at the big man's house. That was just the thing for them to do and I would give dollars (if I had them) to have been Taffy as he opened the curtains and found the young prodigies at it.

I do not care overmuch for the pictures, but the more I look at them the better I like them. That of Ribot smoking two cigars on the door-step and singing *"Allons Glycère"* and the next one when Billee has to sing *"Les Glougloux* etc." are perfectly enormous. The galloping chairs in Carrell's studio also pleases me. Most of the Trilby pictures are grotesque fizzles to my mind—but I do not pretend to be a judge of art.

Part VIII (and last) is as good a close for such a story as one could expect—in fact rather better, Trilby's exposition of her religious ideas being one of the best things in the book—a refreshing antidote for Little Billee's tiresome monologues to Alin's dog, which seem to me to be a little more than any author has the right to inflict upon his readers. The book as a whole is saved by the atmosphere of its opening chapters. That atmosphere never leaves it, though it never comes again with its first freshness.

As for comparing Du Maurier with Thackeray, the idea seems to me utterly ridiculous, though there are a few places where one is reminded of the great William. The pipes and the booze and the songs take one back to *Pendennis* for a moment, but the impression does not last. The "story" comes in and spoils it all. Still the book is a remarkable thing and I am glad for having read it. The style fits the scenes described but like the proverbial ready-made coat, it "fits it too much." And more than that, the English language cannot stand French paragraphing.

I have had a lot of book catalogues lately and find particularly attractive announcements of Thackeray in Cassell's—three or four editions—cheaper than Houghton Mifflin and Co. I am anxious for you to begin reading him because I know that you will take to his novels even more than you have to Daudet's.—I was sorry to see that you did not bid for Coppée's *Disillusion* (*Toute une Jeunesse*) but perhaps you did not know of it. Your sending me that catalogue was like putting oats before a muzzled horse (if horses have muzzles) but I thank you for sending it all the same. I had a good time reading it over and was a little amused at some of the reverend gentleman's possessions in French literature. But then, perhaps they were given to him—Mendès and the like.

I have been writing more music—this time to a little poem by J. W. Riley, which Ford sent me in his last letter. It begins and ends (every verse) with "There! little girl; don't cry!" It is very pretty and simple and I could not resist the temptation. Writing music without knowing how is a harmless amusement—if one doesn't do too much of it. I have done four or five pieces all told, but do not expect to do any more. It doesn't pay—like tragedies!

I am nearly through *The Manxman* and when I finish it shall make an end of reading for a time. I still cling to the *Ebb Tide* and do not expect to change my mind until I read *The Simpletons* or perhaps *Celibates*. With all my admiration for Stevenson's little book, my better judgment tells me that the novel of recent times (that I have read) is *Esther Waters*. It did not make much of a disturbance but it is going to live for all that.

I have the January *Globe* to send you as soon as I read it—also some *Critics* which are unusually good. That review seems to be coming up for some reason, and I hope it will not go down again. The *Globe* is rich—Thorne being omnipresent and not very good natured. "Aaron Stark" came back the other day and brought me one of the best declination blanks I ever saw—and I have seen several. Haven't heard from *Lippincott's*. Glad you liked Musset and still "more glad" that you have begun *Antigone*.—I am sorry to say that I am not impressed by either of the book plates —nor do I wholly like the idea of pasting your motto into, say, *Mlle. de Maupin* or *The Pace that Kills*. The thought of it reminds me of the plate in *The Magic Ink* in the Harvard Library —"for the purchase of books most needed by the university." But this is nothing to the point. I do not happen to care much for the design or for the Latin, would rather have *In Utrumque Paratus* —*Ter in Die*—*Ad Lindorem*—*In Medias Res*—in fact almost anything but *Pro Salute Ammae*—which, for some reason, I cannot stand. I do not mean to criticise your taste at all so do not think too seriously of what I say. I haven't much taste myself.

Gardiner
February 3, *1895*

I had not quite finished *The Manxman* when I wrote last Sunday, so could not give you my final impressions. If you care for them now, I will say that the author proves his greatness by making the book a success in spite of its fearful length. Scene after scene is spoiled by over preparation and half the book is worse than padding. Still it is a great work and Caine is a great man.

In turning from *The Manxman* to *The Blithedale Romance* the contrast is bewildering. How did Hawthorne do it? That is the question that bothers me and I have come to the conclusion that much of it is due to the fact that he was capable of an amount of brain racking and tinkering of which the modern inkspiller has no conception. The fact that the writing of *The Marble Faun* was a five years' job is enough to make a man stop and think. I do not think that I ever fully realized the greatness of Hawthorne until I took up the novel I bought of you. (Did I ever pay you for it?) Not that it is the best, but it somehow reveals the master in a way that is not to be noted in the others.

There is a sense of reality about it which is utterly wanting in *The Scarlet Letter;* and there is a kind of glorification of little things which only a great master is likely to find worth while.

When I leave Hawthorne for my own poor, patient manuscript I feel very foolish indeed; but I get over that and go pegging away—sometimes a page at a time without any trouble—sometimes spending an hour over a dozen words. It seems to me that I have flushed a good-sized volume of my reincarnation story through the water-closet and there is still more to follow. This past week I have been going through the stuff and have gleaned and ground it down to twelve rather large pages—about 6500 words, I should think, and now only have part four to concoct and set down. I think it will take me all this week and then I am going to take a change of air and write a little thing to be called "Saturday," of which you will be indirectly the father, as it is founded on the amiable portrait of one Mr. Hutchings in bed with a pint of rum and a pile of dime novels.

I have left off chewing tobacco and feel as if I had lost the greater part of my diabolical system. But I have more time to think and as a consequence have half thought up a rather elaborate tale which, it seems to me, ought to be called "The Woolgatherers." I doubt, however, if it finds a place with the "Scattered Lines" which I am hoping may someday come together and find a 12mo lodging between cloth covers: it is all too vague for that and seems to ask for rather more space than an ordinary "short story"—Ye gods, how I hate to call them by that name!—and I rather think I shall put it in with another of equal length and let them be a book by themselves. Excuse me for talking about books, but that is almost the only recreation I have now—thinking of the things I am going to do—and [you] must partly understand my feelings.

The thing is wholly out of the question for me, but if I were in your place I should be strongly tempted to subscribe for the Edinburgh edition of Stevenson—if only for an investment. It is a matter of some sixty dollars, I believe, but I cannot see any possibility of risk. You might also lay in a supply of fine editions of Chicago society novels, advertised in the back of the *Chap-Book*, which seems to be coming up a little in the last number. In looking over "The Land of the Straddle-Bug" I drew an inference that Mr. Garland is driving things home. I think you said that you were reading it and that it was worth while. I shall take it up when it all comes and pray that the editor of the *C.B.* may not let another serial story into its pages. It seems to me ridiculously out of place however good it may be.

My posters are piling up, but I have none of any value. Here is the list.

Harper's—Dec.—Feb.	*Scribner's*—Dec. (2) Feb.
Lippincott's—Dec.—Feb. (3)	*Century*—Dec.—Feb. (2)
St. Nicholas—Dec.	*Truth*—Midwinter [?] No.
	Cooking No. (2)

Quarterly Illustrator—(2)
Outing and *Cosmopolitan* (Feb) which do not amount to anything.

If you have any extra Jan. numbers I should be glad to get hold of them somehow. I skipped them all. I now have Bissell and Blanchard at work for me and William when he thinks of it.

There is also a hiatus in my collection of declination blanks. The editor of *Lippincott's Magazine* made it, but he sent me a check for seven dollars to fill the hole. So there is no loss without some gain: I can shake my shoes and laugh (I haven't paid for them yet). I fixed up the sonnet a little before I sent it on, so they did not get it just as the *Dial* people saw it—if they ever did that. The third line now reads "Bleak and unblossomed were the ways he knew," which seems to have some jingle and a little strength. The receipt of my first "blood-money" is now as much a thing of the past as is your first week of school teaching. A check tomorrow for a thousand would not give me the same sensation.

If you have Appleton's catalogue, look up the Gainsborough

Series (paper 25c.) and consider the purchase of Cherbuliez, *Meta Holdenis, Samuel Brohl and Co.* They are all first class and the books are quite respectable and fit for any binding—as I remember Cherbuliez. I was surprised to find Jas. Lane Allen's *John Gray* in the list of old Lippincott's, and so within my means. It was a quiet success like *Esther Waters* and won nothing but praise from the critics. Will send it to you after I read it. You will find some good pictures of Frenchmen in the last *Munsey's* and also (*horesco referens!*) some of Julia Ward Howe and her daughters.

You have struck the right things for a book plate, but I am sorry for the dancing faun. I think of having two old men by a little fire, smoking long church wardens and reading tomes of wisdom,—and the shadow of the woods around them.

I think of all this but shall probably never get it. So if the idea strikes you as a good filling for your square you are quite welcome to it.

[sketch]

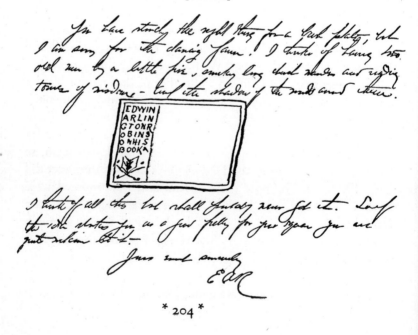

You must not expect much of a letter from me today as I was taken with a bad grouch immediately upon finishing my reincarnation story yesterday afternoon. I do not know why I was taken with it but for some reason I have [been] woefully in the dumps for the past twenty-four hours. If I am not better in the morning I shall be tempted to shovel the snow all out of the yard. Once I was foolish enough to think that I had outgrown such things, but now I see my mistake. I expect to have grouches all my life just as some old ladies have neuralgia. And I even go so far sometimes as to think that I am the better off for having had them; I seem to gain something and come out with new ideas for future work.

I find that I am slowly accustoming myself to a longer period of brain racking than I was capable of a year ago, but I also find that I am seldom good for more than 300 words an hour. Of course I have spurts but not very often. Inspiration will never do much for me. If I am to produce anything I must work for it and then do it three or four times, in the majority of cases. As I said in my last letter, I have worked all the past week on the last section of "A Recognition"—less than 2000 words, but wholly without dialogue. That is the stuff that fills paper and the pockets of popular writers, and is, as a rule, the "ruination" of a short story. Apropos of that subject let me copy a few lines from Ouida's article in the last *N.A. Review* (from Ford's letter):

> "The short story as opposed to the long romance is as the miniature to the fresco. They are entirely opposed to each other. I consider the short story much the more perfect as pure art. It is more concentrated, more delicate, more ideal; that is, when it is excellently well done, like *Boule de Suif*, like *Deux Rivales*, like *Yvette*, like the short stories of Paul Heyse or those of Edmondo de Amicis. But the short story is only adapted to pathos (this is what I have always lacked the courage to say); when humorous it is odious; and it

never could replace the long romance if intricate events, complicated characters (?) or if the portraiture of contemporary society is to be undertaken . . . I repeat, I consider the short story [is] the most exquisite form of fiction, as the sonnet is of poetry; but the *Iliad*, the *Inferno*, the *Orlando*, or the *Tempest* could never be put into a sonnet, and no more could *Gil Blas* or *Waverley*, *Adam Bede* or *L'Impérieuse Bonté* be put into a short story."

All of which is very good sense to me but somehow *L'Impérieuse Bonté* is not in my list. In other words, I never heard of it before. If you know anything of it, kindly tell me in your next letter.

Ouida's words are all true but not for the American people. The short story as a work of art has never taken a great hold in this country, as the standard set in the leading magazines will easily show. If the reading public ever comes to learn that the New England misuse of the English language is not a dialect there will be some hope for American fiction—perhaps. Are we getting such a flood of it now because it is the thing to write or because it was all written and accepted years ago? And there is something still worse than that,—the small society talk that monopolizes the other half of nearly all the stories now written in this glorious republic. But don't mind this—I have a grouch. Also excuse the *Ego* in this letter. It always crops out when I am not feeling well—and often, I fear, when I am. Yesterday I read Book I of *The Excursion*. Whenever you take a notion to do the same thing you will experience a revelation. The fact that you can read Cowper is enough to ensure my saying this.—Just now I have a great desire to read Bourget's *Un Saint* and Daudet's *Fromont Jeune et Risler Aîné*. Think I shall have to buy them as text books.

[P.S.] Does this read any easier than my past letters? It is written with something quite new to me—a glass pen. I suppose you know all about such things.

I have been sick all the week and am afraid that I haven't much to write save to tell you that I have bought two or three books and have read a little and have written that little marionette thing that I have spoken of once or twice in the past. I call it "Lachesis" and do not think it amounts to anything in particular, perhaps because I wrote it so quickly.

I have been reading *The Excursion* and find that I am just beginning to feel the value of the book of Wordsworth that you gave me. Hereafter it will be a part of my life. Of course a great deal of it is slow and of not much value; but the general tone and effect of it is so clear and wholesome, not to say magnificent, that we must all own its power to some extent. In my private opinion his "Ode on the Intimations of Immortality" is worth all the rest of his work put together, but I am only one man, and not much of a man either—today.

The books that I have bought are in French. I borrowed four dollars of Dean and sent to Jenkyns for *Une Vie* (De Maupassant) *Fromont Jeune et Risler Aîné* and *La Petite Paroisse* (first edition)—Daudet. These are three stocky volumes and I expect great harvest from them before long. I also ordered in a cheaper edition *Les Ruines* and *La Loi Naturelle* (Volney) and *Voyage autour de ma Chambre* (X. de Maistre). I have always wanted to read "Volney's Ruins" and now I have a chance. The book is rather inviting in its appearance—in fact they all are. *Fromont Jeune* is illustrated, but not by Myrbach, who did *Jack* so well in the "Guillaume" edition. And by the way, that Guillaume edition is all printed by somebody in English—with the original pictures.

I seem to have nothing but books to write about today so will go on and tell you about a volume you may possibly care to purchase—or try to. I remember some ten or twelve years ago of an old man calling upon my father and selling him a book which he had spent half his life in writing. The man was the Rev. David Q. Cushman and the book was his history. The title page reads as follows: "The History of Ancient Sheepscot and Newcastle, including Early Pemaquid, Damariscotta and other contiguous places, from the earliest discovery to the present time: together with the genealogy of more than four hundred families. BY Rev. David Quimby Cushman, Member of Maine Historical Society and Member of the New England Historico-Genealogical Society and Member of the Sagadahoc H.S.—Bath: E. Upton and Son, Printers, 1882." The book is well printed and bound and has 458 large pages. Someday it is going to be as scarce as Hanson's *Gardiner* and infinitely more valuable. I do not know the price of the book—for all I know it is out of print—but I have a dim impression of seeing my father give him two dollars— though it may have been five—or one. If the thing should happen to interest you, of course you have only to write to E. Upton and Son, Bath, and find what information you want. Or possibly you know all about it and its author to boot.

I have nearly finished *John Gray,* which is a very good thing though a little strained in places. Sometimes I am tempted to give James Lane Allen the place next to Hawthorne in American fiction, but somehow I lack the courage, or something else. If he doesn't belong there, he does very near it.

The last *Critic* is mostly taken up with the sale of the Foote collection. The most valuable book in the bunch was a very rare copy of *The Temple,* by George Herbert, which went for $1050.00. Lots of others went from $200 to $800. I will send you the copy tomorrow and will now ask you to bring it back with you when you come. There is now and then a copy that I shall want to save.

The *Book-Buyers* came last evening and I was mightily glad to get them. Send anything that happens to fall in your way and I will preserve it most carefully. Have you heard anything about the "Whistler number" of *Harper's Magazine* (March 1894) being worth thirty or forty dollars?

[P.S.] I hope you may find something better than Aldrich's for a book plate.

Gardiner
February 24, 1895

You will be glad, I think, to learn that I am more than a hundred pages into *The Greater Glory* and that I am enjoying it more than a little. It is ahead of *God's Fool* but did it occur to you that the author's style is a little more affected—a little more *décadent*—than in that book? It seems to me that Mynheer Schwartz really sacrifices strength by his freakish use of periods. Of course that really has nothing to do with the language, but one cannot get over the impression that such business makes upon the mind. For some occult (?) reason, Joe doesn't find the book readable; prefers Marie Corelli.

Did you tell me that [you] once read Maistre's *Voyage around my Chamber?* I have just read it and have no words to tell what I think of it. There is nothing really great in it, perhaps, but there is something that appeals to me more strongly than any [thing] that I have read for a long time. It suggests *Tristram Shandy* and *Sylvestre Bonnard* but still remains original. Some of the epigrams are fine. I suppose it has been translated into English and I should advise you to get it. I know you cannot be very familiar with it or you would mention it once in a while.— The second part ("The Nocturnal Expedition") I have not yet read, but it looks as interesting as the first.

As soon as I finish Maartens I shall take up Volney's "Ruins." I have always heard of "them" and have always wanted to read them. They seem to be a history of almost everything from the beginning down—and all in considerably less than three hundred small pages. There are (included) 50 pages of notes which seem to contain a world of interesting stuff. I mention the nature of the book thinking that it may interest you for its historical value. And I will say here, by the way, that you can get any information you desire concerning English translations by writing to Schoenhof's or Brentano's.

I am aching to have you read *Pendennis*. I want to hear you talk about it and have your opinion of its merits as compared with those of *Trilby*. And speaking of *Trilby*, let me quote you a few lines from a letter I got the other day from Latham. They will interest you as much (and more, I think) than anything I can write today: "Yes, I've read *Trilby*. I haven't got it very bad—it is spread out too thin. The first hundred pages will do, but when you get to talking Darwinism to your dog Tray etc. . . . I have almost given up fiction—you can't do everything; and as for a book that pleases, Goodwin's *Moods and Tenses* isn't the worst. . . . The last book I have acquired (I bought it yesterday morning) is Barrett Wendell's *English Composition*. Was there ever a more interesting book written on the subject?—I am working somewhat intermittently at several subjects: Greek drama, Italian and the science of language. Have you read Max Müllers lectures? They are fascinating enough for me etc. . . . Can anything shrivel up a man more thoroughly than reading the same books with his classes year after year?" (This in reference to the classics in lower grades. I should hate to believe that L. would apply it to Virgil).

My posters are standing still but there are two declinations due me—one from the *Cosmopolitan* and one from the *Youth's Companion* (Quatrain). My work is going on in the same way only perhaps a little faster. Last week I wrote and copied "Alcander," a sketch of about 3500 words without a line of dialogue. I rather like it myself but do not think that you will find it worthy of the man who suggested it—Mr. Hutchings.

I had an idea that I warned you that there was no story to *The Marble Faun*. If you will think twice you may find something in [it] that invites comparison with the *Ebb Tide*, though the thing seems absurd at first. It makes no difference to me whether Hawthorne has any definite story to tell or not as long as he doesn't write "Note-Books."

I am still browsing through *The Excursion* and am glad for the chance. My great trouble is that I am rotting for human companionship. I have made an inward resolution, however, to get to Boston for a few days in June, and the prospect buoys me up strangely.

Your term must be more than half through. When do you expect to get this way again?

P.S. I do not know or care anything about the Bronze Horses of Venice but you may find something about them in Mark Twain's *Innocents Abroad*, Howell's *Venetian Life*, Reber's *Mediaeval Art*, Ruskin or somewhere. I have not seen the *Bibelot*, but think I shall subscribe for it when I get another half-dollar. I am sorry that you did not see O. B. Clason.

Gardiner
March 3, 1895

This is a pale blue day and there seems to be no sun to speak of. I am glad to say, however, that I am not in the blues myself but on the contrary rather radiant over something—though I haven't the slightest idea of what that thing is. I think it is the knowledge (or at least the belief) that I can do anything, in my own way, that I undertake. Last Monday I began "John Town" and now it is done. Up to Thursday it seemed hopeless and even now it may not be good for anything, but it is done and that is something. It seems to me to be as good as any of my stuff, but I have lost all faith in my own criticism. If I keep on at the rate of one tale a week I shall have a mess of them before long.—But then, I cannot do that, for I have written all the short pieces I intend to for a time. My next work will be to fix over "Theodore," "Lévy Condillac" and the "Three Men and their Wives" (the last two of which you do not care for, I think). Some day I may come to that opinion myself, but just now it is impossible for me to believe it. I shall peg away at these things all summer (forenoons) and in the fall I shall make a large attempt to do something with them.

Your little story of the two friends has made a great impression upon me—as great as that of your friend H— [*sic*] whose college career was such a failure. I have salted him for future use and know just what I am going to do with him. I have never said much to you about it, but I think, if I am good for anything, that I may owe you something for it some day. As for this other case, it seems to me just the thing for a three part story of say 12,000 words or so. I have so much material in my head, and good material too, that the weight of it makes me dizzy at times; and then there is that fear that I may not do anything after all. My worst and most persistent enemy, though, is a constant inclination to write poetry. Sometimes I am half afraid the damned stuff will kill what little ability I have.

The other day I took up *Fromont Jeune* and read the first book,—which is really a prologue and a masterpiece of artistic fiction. After that, the book cannot help being great. There is a chance for all sorts of diabolical occurrences in the coming pages and I have no doubt but that Sidonie will bring them around. She seems thus far to be a combination of Becky Sharp and Dolly Varden, with a very large percentage of Becky. I am getting more and more convinced that Daudet is the greatest artist in fiction now living—and his art never crowds out his humanity. I have always been a little suspicious of *Sapho* but shall probably read it before long and find out what it is like. I have always attributed its tremendous sale to the risqué characters of its pages, but I may be doing its author a rank injustice. Have you ever read the book?

I know nothing about *The Melancholy of Stephen Allard* more than that [it] is published by the Macmillans at the rather disquieting price of $1.75. Nobody mentions it here in Gardiner that I know and whenever I speak of it I speak of a thing totally unheard of. I fancy the book may be something after the style of Daudet's *Robert Helmont—The Diary of a Recluse,* another book I am anxious to read.

I am crowding my days a little too hard lately and the natural result is that I am beginning to lose sleep. I am becoming filled with an utterly insane desire to get out of bed at six o'clock in the morning and would do so were it not for two rather dull hours to live through before breakfast. It will be all right when warm weather comes and a fellow can get out of doors but just now I have nothing to do but to blow my clarinet; and it is not good for one to do too much of that on an empty stomach.

Regarding that number of *Harper's,* let me say that you took, or mistook, Whistler for Whittier. I mean the number that contains the third installment of *Trilby* and has to do with a character who is a "guy" on Whistler,—Joe Somebody I think, who is not in the published volume at all. The sale of the magazine was stopped at W's request and I have heard that it is now practically impossible to get one of them.

I have received the first two numbers of *The Bibelot* but can't say that I think much of it except the covers. And what the deuce does the publisher mean by printing Blake's best known poems as things "not generally accessible"? They are just as accessible as any other poems, although they have never become popular. The third number will be interesting, as was the second and I hope the paper may be changed before long to hold its own with the covers. I detest the type he has chosen for printing his poems, but that, I suppose, is Mr. Mosher's own business.

Joe and I were going to eat beans with your father and mother last evening, but the event did not take place on account of your mother's bad cold. She has been unfortunate this winter in that respect and I trust the coming [spring] may bring a change. I very seldom have a cold that is of any consequence, but I know what they are and how to sympathize.

Shall send you *John Gray* this week and feel sure that you will like it. I see that *Critic* praises *A Kentucky Cardinal,* by the same author. He deserves it.

Gardiner
March 10, 1895

I did not write you a letter yesterday, because I was not in the mood for anything of that kind. I am afraid that I am not today, either but can at least let you know that I have just read Hamlin

Garland's little obstetrical story in the *Chap-Book,* and that I rather like [it]. It is strong and true to life, according to my notions, but is a thing to play the devil with readers who are ignorant and naturally "easy." I cannot say that I agree with Mr. Garland's ideas of realism—what it should be, but the story is good and I am glad that the *Chap-Book* was on hand to print it —though a paper of that sort is not the place for a serial story.

I have finished *Fromont Jeune* and shall next take up *La Petite Paroisse* which the new paper, *Vanity,* calls one of Daudet's best things. I had intended to put off reading it for a time but have changed my mind. The book deals with the old story of a woman's infidelity but that is a subject which, if treated by a master, can never wear out. De Maupassant's *Une Vie* touches infidelity of the kind and the book seems to be a great perform- ance. I haven't read it, however, so cannot tell you much about it. But you must have *Fromont* in translation to read this sum- mer. A translation would probably have an entirely different title from the original, as *Fromont Junior and Risler Senior* would not sound so well in English. But I won't say anything more about this summer until I find out whether you are going to get married or not. If you do, you must not ask me to go to the wedding (I said that a year ago, I think) nor expect any wedding present for a time. I am almost on my sacrum, but I hope to get righted, or right myself, before very long.

Do you think a great deal of *Peter Schlemihl?* I sent for it, with Lessing's *Nathan the Wise* in Cassell's Library and read it the other day. It doesn't seem to me that there is quite enough in it to warrant its reputation, but I suppose there is. I fancy the trouble all lies in the fact that such figurative extravagancies seldom appeal to me. I cannot appreciate them—not even *Gulli- ver.* There is a kind of romance that I like but I cannot define it. I like *Paul and Virginia,* and I like *Picciola;* I like *Atala* and *Undine*—in other words I like the romance of the commonplace —without any guns or swords or cavaliers to speak of. Of course this doesn't exclude *Peter,* but for some reason I was disappointed in reading it.

Yesterday Joe and I went over the Iron Mine to call on your father and mother. The walking was damnation itself but the day was glorious. So is today for that matter.

I shall be glad when you come this way again as I am in a bad way for Theocritus, I think. I haven't used any tobacco for six weeks and have about concluded to stave it off for an indefinite time—a year, perhaps. I think I do a little better work without it and sleep better—though it may all be fancy. There is surely no "great change." Have made two additions to my collection of declinations—*Cosmopolitan* and *Youth's Companion.* Think I may as well stop now and wait till the Lippincotts print my "Poe."—If you think of buying *St. Ives,* why didn't you send your name in for a first edition?—or wouldn't that work?

I have lately caused a lawyer in Omaha to read *Jack* and *The Manxman.* He doesn't think that Cain succeeds in making a man of Philip—if he tries to.

Gardiner
March 17, 1895

You may have thought it strange that I said nothing at all about your father and mother's sickness, but they told me that you knew nothing about it and after that I felt that I had no authority to mention it. Miss Patterson told me yesterday that they are both getting along finely now, in fact they were out of the worst of it last Sunday, when Joe and I went out. We are going again this afternoon.

I find that I have been reading too much of late. My eyes tell me so. Last week I did not read so much—only Lowell's essays on Carlyle and Lessing and Swinburne's Tragedies and half of Stevenson's *Inland Voyage.* Of "Atalanta in Calydon" Lowell says, "These are not characters, but outlines after the Elgin Marbles in the thinnest manner of Flaxman. There is not so much blood in the whole of them as would warm the little finger of one of Shakspear's living and breathing conceptions."—And I think he is right, though he goes on to praise the choruses more than I possibly can. The first, "When the Hounds of Spring," is great but the rest are nothing, to my mind.—Of Lessing he says, "Wherever he sat was the head of the table." Which is enough praise for any man.

The essay on Carlyle did not strike me as of much value, literary or critical. Carlyle seems to be a hard man for the critics to handle. I wonder what Minto did with him in his *English Prose?* Are you acquainted with that book? It is rather ponderous in its treatment but pretty good stuff to be acquainted with, I fancy. Saben had it [in] Cambridge and I used to look into it occasionally.

The other day I received a blank "life-book" from the Secretary of the Class of '95, Harvard, for me to fill out, but I do not feel like responding. The circular that came with it says that it is sent to all past and present members of the class and to such Special Students as have had social connections with the class—whatever that may mean. There is also, and infinitely more to the point, a request to contribute as much as possible to the Class Fund, which ought to exceed $12,000. If I should give them $5 a year for the next 5 years I should feel quite free to go to all the Commencement Dinners and the Triennials—as far as right is concerned—but my conscience would be somewhat in the way. It is too much like sham membership, and the whole thing surprises me. I am in doubt as to how to reply. The blanks were evidently sent to me for what money I might return—or I suppose they were—and I do not just like the notion of associating a thing of that kind with Harvard College—which is the object of almost the only patriotism I possess, notwithstanding the fact that I was there but two years, and then as a Special.

Here is a rather striking epigram from *An Inland Voyage:* "To know what you prefer instead of humbly saying Amen to what the world tells you you ought to prefer, is to have kept your soul alive." This is in the spirit of the whole book, which I am sure

* 216 *

you would like amazingly. Perhaps you have read it, but I have never heard you speak of it. It is a good thing to begin a reputation with and contains, as the author states in his preface, "not a single reference to the imbecility of God's universe, nor so much as a single hint that I could have made a better one myself." There is a good deal of high grade humor in it and some rather wise reflections on life,—like unto this: "He who can sit squarest on a three-legged stool, he it is who has the wealth and glory." "The slug of a fellow, who is never ill nor well, has a quiet time of it in life and dies all the easier." These are observations, not complaints.

I have finished up "A Little Fool" and have rewritten the first part of "Lévy Condillac," which I like immensely—better than you ever will—or anybody else, I fear. I have always sworn to myself that there is the germ of something worth while in that first sketch of mine and I cannot get over the impression. If these things of mine ever get before the public I shall await the criticism of that piece more than any other. I may be laboring under a delusion regarding its significance, but I shall not believe it yet a while.

This letter is dull, unoriginal, and slow—just as I feel. I enclose a quotation however which will make up for all that.

The *Chap Book* came this morning and I have read it. If Mr. Mabie's contribution is a fair sample of his work, he is the master of a drool that is overwhelming. All that he has to say could be told, and much better, in one well-balanced sentence.

Old World Lyrics is all safe. I will bring it up to you when you come home. I like your quotation from Goethe.

Gardiner
April 14, 1895

Your letter and the *Book-Buyer* came last evening and paid me well for paddling down town through the wind and rain for whatever I might find. I like the *Book-Buyer* for what it is, but it seems to me that one might naturally look for a little more

I am glad that you have taken up *Pendennis* at last and [am] anxious for your opinion of it in your next letter—or whenever the time comes. Have you got to the Chatteris Bridge scene yet, where old Bows tosses his burning cigar stub over into the water and leaves Pen to walk home thinking? Andrew Lang and I are very fond of that passage and I am glad to be able to say that my admiration for it was as strong before I ever read a line by Andrew as it is today. I have read the book four or five times and shall soon be ready to read it again. There is something in the touch of the master that cannot be mistaken or explained, and—at least I find it so—cannot always be seen in a first reading; but I don't suppose there is any use in preaching that to your recent resolution.

I am going to read *Sapho* when I get a good chance and am glad for your words concerning it. I have never been able to believe that the book is "smutty" as the word goes, and I think you are quite right in saying that Daudet could not write a novel of that sort. To me he is a mighty moralist but a French moralist with all the term conveys—or, as some Harvard instructors would say—connotes. There are lessons in *Jack* that I have never seen brought out with half the clearness or fire that Daudet gives them and the same is true of all the serious works of his that I have read. He is never tired of dwelling upon a person's bringing up, that is, of his general surroundings during the age when the mind is most susceptible to impressions. That, I take it, is the first idea of *Sapho* as it is of *Jack* and *La Petite Paroisse*. Then there is always the compensation, or retribution, which ought to suit your ideas to perfection. In *Fromont Jeune,* though, he makes the doings of the sinners blast the lives of two innocent and (to me, Henry James's word) adorable people, leaving the sinners themselves to the disposition of the reader. The more I think of *La Petite Paroisse* the more I am convinced that it will hold a place with the author's best works, but I doubt [if] it ever becomes as popular as some of the others. It is built upon a wholly different plan from the earlier novels and nearly all of the "story" is brought up after the incidents themselves have taken place. Even the pathos is largely implied, though the reader feels it from the beginning. It is a sad story with a happy ending and the happiness is all kept back until the last page. Ordinarily such a dodge as that would tend to make a novel weak, but Daudet has taken care of that. The only thing to trouble the reader is the question whether a man can be happy with a wife whom he knows has been unfaithful even though the paramour be dead. The reader must settle that according to his own notions.

Lately I have been reading Wordsworth's *Excursion* and now am nearly through it. I never half realized before what a magnificent thing it is. You must read it sometime. Excepting that, I haven't read much of anything but some stories by Catulle Mendès over again. They are wrought with a cleverness that is perfect but they are absolutely un-moral.

This is not one of my letter-writing days, so you must not swear if I am duller than usual. The day is great and all that, but my thoughts are slow and I fear that I am not in the best of spirits. In the last *Critic* I notice an announcement of *Fromont Junior and Risler Senior* published by the Lippincotts at two dollars. The price is a little stiff but the book is worth it.—Rand, Mac-Nally and Co. sell *Numa Roumestan,* Illustrated, in English for $1.00. The *Critic* has taken my Hardy sonnet but I think I said so in my last letter. It would be a good thing for me if I could go through some treatment to make me remember what I say to my correspondents.

Gardiner
May 5, 1895

The French book came yesterday and it is very nearly what I expected. Some of the selections ("La Grève de Forgerons" and De Maupassant's "Le Parapluie," for example) surprised me a little as examples of difficult French, but Zola, Rosny and De

Goncourt are where they belong. The book will do a great deal for me if I have a mind to make a study of it this summer, and that is what I intend to do. I am very much obliged to you and will request [you] to kindly charge the cost to my account. I enclose postage.

Yesterday afternoon I finished my first complete reading of the *Excursion.* A man must read that poem before he knows Wordsworth; it is the man himself done over into words, and magnificent words, too. I shall take up the *Prelude* right away and then the *Recluse.* These poems are to be read slowly and with no sense of time. That is, a man must not be in a hurry. The same will apply to Montaigne. Speaking of him, there is an article in the last *Chap-Book* by Maurice Thompson which is refreshingly worth reading. It hits the old fellow the best of anything that I have ever seen, I think, and I sincerely hope that the story of the nuts and the little girl may be true. I care infinitely more for them than for the man with the three dogs and the giant fireplace.—In the same number there is a poem by Bliss Carman which has an unquestionable touch of greatness in it. And there is a sonnet by Hugh McCulloch which has nothing of the kind. The thought of it is either an unfortunate accident or a conscious dilution of the passage in Keats's "Lamia":

"He answered, bending to her open eyes,
Where he was mirrored small in Paradise."

I have been doing some labor of late—too much, I think. This (Sunday) morning I was up at five o'clock. At six, or before, I was at work in that cursed raspberry bed of ours and at half-past seven I had breakfast. It is impossible now for me to sleep much after four o'clock in the morning and almost impossible for me to keep from getting up. I sleep well enough the first part of the night though, and that is when sleep counts—at least, so say the medicine men.

At last I am the owner of Hill's *Foundations of Rhetoric* and

I feel much better. If I could now get hold of the person who walked away with my *Rhetoric* itself, I should feel still better. I have a great faith in the professor's judgment and I have seen the man and heard him talk, so his books are perhaps worth more to me than they are to you.—I have finally changed the title "Christmas Eve" which you so detested to that which I mentioned, "The Ruins of Bohemia." The last fills the bill and is rather better, I think, though it is not so good as "The Black Path," or "The House Across the Water."

This is a gray day, with no sign of any change. There are no ideas in my head and I think the sooner I put an end to this letter the better it will be for you and me alike.—Did I ever acknowledge receipt of the second *Bookman*? I enjoyed it very much, though I don't think I care over much for Prof. Peck's poetry. The thought was all that made it tolerable.

Gardiner
May 12, 1895

I have been reading the *New Testament* (Matthew and Mark, which are pretty much alike) and am just beginning to realize what the rising generation is losing by letting such reading go by. For we all know well enough that the "scriptures" are the last thing that a fellow takes up nowadays, though it comes natural, for some reason, for a girl to know all about them. I have found that I can satisfy myself very well with the Big Book and I doubt if I read much else this summer save that and some French novels. The combination may point to certain paganistic tendencies on my part, but is far better to read the *Bible* as mere literature than to read most of the stuff that is printed in these days for anything at all.

When I look over recent book lists and see the titles of some of the stuff put out by our leading publishers it makes me tremble for humanity. But yet, I do not think it can last; I have too much faith in humanity for that.—I am waiting patiently for Mr. A. T. Quiller-Couch to have his innings. It is a mystery to me how he can be so shamefully neglected by a reading public which buys seventeen editions of a thing like the *Prisoner of Zenda;* for any man or woman who cares for a good and wholesome romance must find "Q" infinitely superior to Anthony Hope—that is, if I am any judge of fiction. To my mind there is nothing outside of Stevenson that can be compared with *I Saw Three Ships* and I am told that *The Blue Pavilions* is much better than that. "Q's" short stories are almost unapproachable in recent literature—keeping up a better average, I think, than even our common idol, Kipling. "Q" never wrote anything so good as "The Children of the Zodiac" or anything better, perhaps, than "Georgie Porgie" or "Pambé-Serang" but I am sure that he has never written anything half so bad as the "Mutiny of the Mavericks" or so magnificently dull as "The Bridge Builders." This last named piece is literature of a high order and as such I can admire it; but from any other point of view it seems to me a total failure. I am still of the opinion that if Kipling leaves any name to posterity it will be almost wholly for his poems. He is the greatest poet now writing English and I have said so ever since the death of Tennyson; but he has got to free himself of that habit of over loading his lines— as in the proem to *Many Inventions* and the dedication to *Ballads and Barrack Room Ballads,* and even here and there in the "East and West," before we can know him for what he really is.

The French book you procured for me I find a very valuable companion. I do not think much of such books as a rule (but that is only because I need them) and yet I am beginning to see the good that may be got from them. They serve as one more proof that there is no royal road to the learning of the French language—or any other. As long as a man reads French or German "to get the sense of it" just so long is he prostituting his intellect to the thinnest of thin pleasures. Skimming through a French novel with no imaginative sympathy whatever and with no regard for literary touches and other individualities of style is not only insulting an author but doing an injustice to one's self. It is far better to read a good translation of a book by a foreign author than to slop through it after the manner of the bright young ladies who read French a little, German a little, sing a little, play the piano a little and do nothing at all with anything like completeness. There is too much of that kind of thing going on now and if I had the bringing up of a girl I should make her do one thing well if that thing were only to take good care of her eye-brows.

The last *Critic* has a fairly good review of *La Petite Paroisse*, but [the] writer denies M. Daudet the privilege of drawing an individual. He has a poor word for *Rose and Ninette* and for that reason he must have [read?] that book, I think, from the same point of view. To a man like Richard Fénigan the story in question is quite plausible. As a [word illegible] the book is without value nor can I conceive of a man with Daudet's insight ever dreaming that it would be taken as such. Every man and woman who writes for the *Critic* seems to be cursed with a flippancy that I am getting very tired of. If possible, it is worse than the patronizing ease of Wm. Morton Payne in the *Dial*.

It is "blowing up" a storm now and I hope it will rain a week to give the burdocks and myrtle a good start in my raspberry bed. The grass needs it too.

[P.S.] I cannot find the *Atlantic* poster. No one has seen it.

Gardiner
May 20, 1895

The more I read of Mr. Mabie in *The Bookman* the more I think of him. It is not a safe thing to damn a man for one short piece like that of his in the *Chap-Book*, but I am afraid that we are both too liable and too willing to do it. I am, at any rate, and hereafter shall try to improve my ways and conquer some of my prejudices. Were circumstances favorable I should immediately take up Mr. Mabie's books and then those—or some of them— of Mr. Cable and Mr. Howells—two men, and great men, as men go nowadays, of whom I know next to nothing. In spite of his weak whiskers, I am beginning to believe that there must be something to the author of *The Grandissimos* and *Dr. Sevier;* and Howells, I doubt not, is really good for something, even if he does write "literary passions" for the *Ladies Home Journal.*

I am in the middle of St. Luke now and find him magnificent reading. I am going through the *New Testament* and then I shall probably go back to the *Old.* It is high time I knew something about the *Bible,* if only for the sake of mental decency and I am positively glad to feel that my conscience, or rather pride, has at last turned against me. There seems to be no place in my brain for much reverence but the reading can surely do me no harm.—Yesterday I raised forty cents and sent for Renan's *Vie de Jesus* (*édition populaire* in 12). That may not be the most advisable accompaniment for the reading I have laid out for myself, but I have always wanted the book and now am going to have it.

You had better keep a good eye out for translations of *L'Armature* by Paul Hervieu, *En Route!,* by Huysmans and *Le Desert* by Loti. They are all attracting an unusual amount of attention and there must be something in them.

Joe and I went out to see your father and mother. They had been to the rededication of the White Meeting House and your father described the whole occasion as a hell of a time. The most interesting feature of the thing was, according to the description, the attitude of Long John Henderson who stood facing the congregation and waved a large hand of welcome to all who came in.

Speaking of the *Bookman* and Mr. Mabie, can you tell me why the picture of Mr. Lowell "always studying Dante," with a magic ring of books around him, is not a pleasant thing for me to consider? I am afraid I am a little sour on Lowell, in spite of all that I can do. I cannot take him for a great man as I can Bryant, or even Longfellow—who, were it not for his sonnets, would immediately fall in my estimation, to second rank of American poets.

I sent my quatrain to the *Chap-Book* the other day but do not anticipate its acceptance. But it seems more natural to have it "out" somewhere and I am one of those happily constructed people whom declinations do not disturb. I have had too much practice in that line.

I am now turning our friend "Theodore" inside out, completely rewriting him. I do not expect to do any more original work until next winter—nothing now but copying and tinkering with an uncomfortable feeling that I am not yet ready to publish anything. But I shall try it all the same, even if I have not much hope.

Gardiner
May 26, 1895

I have a feeling that I ought not to write to you today, because I am wholly out of the mood and strangely destitute of ideas, but I have a feeling of pride, on the other hand, which tells me that I shall feel better for the writing, even if it be at your expense. Were I a little more courageous I might write with a deliberate intention of destroying the sheet as soon as it was covered, but I'm damned if I do that today, even for you. I purpose to keep right on in just this style until I arrive at the bottom of page 4, when I shall fold the matter up, seal it, and let it go. I shall not take the trouble to read it over (I seldom do that for anybody) but shall trust to your own ingenuity in filling blanks and deciphering hieroglyphics, in the making of which I own no master.

I am in a peculiarly reminiscent mood today, and I think the cause of it lies in the fact that I shall hear no more of Reece's Band, which, as you know, has been with us all the week. At the end of the closing concert last night they all stood up and played "Auld Lang Syne" in a way that sent seven distinct kinds of crinkles up my spine and through my hair. When it stopped and the men began to put up the instruments I felt as if an epoch in my life were over. You don't like lives with epochs in them, [but] you must grant me one this time.

Last evening's programme was particularly fine from the *Tannhäuser* overture to the "Miserere" in *Il Trovatore* which I played (?) you that evening you ate eggplant. It was taken by a trombone and a cornet with a subdued accompaniment by the band, which kept up the anguish and the tension of the scene in a way that was almost beyond belief. I have heard the opera, but the spirit of the piece was not brought [out] by the human voice as it was last night by wind instruments. But then, instrumental music was always more to me than vocal, and I have no doubt that it always will be. This band had the greatest clarinet arrangement I ever saw—seven of them, with bassoon, in a band of 25 pieces is a pretty good showing.

Renan's *Vie de Jesus* has arrived and looks like most attractive *reading*. My *New Testament* work is going on well and I must say that I enjoy it. That, with five or six French novels, will constitute most of my reading for many weeks to come. It would be a good thing for me, I think, if I could cultivate your interest in posters, or something of that kind, but it [is] an absolute impossibility for me to do it. There is no place in my brain for collections now, though when I was a kid I used to be collecting everything from bugs to buttons. The only things that I could possibly collect now with any ardor would be first editions of *recent* books. But they all cost money, and money is a substance which I designate with a very small "x." There was a man and he had naught, and robbers came to rob him. I am that man without the robbers. They all know better.

In *The Story of an African Farm* the chickens were wiser than human beings; and I wonder now if my six hens are wiser than I am. They are saying something down there behind the barn that I cannot understand, and for some reason they are making me think of the whole scheme of life and of its final outcome. A man is more than a hen, but a hen knows something of which a man knows nothing. I'll bet they know more about the weather than all men and women in the world. Sometimes I think instinct is only another name for divine knowledge and sometimes I don't think much about it anyway. Today my thoughts are all mixed up and the smell of wet lilac-blossoms coming through my window makes me a little sick. I wonder if Pierre Loti could stomach them in his study?

[P.S.] I shall see you at the end of the week—saw your father and mother this afternoon.

Gardiner
June 9, 1895

I have [been] trying all day to screw up courage to write you a letter; but my room has been too confoundedly hot to permit of any prolonged thinking so I have let the day go by until now— six o'clock, or thereabouts. I have been reading Schuman some prize bits from *Degeneration*. He seems to enjoy the book and is inclined to be of the opinion that Nordau could not write so elegantly and so lingeringly upon sexual aberrations without being a victim himself to one or more of them. Did you read the chapter on Zola? It is pretty good work and sound, too, I think; only it is overdrawn and unnecessarily vituperative—if I may use two big words together.

I had a letter yesterday from Ford, in which he speaks of Barrett Wendell's *William Shakespeare* as "quite characteristic of the author, paradoxical, impertinent, and little, and yet interesting in a way." If you had ever had the slightest acquaintance with Wendell, these three adjectives would strike you as they do me—almost like magic. What I have just quoted is so far the best thing that I ever knew Ford to say, that I shall have to tell him so in a letter. I have given up my trip to Boston but shall partly make up for it by spending next Sunday in Exeter where I shall have a good talk, and, I hope, some good beer, with Ford. If he were to be married, however, I should stay at home and make the best of it by myself.

Sometimes I am half afraid that you do not, that is, cannot, understand my feeling as to attending your wedding. But I shall not attempt to make any explanation upon paper, for I am sure that it would be labor wasted. I only know that it is better for me to stay where I am, and also better for you. If you cannot understand what I mean by the last clause, I will tell you when I see you.

Now, old man, I am going to preach for just about six lines or so. You have always had pretty much your own way and have been forming the habit for the past twenty-five years of exercising a devil of a lot of authority, especially at home, without the smallest suspicion of what you were doing. You have no desire to hurt the feelings of anybody on earth, but you are the victim of a mild form of impulsive selfishness, which it will be well enough for you to bear in mind. If this sounds stronger in writing than I intended it to, let this little apology be enough to assure you that I am quite honest in saying what I do, and would not, if I could, say anything to hurt your peace of mind or give you the slightest possible chance to doubt my sincere friendship and general admiration for your character, ambitions, intellect, and hair.

[P.S.] I like Theocritus—especially "the blunt-faced bees."

Exeter, N. H.,
June 15, 1895

Ford has gone to a Faculty Meeting and so I am here alone in his room to pass the time as best I may. It has been a long time since I have written a letter in the evening but it seems to me that I ought to send you one more before you are married so I shall run the risk of straining my eyes and tell you that I am somewhat taken aback by this visit. Ford is just the same and is obviously glad to see me; but his prosperity fills me with something between discouragement and dismay. I say his, but I must mean his and yours together.

A man who is earning his living, to say nothing of holding a position of responsibility and respect, has a peculiarly depressing effect upon me just now. It may make you laugh to think that you have often been the cause of such feelings in my mind, when you consider the relations we have had, but it is true all the same.

I know I am a damned fool to be disturbed by the progress of others, but I can't seem to help it. I am beginning to get desperate, though there is perhaps no good reason why I should.

Ford goes to France in a few days and will have, I suppose, a good time. He has unusual advantages, among others a personal invitation from Paul Bourget to call and see him. He made Bourget's acquaintance last year at Harvard. The possibilities associated with such good fortune as that make me mightily glad for him, for he is a fellow who deserves all he can get. Just now he seems to be getting considerable, but it may not always last. His position here is much more prominent than he ever gave me reason to suppose, but it is all through influence and almost phenomenal influence at that. Next year he drops History and takes German in its place. That language with French are the two things he cares for.

But you don't care about Ford, for you don't know him, so I will come back to familiar ground. How do you feel about it anyway? And how is your courage? If I were in your place I think I should be tempted to skip the state. But then, you are not troubled much with my uneasiness over small things, like getting married, so you will get through it all right.—Accept my best wishes, and read this stuff if you can. I shan't try it. To have written it with a pen so fine as this is all you can ask of me.

Gardiner
October 6, 1895

I must ask you to pardon me for not writing before, but I am afraid that I cannot give any very good excuse for my negligence. All I can say is that I have not been in the mood and that, after all, is more of a reason than it seems at a first thought. My ears have been knocking a good deal, but I don't [like] to say too much about them—especially in letters—so will let that matter drop.

I am glad to know that you are well fixed and contented in your new quarters and I trust that your experience in college is none the less congenial. Your few words concerning Professor

Goodwin lead me to think that he is a good fellow as well as a great scholar. I never heard him spoken of before as "a really great man," but I suppose he is that—in his line, at any rate. To me, there is only one of the really great sort at Harvard and of course you know who he is—possibly you went to hear him speak at the Freshmens' reception in Sanders. The *Crimsons* you sent were like old friends, and I hope you will keep on sending them —that is if you are a subscriber—and please let me know if you wish to keep them. It is twice as large as it used to be but I cannot see that there is much more reading in it. But advertising pays and I don't blame the editors for their change. As time goes on I suppose the reading matter will increase, for an editor, and above all a college editor, likes to air his English—however good or bad it may be.

I am coming to Cambridge some day this week or next so I shall have a chance to smoke a pipe with you and have some talks. I am through the Messenger's long speech in *Antigone* and the rest will be plain sailing. I have omitted the Hyporchema, however, as I want my time for it—also Jebb's version. It is the most mixed up mess that I have yet found, and I want all the legitimate assistance I can get. You will be glad to know that I am more enthusiastic than ever over the play and am pretty confident that it will amount to something some day. To be sure, the time and work I have spent on it would be ample to write a book, but I do not regret what I have done. I am a great believer in solid foundations, and what could be better than a creditable translation of a Greek play?

If there is anything you wish me to bring with me, write me a letter Monday so I shall have time. I went out to your place last Sunday and found Joe and his spouse-elect there before me. I shall probably go out again this afternoon. The notion of going to Boston this fall tickles me exceedingly. I need something of the kind if ever a man did and I have struck my usual luck as regards rooms. Butler tells me, in one of his short spasmodic letters, that he has a room on Bowdoin St. that will feel better for my living in it. So, with that and some college rooms, I shall not have to bother you.

I am glad that you will have a chance to meet Ford and Hubbell (who, by the way, is a student in the New Church Divinity School) and I only regret that Latham is too far away to be called. I had a letter from him the other day acknowledging *Une Vie* and telling me of various things. He is getting to be an enthusiast on the subject of moulding the young mind and I am mighty glad of it. He is a fellow who might have a tremendous influence over an intelligent young one and it is very gratifying for me to know that he is bringing it to bear in the right direction. There was a time when I feared the contrary, for he used to be full of whimsical precepts that might play the devil without his meaning that they should.

Judging from the weather we are having here, Cambridge must have been in its glory during the past fortnight. A native will tell you that that time is in June, but October is the month for me. I like the red leaves. Red leaves makes me think of *Degeneration* and that makes me think of Lombroso's article in the last *Century*. To judge from some extracts I have seen, he comes down upon his disciple pretty hard in places. You have probably read the thing for yourself by this time. I do not read much of anything now, as my eyes have given out again. *Une Vie* must have been a little too strong.

I have [been] composing some more *"miousic"* lately and am now doing a sort of Funeral March with two themes—or rather it is doing me. I have the music all settled for a ballad, which, I trust will some day be a Tavern Song. Do not think by this that I am beginning to serve two masters, for I have dabbled with notes all my life and probably shall as long as I live. I have no faith in any of it, however, save the ballad just mentioned, which, I think, has a little character and some originality. The words are not yet made, but they will come with time.

I had a letter from Thorne the other day in which he incidentally enclosed a clipping from the *New York Sun*—a reprint of my "Miracle" business, which you know. "Kosmos," which will appear in the *Globe* for October 18th, is crazier than that. You heard me read the first draft of it—which was not much like its present form—and did not care a damn for it. I doubt if you like it any better this time.

With my best regards to Mrs. Smith, I remain. . . .

Gardiner
November 10, 1895

I am afraid that I can't write you much of a letter today but I must send something to partly make up for the long delay. I was out to eat beans with your father and mother a week ago last night and had a good smoke in the evening. Joe and I may go out this afternoon if the wind does not discourage us. It is blowing now like the very devil, but it may stop sometime.

It was my impression that I once referred to my own surprise at finding Lanman so young a man; but I suppose I did not. Did it strike you disappointingly?—I am making all sorts of poems nowadays, and do not dare to stop for fear I might realize what a damned fool I am. That is not a pleasant experience and I do not intend to go through [it] more times than are necessary. The stuff will be put together, I think, by the first of February.—Schuman's sonnet in the *Bookman* was to him like a long drink of the stuff that Ponce de Leon didn't find. You see he had [heard] nothing of it since he sent it on in June and had long since given it up. I am glad for him, for it is a good thing in a good place.

I have not read anything since I got back and have done little save to torture my gray matter with this scheme of mine. I doubt if it amounts to anything but do not let that discourage me.

Your father is better from his last trouble (that fall in the cart) but I can see that he is slowly breaking up. I tell you this because I want you to keep it in mind—not because I think there is any sign of immediate change, for there is not. He says the government ought to appoint a committee to knock men on the head when they are fifty years old. Give my regards to Mrs. Smith, and beware of alcohol.

Gardiner
November 26, 1895

You will, I fear, threaten to strike me off your list when I tell you that I do not yet know how either of Saturday's games turned out. I did not think to get a Sunday paper, there was nothing about them in our delicious little daily, and this morning I forgot it again. And yet I deny all relationship with your five year man. This makes me think of the morning after the New York state election when I met Sumner Soule on the hill. "Well," he said, "how did she go?"—"What?"—"New York."—"Don't know." —"Well, my God, young man! . . ."

I hope you will keep on sending me *Crimsons* whether I acknowledge them or not. They fill a little place in my life that would otherwise be empty. They seem to take me back somehow to the time when I used to sit and smoke in my room at Beelar's and hear Saben come pounding up the stairs, or maybe Latham with some damned sour-bellied criticism of Andrew Lang.

I had a small letter from Hubbell soon after my arrival in Gardiner and one from Ford, who tells me that he will spend Sunday with me if I want him. It makes me feel good when such a fellow is willing to ride five hours in the cars and back again for the sake of a few hours with me and my notions and I am wondering "as to how" I shall be able to entertain him. I have decided to let him entertain himself and me at the same time. Nothing like a little ingenious forethought.

I ought to ask your pardon for running my friends into your letters as I do, but when Latham writes me that he is not reading anything but Greek, and stuff pertaining to Greek I know you must have a kind of brotherly feeling for him. He thinks Moulton goes altogether too far in his mechanical distinction of tragedy and comedy and I am inclined to agree with him—though I only

* 235 *

looked through that portion of the book.—I have stopped *Antigone* on account of my other work, but you need have no fears of my stopping it altogether. If, by any strange chance, I manage to do anything to live a year or two, it will be that Greek play— that is, unless I am tremendously mistaken.

Your letter last evening did me a world of good and I only wish that I might give you a decent return for it. But I cannot today, and God only knows when I can. What little faculty I ever had for letter writing seems to have left me this fall. Perhaps it is on account of the hard pull my pomes are giving me. If that little book ever goes out, I am half afraid that I shall go with it. I never had such a damned time in life with anything as with some of those verses which ought to go like bees and things and which want to go like camels. It is hunting for hours after one word and then not getting it that plays the devil with a man's gray matter and makes him half ready to doubt the kindness of the Scheme.

I had already read the clipping you sent me. It was copied in the *Reporter-Journal*. Sometimes I wish the tiny town on the Kennebec and all the people in it (myself included) could be blown up among the Asterids or picked off with one of Jules Verne's comets. When I feel that way I almost always go and have a smoke which doesn't taste right. I am glad you are coming home pretty soon because I want to see how you look. You seem to be enjoying Harvard, and I am glad of that, too.

I see by one of the *Crimsons* that Jamie is trying for the *Advocate*. Hope he'll get it, for it would put him in the way of meeting some very good fellows. He must have talked through his hat about my song, for he never heard it. But then, he thinks I am something pretty strange just now and is a better friend to me than he will be in two more years. There is a pathos in a younger fellow's friendship that well-nigh kills the pleasure of it.

P.S. You will find the Thomas Hardy sonnet in the *Critic* for November 23—Holiday Number.

I was glad to get hold of the *Philistine*—particularly for the "Dipsy Chanty," which I think one of the best things Kipling has done. It is not so good as the "Bolivar" or "There's a Whisper down the Field" but of course a man can't always be at his best—that is, his very best.

I followed your suggestion in regard to the *Chap-Book* business and sent them a page of stuff about the Rosny books. I haven't the slightest thought of their printing it but I suppose there is the ghost of a chance. A "V" would come in handy just now but I am afraid that I must do without it—at any rate from that source.

Ford spent last Sunday with me and his coming was as you may imagine something of a change for me. I think it did me good though he was probably a little surprised to find what a seed I have developed into. My only hope is that someday I may sprout and make some leaves. The poetry-book is getting on and will be pretty well shaken out by the first of February—sent off, I hope. When that comes back I shall be stirred up for a few days, but not for many. It isn't worth while. And on the other hand it isn't half so easy to put such things out of one's mind as it may seem to you who have never had the experience—as far as I know. You may be a *literatus,* "on the quiet," but I don't believe it. You have more respect for your brains.

Do you hear anything from Butler nowadays? I haven't had a line from him since he sent me his book-plate—five or six weeks ago. And how about James' piece in the *Advocate?* I fancy it was about the dead men outside the wall, which was a very good story indeed. I never saw his writing of it, but I imagine he did it pretty well.

I have been rebuilding that sonnet translation of Horace's ode to Leuconoë. How do you like these for the opening lines?—

> *"I pray you not, Leuconoë, to pore*
> *With unpermitted eyes on what may be*
> *Appointed by the gods for you and me,*
> *Nor on Chaldean figures any more."*

I may get the thing to partly satisfy me some day, but I rather doubt it. I have spent the last three weeks mostly in rewriting that story of mine, "The Night Before"—you may remember it— in blank verse. "Look you Domine, look you and listen etc." I don't know what it all amounts to, but there are some pretty good passages in it and they may lug it through. My songs are corkers —particularly Edward Alphabet:

> *"Look at Edward Alphabet*
> *Going home to pray!*
> *Drunk as he can ever get,*
> *And on the Sabbath day!—"*

and so forth. You may not think it from the first lines but the poem is an argument against the present attitude of the females. I also have a piece of deliberate degeneration called "Luke Haver-gal," which is not at all funny. Then there is old John Everel-down who had all the women of Tilbury Town under his wing, or thought he had. The "Tavern" part of my book is not like any-thing I ever wrote before and I doubt much if I ever try anything like it again. The songs have been for the most part villainously hard to make.

I think I shall have to [go] out and see your father and mother this afternoon, for I haven't seen them for nearly a month. Some-thing has turned up every Sunday to stop me.

Monday morning.

I was out to your place last evening and had a good smoke with your father. He is going through my set of Marryatt and thinks them great—particularly *Japhet* and *Midshipman Easy.* If I had

eyes I should read them again myself, but as it is I cannot. I am
going through a school edition of Loti's *Pecheur d'Islande* which
is very good but rather suggestive of short life. To use Bennell's
phrase, "it smells of mortality."

Hope to see you now in a few days.

Gardiner
February 7, 1896

Your father said he was sorry to have the books go out of the
house, because he wanted to read them himself; but I suppose
they were sent all the same and you probably have them by this
time. Three or four days ago, I took the liberty to borrow Henry
James's *The Lesson of the Master* and have read it to find that
H. J. is a genius. No smaller word will do it for the man who
produced such work as this. Did you read it? If you didn't, you
must. If there is any more of his stuff out there let me know, and
I shall try to read it, though I must take a rest for a time. The
reading of a book is an event with me and a luxury that I cannot
indulge in very often without paying for it ten times over. So I
fiddle now instead of read and I suppose I make some cruel
noises; but as long as I get a little fun out of it I don't care much
for the effect my diversion may have upon others. It is fiddle or
nothing with me now, as my literary machine is all out of order
and I have given up all such business for two or three weeks at
least. The past three months have been a grind with me, and, as
far as any immediate reward is concerned, have probably been all
for nothing. That, however, doesn't affect me much, as I have
partly succeeded in looking at such things as steps to what I am going to get later. I may never get it, but I can climb and make myself believe that I shall. Anticipation is more than half of life
anyway, and this is particularly true of a life like mine, which is,
in reality, almost wholly selfish, however much I may dislike to
say it.

Do you ever see Butler nowadays? I have heard nothing from
him and do not know whether he is dead or alive. I have a sort
of presentiment that things are not going as well with him as they

might,—but then, I know that to be the case. It has been so ever since I knew him.

Your examinations must be pretty well over by this time, and you of course know about how you are coming out with them. You have been fretting a good deal over them, but I have thought all along that there was no need of it. Was I right or wrong? Examinations are queer things sometimes, but as a rule a man can tell whether he has failed one of them or not without waiting for his mark. Have you been to any of the operas, or don't you care for that sort of thing? You had better go once—*Martha* or *Traviata*—if you want something sure—for the sake of being surprised. There is no resemblance between these performances and those of an ordinary theatre company. I can't tell you what the difference is, but you will soon see it if you go. Or, you can be a "degenerate" and hear Wagner, as I think I should do if I were in your place.

It is warm and sloppy today, and I am correspondingly lazy and indifferent. It is one of those days when a fellow is particularly aware of his liver and falls to wondering what it is for. Rain all night and slush in the morning. I fancy you have the same there, and, if so, I can picture you to myself trying to paddle through Cambridge streets. The drainage there is beautiful, if only for its picturesqueness. The memory of certain spring mornings there will never leave me—especially the scene around Memorial Hall. There were times there when we had to swim for our breakfasts, and swim back again for recitations.

Are you reading anything now? There is more or less talk about *A Singular Life* but I doubt if I ever get up courage to tackle it. By the way, you needn't send me the *Bookman* any more. I am just as much obliged, but I can read Schuman's. And please do me the favor to destroy the letter in which I made remarks about his friendship. Not that I have changed my mind, but a man has no business to write such stuff. A line in your next letter to the effect that you have done this will be a relief to me. I don't like to have such stuff floating around.

I am glad you are at the point where you think you are getting somewhere. I have had no fears for you myself, but I know that fussy nature of yours pretty well and was more than half afraid that you would never be sure that you are more than a third rate man. It is rather amusing to us who look on, but I suppose it is no joke with you. It is needless for me to say that I shall be glad to have you send me your marks when you get them. Marks do not amount to much in themselves but they amount to everything when a man is working for honors.

A whim took me the other day and I joined the "Society of the Philistines." I don't know why I did it, any more than I know why I do a good many things. I suppose you have a *Philistine* poster in your collection, but I'll send you another if you want it.

I have got to work again and my "book" is fast nearing completion. If nothing happens I shall pack it off sometime this month, but my expectations are not much. I still think that I shall have to print it myself and then give it away—if I can. I have not lost any faith in the stuff, but I am afraid I shall have a hard time in making others look at my work with my eyes—that's all. I am not "stuck on myself" by any means, but I am cheered sometimes by the conviction that I am not a total damned fool. That is something for a man to say in the first person, I know; but I shall keep on saying it as long as I have breath.

My liver has made itself known again today and I feel rather out of sorts. I went to a church supper last evening and that may have something to do with it. I should not have gone, but Charles Longfellow persuaded me that it was the thing for me to do, so I went. Charles is here for a week on account of his nerves. They work him like an ox there in Hopedale and it [is] half a wonder to me that he stands it. Just now he is very enthusiastic over Stone and Kimball's *Poe*.

I called on Jones the other day for the first time and had a very good time. He gave me a Tom Reed cigar, and we talked about Zola. I think I shall have to go again, for it does me good to meet such a man once in a while. He is full of queer ideas of life and death, but he is right in believing that a man should think of life. Death will take care of itself. He cites Maupassant as a splendid example of the triumph of mind over matter. He died young and crazy because his life was false and immoral, he says, and I am inclined to believe him. He defends Zola for the truth and sincerity that lies at the bottom of his nastiness.

Well, I'll go down now and get something to eat. I'm not hungry but I'll feel better for going through the movements, I suppose. This [is] not one of my letter-writing days, so you must excuse me again and write when you feel like it.

P.S. Stick to that big perpendicular handwriting you have lately adopted. It is one of the best things you ever did.

Gardiner
March 7, 1896

It has been some time since I have written a letter for you, but I hope you do not think that I have forgotten you. All my correspondents are waiting as you have been, and some of them, I fear, will keep on waiting until I get into trim again. Since I finished up my poems and sent them away I have done nothing but exist and read postage-stamp catalogues, which, by the way, are tremendously exciting. Postage-stamps always had a strange fascination for me, and now I think I shall go into the business again—in a small way. I need something of the kind and can think of nothing else that will fill the bill. Posters are absolutely out of the question, as they do not mean anything to me. Stamps on the other hand, particularly when they are unused, appeal to my sense of beauty—or something—as nothing else will do it. If you are at a loss to understand me, you might go to the Post Office and buy a well-centred specimen of the present issue—say from 1¢ to 10¢ and spread them out on white paper. I think they will give you some new ideas, as Joe says, and make you sympathize with me. The most alluring stamps however are the British Colonials—that is, some of them. There is something in the color of them that we cannot seem to get. I have often wondered why it is that England doesn't make her own stamps after the same models.

But I won't say any more about stamps. I'll tell you that I am reading your copy of *The House of the Seven Gables* and am completely soaked in it. At first—for the first hundred pages—it seemed to me that Hawthorne was no[t so] sure of his way as in his other books; but that impression has all gone now and the book runs like oil—some ancient oil, full of strange lights and odors. This may sound queer to you, but I am telling you how the thing impresses me. I am ashamed for never having read the book before, but I am reading it now and that is enough.—I expect to hear from my poems almost any day; but as I know well enough what I shall hear, I am in no great state of trepidation over it. I still believe that Kelley will be the man to print them and am almost beginning to hope that he will. If the book should make its way then, my satisfaction would be proportionally greater. I am sure of one thing, however, and that is that they are to be printed by somebody. It is a good deal to get as far as to feel that. The book will contain something like a hundred pages and will be called *The Tavern and the Night Before.* You see I was bound to wring the "tavern" in somehow, and I think I have done it fairly well. In fact, if the publishers, and then the public, are as well satisfied with the contents as I am with the title, there will be no further trouble with this first venture. But that is out of the question, I suppose.

I am glad you got your two A's and hope you will get more of them. They signify rather more than you seem to realize just now, but I knew well enough that you would get them. I am pretty sure, too, that you will eventually change your attitude toward Greenough, though maybe not till you are out of College. There is a bump of persistent egotism somewhere on your cranium and I am glad of it. It will make things all right for you in

the end—about the time you get the money I owe you.—Write
when you feel like it.

Gardiner
April 4, 1896

I haven't done much writing—letter-writing, or anything else—
lately, on account of a protracted attack of something very like
the disease that made life such a disinterested hell for "Little
Billee" in *Trilby*. All the difference is, there seems to be no particular cause for mine. I am getting out of it now, though, and
am beginning to ache for some human companionship. Think
I'll have to go out and see your father and mother. I haven't seen
either of them for nearly six weeks, for the same reason that I
have hardly seen anybody save such people as have fallen in my
way. The way in which my few correspondents are acting leads
me to half think that they are all in the same condition that I
have been, or something like it.

When I sent my book away, about a month ago, I thought that
I should think it a small matter when it came back; but I may as
well confess that I am in no mood now for such a thing to happen, though it undoubtedly will happen, and that before a very
long time. I am bound to hear from it one way or the other in
a week or two at the longest. Its return will hurt a little, considerable, I fancy, at first; but I shall keep on having the same
faith in myself. That faith has become chronic now, like the
business in my ears and I accept it for whatever it may be with
a kind of optimistic desperation, if you know what that is. In
the meantime, *tempus fugit* and my poor prose is dangling.
Can't seem to do anything since I finished the rewriting of "Alcander" a week ago.

You say that your summer's work is to read Homer, and what
do you mean by that? Is the work appointed or just for your own
satisfaction? Something in your letter made me wonder if you
intended to spend a second year at Harvard. I rather had a notion that you were going to Germany, though I don't know just
why I should have thought so. But whatever you do, I am mighty

glad on your account for this year in Cambridge. Bowdoin is all right as far as it goes, but there are some things (not laid down in the curriculum) that a fellow can't possibly get there. If I had spent your four years at Brunswick, however, I might not think as I do, so pardon my ignorance if you do not agree with me.

I am glad you are getting to like Hubbell. There is a passing (I hope) touch of something like asceticism in the man just now and I am free to say that I do not fancy it; but the fellow at heart is truly human and intellectually generous. It is also a good thing to remember that he danced on tables after a Springfield game and climbed a waterspout for a drink of something without any demons in it. The peculiarly labored phrasing is probably due to elocutionary training. Tryon has it just about as bad, but I don't think he is aware of it.

How did you come out with your other two examinations?

If you are still in the book buying business I should advise you to gather in a copy of Lamson Wollfe and Co's *Magda*. It must be great reading, especially before seeing Duse. I have an idea that Sudermann is bigger than the world knows, but then I don't know anything about it as I have never even seen one of his books.

Gardiner
April 8, 1896

I was out to your place Sunday and again yesterday afternoon. As you know by this time, your mother has been very sick but I am glad to tell you now that she is sitting up and out of all danger unless from some possible relapse. That, however, is hardly to be expected and I do not see any cause for you to worry.

I did my best to make her realize her mistake in feeling so indifferent toward everything, but I don't know how well I succeeded. Her greatest trouble just now seems to me to be a general lack of interest in the world and all in it—a kind of discouragement brought on, I suppose, by her unsatisfactory recovery from her sickness last year.—Your father doesn't say anything about himself, but he has a hard time getting around on account of his knees. He says he is going to Bar Harbor this summer and get a job as cook in the biggest hotel in the place.

I write this, thinking you might like to know just what I think of the condition of things.

[P.S.] No news from *The Tavern*.

Gardiner
May 13, 1896

I must ask you once more not to think that I have forgotten you because I have not written. This spring has been a long, queer season with me and I am glad that it is gone, though I am aware that such a feeling is hardly in accordance with what I try to believe are my honest views of life. My religion seems to be a kind of optimistic desperation and the deuce only knows what will come of it. I am trying as hard as I can to get over my almost helpless dependence upon my friends, but I find it sorry work. I say to myself that I was not made to live in solitude (and my present life amounts to little more than that) but I keep on wondering if the fates are not taking care of me, after all. If it were not for the solitude that I have been through I should not now have the "dog-gone fool notions" (I like to quote Jones) that are in my head; and if it were not for those notions I should not have my present ambitions to be something big. I don't much think that these ambitions will ever be realized, for I am getting more and more to know my limitations; but for all that, I like to keep on hoping in a sort of blind way, even if I have to stop every now and then to consider how my life is running away from me. You don't know what it is to be twenty-six years old, and still a little child as far as a prospect of worldly independence goes. You may not be exactly free just now, yourself; but you know what you can do if you are driven to it and you know that you can do that thing well. Yesterday I had to put down a carpet, but had to stop on account of my head—which will go to show about how much I am good for when it comes to scrubbing for myself. I don't know enough to teach, and any kind of business would swamp me in a month. All I have to look forward to in the way of worldly prosperity is a distant vision of a time when I may possibly earn two or three hundred dollars a year by writing. That time, however, is very far away and I don't waste a great deal of nervous energy in thinking of it. It doesn't pay.

My first venture with the book has proved a fizzle, as I knew it would. I was so thoroughly satisfied that the stuff would be rejected, that the information hardly touched me. One peculiar thing in my make-up is that I don't seem to have any capacity for discouragement, no matter how much I may be running over at the heel. I have done a few things which I know are worth while and that is a great deal to be sure of. If printed lines are good for anything, they are bound to be picked up some time; and then, if some poor devil of a man or woman feels any better or any stronger for anything that I have said, I shall have no fault to find with the scheme or anything in it. I am inclined to be a trifle solemn in my verses, but I intend that there shall always be at least a suggestion of something wiser than hatred and something better than despair.

All this, no doubt, will make you grin, but I assure you that I am getting to be pretty much in earnest. As far as common pleasure goes—the kind that makes people laugh, I mean—I don't see any more of it in the future than there has been in the twenty odd years that are behind me. My fun has got to be of another sort, though I hope, for your sake, that it won't always be in the writing of letters like this. A man has no right to wreak himself on a friend in any such wholesale way, and I'll try not to do it again.

Gardiner
May 22, 1896

In my reply to your wholesale damnation of Harvard, I suppose you naturally expect me to dig both heels into Bowdoin; but I don't think I should gain anything by doing that, though I could accomplish the feat without any conscientious scruples. Barring the great and inevitable seal of the plough and milking stool which is peculiarly characteristic of the Lewiston institution, my objections to Bowdoin are precisely the same as those which I have to Bates. I cannot see that either college does anything at all to develop the mental intensity of a man or to awaken his latent comprehension of the "greater glory." As far as my observation has served me, Bowdoin and Bates leave their men just as they receive them—making, of course, due allowance for four years of natural human growth. In Bowdoin there is perhaps a peculiar danger of succumbing to the innate rowdyism of the place, but that danger is nothing to the tragic certainty of being branded with the great seal of Bates. The Brunswick college is a kind of rural miniature of Yale, while a miniature, rural or any other, of Harvard would be an absolute impossibility. It is the human largeness and not the local smallness of the place that puzzles and too often finally disgusts so many of its transplanted students. They wonder at its imperfections and its shams because they have never brought themselves fully to realize the shams and imperfections of the world; and thus they sometime "loathe" it because they, in the well-meaning provincialism which is the natural heritage of a place where a fascinating but withal narrowing "college spirit" is the great fetish, really loathe the world without knowing it. Disillusions are devilish things, but I am afraid that there is one coming to you that will make you sick to think of; and that is, that a time is coming when you will be compelled to confess, away down in your bowels somewhere, that your one dissatisfied year at Harvard has been more to you than the whole four at Bowdoin—though of course it was then that you had your fun. As far as "pulls" go, I think you will find that all colleges and all planets are just alike. You had several pulls at B. and I have no doubt but that you have or can get just as many where you are. When a college "pull" is analyzed it generally means that a man has done something that has been appreciated. The pity is that some men do things that are not appreciated, and then there is no pull.

I suppose this is all pretty big talk for me to make, knowing as

I do my own limitations; but even though I be an incurable clod-hopper I have the satisfaction of knowing that people will not invite me to the damned times they have. This is a good deal to me, more than you can begin to realize. I suppose I can stand more letting alone than any man who ever breathed. Two or three good friends (if I keep on writing letters like this, I may lose one of them) and some oatmeal porridge are the things that keep me going.

I have written a sonnet to Paul Verlaine and another one called "The Dead Village." I have been a wallowing degenerate ever since I painted the dining-room floor last week. And I didn't paint the whole of it, either. There are seven shades of yellow in it and I have a symbol for every devilish one of them.

Hurry up and come home.

Gardiner
June 7, 1896

I am glad to know that you feel you have got something to pay for your year at Harvard, but am still sorry that you are so thoroughly disappointed in the place. That, however, is your own affair and has nothing to do with my high opinion of you as a man and a "scholard." Why don't you go to Athens and immortalize yourself by reading nail-holes on some old temple as Mr. — [sic] did by reading those on the Parthenon?

I have often wished you might go to a "Pop" concert with Professor Goodwin, but I suppose such a thing is hardly to be expected. It would be a good thing for the old man, though, and incidentally a good thing for you. He would doubtless expand during the intermission. Something makes me think that you have made an impression at Harvard in spite of all your hard feelings, and I feel pretty confident that Allen, Goodwin, White, and your particular friend Greenough have their eyes on you for something out of the ordinary. I do not say this to give you a momentary sense of pleasure but because I believe it to be a fact. Perhaps you are not aware of it, but you have changed tremendously during the past two or three years, and it is for this reason that I think it was a glorious thing for you that you were not able to go to Harvard, or anywhere else, before you did. The Rockland change was the thing you most needed and it did its work to an extent that you can never realize. Bowdoin is all right for the ordinary everyday student and good fellow—particularly the good fellow—but it is not the place for men like you. I know I can not make you agree with me in this, but for all that, I cannot resist the temptation to write what I think. I am not foolish enough to suppose that any words of mine can turn [you] in any way against your Alma Mater and that is why I feel free to say "just what I dam' please." Even if you feel yourself that Bowdoin didn't give you a fair chance, there must always be that sense of motherhood toward the college. When you are gray-headed you will have it just the same, and it is right enough that you should.

Jones and I were going to Togus today, but this rain will spoil the plan. Jones is a tremendously good fellow, when you get to know him, and I get a great deal of satisfaction from an occasional visit to his room. His philosophy is great and his hospitality is perfect. In short, he is a gentleman in the very best sense of the word. He calls the gold men "dog-gone robbers" but I can easily excuse his politics.

I am mighty glad that you are coming home, for I have been damnably lonely of late. I don't see much of anybody and am anxious to get out under that apple tree again. I was out to your place last Sunday and had [a] smoke with your father by the shed stove. I enjoyed myself very much, but I don't know how it was with him. I cannot get over my chronic fear of bothering people, and it may be a good thing for me that I can't.

I don't hear anything from my book, and am making definite plans as to how I shall print it on my own hook. It won't be a very imposing volume but I have a little hope that the inside of it may be good for something. If I am wrong in my ideas, the sooner I find it out the better.

I enclose a sonnet which appeared in the *Transcript* the other day. I cannot see that it amounts to anything, though it may be a trifle odd.

Gardiner
September 11, 1896

Your letter came this morning, and now, after this long delay I'll try to send you mine. The reason why I have not written before is that I have been so damnably out of sorts that I hardly had the courage. I was afraid that I should make a fool of myself. That confounded little book of mine (you must be getting sick of the sound of it by this time) is raising the devil with me. You can't understand my worry over such a trifling thing, and I am glad of it; but the fact still remains that I am puzzling my life away to find out whether the stuff is worth printing. I shan't puzzle much longer, though, as the whole thing goes off to Riverside, for better or worse, tomorrow morning.

I am glad to hear that you are enjoying yourself—or yourselves —and I rather hope that I may get over there myself sometime. But that all seems so far in the distance now that I feel childish to think of it. I should like to prowl around Hamburg and drink *ein bier* now and then, but I could never kindle any enthusiasm for the military spirit which is so rampant with the German people. The whole thing always went against the grain with me and always seemed in complete opposition with all human and spiritual progress. The result of it in Germany is not far to seek. It breeds, almost in infancy, an unnatural recognition of authority which is really nothing but an unwarrantable despotism softened a little by tradition, and piles on top of that an hereditary love of externals (or rather a worship of them) which is, to my eyes, anything but impressive or desirable. I am just beginning fully to realize that America [is] the hopper through which the whole civilization of the world is to be ground—consciously or otherwise. I am not much of an American, either—in a popular way; but I am glad to feel an inkling as to what the western continent was made for. So you may keep your red flags and (pardon my intolerance) your photographs. Souvenirs and "points of interest" are worse than the measles to me, and always will be, though I cannot tell just why. I recognize the value of such things (both historical and sentimental) but unless a place is so familiar to me that I can supply the natural atmosphere and color, the effect is wasted. This condition of things is significant, no doubt, in considering my acceptance of life as a state of "quiet desperation," as Thoreau had it. All I can see to life, as an occupation, is a kind of spiritual exercise (or at least a chance for that) by which we may, if we will, put ourselves beyond it. This may be paradoxical and unsound, but I don't like kodaks and I never shall. They are always the next thing to tourists' "views"— shut up in stiff covers and running out for five yards if you drop them. I don't think I'd ever make a tourist anyway; I'd get stuck in a comfortable house somewhere, and stay there till the weather changed.

I go out to see your father and mother once or twice a week and am glad for the chance to do it. It gives me a queer feeling at times and makes me wonder when the next sawdust ride is coming, and all that; but the place is there and so my imagination gets fed. Last Saturday night my system got fed also—on beans. I was too late to eat with your mother, so I had Prince and Jack instead. Jack had part of my beans, but the dog didn't get any. He kept his muzzle under my elbow all the time, but your mother drew the line at my feeding him. She said he had had enough and his respiration proved it. While I was eating, your letter came—which, of course, was something of an event. When it came to "tell Pa I'm sick," "Pa" seemed to derive a most unchristianlike pleasure from the information and I have fancied that he has been more hopeful ever since. He talks now about the parsnips he is going to raise next year and tells your mother that he is going to send her on an excursion to New York as soon as he gets away from that damned bed. I don't know what he intends to do while she is gone, but I rather fancy he will take that time to make up the smokes he has lost. He says they have got to be made up sometime.

Bliss Carman, writing to the *Critic*, in the third person, pays his respects to bicycles as follows: "He cherishes a black, bitter, benighted bigotry against that harmless but undignified convey-ance, and seeing trousered women ride through the streets of Boston, he is given to curse. Not while he has strength to dip a paddle in a mill-pond, or intellect enough remaining to count a stack of poker chips, will he forsake these infinite amusements for any base utilitarian thing as wheels [*sic*]. Bicycles are only fit for children and letter-carriers. The moment a gentleman puts his leg over one of them, he becomes a 'gent.' "—I do not agree with Carman, but still there is something in his words that appeals to me in a way. You will probably understand what I mean and appreciate my lack of real bicycle enthusiasm. I like almost any kind of a machine, however. I cannot find the poetry of motion in a "social dance" but I can see lots of it in a locomo-tive going about a mile a minute. This maybe accounts for some of my noisy verses which Schuman doesn't seem to care much for. When my book appears (I did not intend to mention that thing again) there will be in it "The Chorus of Old Men in *Aegeus*" which I fancy is pretty loud in places. As a whole it is unsatisfactory, but I am going to let it go, all the same. I am not old enough, intellectually, to print anything yet, but somehow I can't resist the temptation. It's a good deal like rum, only a little worse, if anything. I hope you'll never be afflicted with it—not for two or three years, at any rate. Then I want you to think over the Lucretius octaves.—I have thrown out "The Mole."

Sunday

This is a cloudy, disagreeable day and I am feeling all out of sorts—or as nearly so as I permit myself to feel. I bought a Sun-day *Journal* this morning and have felt condemned ever since. There is something in a Sunday paper that is positively awful. A man buys one, becomes disgusted with himself for so doing, and swears he will never do it again; but the chances are that he will do it, and go through the same feelings, and so on. I am on the road to a cure, though, and it will be many weeks before I buy another one of the things.—I can't do much of anything to-day but smoke, and wonder what the deuce is coming of it all. If you were at home I should put on my hat and climb over the hill to talk with you;—but that is wasted sentiment and I am glad of it—for your sake. You are in a way to spread your wings now and I expect you to fly pretty high before the ground gets you. Don't feel in too much of a hurry but just wonder once in a while, and in a healthy way, where you will be in about five years. In the meantime do all you can for yourself and trust in the powers. There is no charge for this, but I want you to be-lieve, or try to, that I am not fooling. There is wisdom in my words (sometimes) even though I may be an ass in the way of personal accomplishment.

More political honors have been thrust upon me, and I am going to make two dollars tomorrow. Ward clerk again. If I don't look out I shall be a prominent citizen before long. The Clason reign has given me great hopes as to my value to the public, if I ever had a chance to show it, and I even indulge now and then in dreams of a time when sagacious men will call me Solon. When a fellow marks a voting list and chews tobacco there is a tendency to think of these things, even though there be two sonnets and a villanelle in his head at the same time. The American air is full of politics now just as the German air is full of patriotism. I think I like the American article a little better, because it appeals directly instead of indirectly, to my sense of humor—which is about the only sense I have. My book of poems (there it is again) is one of the funniest things ever written by a mortal man. I do not know of anything funnier unless it be *Werther* or a *Life of McKinley and Hobart*.

I am sorry to tell you that the hammock tree in your yard has collapsed. As I looked at the ruins of it, it seemed like a symbol of a good time gone and the impression made me feel very queer indeed. It intensified my old realization of the fact that I must be up and doing and put old things away. My spiritual and intellectual activity (if I have any of the latter) are all for the future, but somehow my human life is all for the past. In other words, I lack the stamina which goes to make a successful man of the world. This is probably news to you.

Give my best regards to Mrs. Smith and write whenever you feel like it. I shall not be so slow in answering again.

Gardiner
September 27, 1896

I sent a long letter to Bonn about a fortnight ago, but as you are jumping around so much I doubt if you ever get it. When you get fairly settled I shall have better courage to write, even if I have nothing to tell you. You see my life is a pretty dull grind just now, and I fancy my letters must reflect it more or less.

Lately, I have been hard at work on the *Antigone* and have done nearly 400 lines of the new version, which, by the way, is a vastly different thing from the old. I find, though, that I am letting the play run away with me, and must somehow contrive to get rid of it for a time. It chases me day and night, and I am often two or three days in getting a passage into anything like a satisfactory condition. I am daily getting to think less and less of literal verse translations and am rather inclined to think that my performance will scare you when it takes on its final dress. As a scholar, I doubt if you will be able to enthuse over [it], but all I can do is to work in accordance with my own ideals, and do that work to the best of my ability. If I make so free with the text that you will be unwilling to identify yourself with the work, I want you to say so; but, on the other hand, I don't want any such thing to be necessary. The scheme was originated by you and I should hate to have a "split." But I am now thoroughly convinced that no man can follow out the plan of Plumptre and make an adequate translation of a Greek play. If the translation is to be in prose, I do not see any necessity of making the lines metrical, as P. has made them.

I was out to see your father and mother again last night and found them in pretty good spirits, though I think they have altogether too many callers. Your mother seems to be too busy with taking care of other people, but this may be just a notion of mine. I am, as you know, rather likely to have such things. The great trouble with your father is that he is too anxious to get well. The removal of the flat-iron has made him rather too confident, but who the devil can wonder at it? My greatest wonder is that a man can lie in his position for nine weeks and be alive to tell about it. But now, if nothing happens, he will soon be sitting up with a pipe in his mouth, and I am as anxious as you are for that day to come. If I couldn't walk out over the Iron Mine once in a while and find someone there that I could talk with, it seems to me that I should rot.

Joe doesn't come to the house any nowadays and I consequently see very little of him. It must be that I am not the sort of fellow that he cares to run after any more, and, when I think it over, I don't much wonder at his absence. If I keep on, I shan't be company for either man or beast; and you must not be surprised if you find me completely gone to seed when you get back to America. I am beginning to have the feelings of a man who has undertaken too much, and the feelings are not pleasant. When I finish the stiff winter's work that I have laid out, I can give you a better impression of my faith in myself. Until then, I shall try to be decent, and talk about other things.

I have two novels by Daudet to read when I get around to them, and they will doubtless help me over a good many knocks [?]. Daudet is a big man, and I tell you it gives a little fellow like me some queer ideas to read him. He is an awful worker, but that is not the whole of it.—Speaking of novels, the reviews are making a great fuss over King Noanett by F. J. Stimpson (I don't know whether there is a "p" in it or not) but I haven't read it so can give you no opinions of my own. I may read it if I ever get hold of it, and then I'll tell you what I find in it. The Dial gave William Watson's Armenian Sonnets a rather nasty wipe in the last number, and I was rather surprised to see it.

When I say the *Dial,* of course I mean William Morton Payne—his name and all that goes with it.

The leaves are turning red and the year is evidently growing old. When I walked home from your house last night everything looked so damned solemn and solitary that I couldn't help feeling glad for you away there in Berlin with your head full of Greek and Latin and your bowels in good order. Mine have been a little tight of late, and they may have had their effect on the landscape.

I dug my potatoes yesterday and found them rotten. I was not surprised to find them so. Tomorrow I am going to gather some apples. There is one to about every ten feet of tree-space and the devil only knows how I shall get them. Now I'll go and have a smoke and read the local *Herald.*—Bryan spoke in Bath last night, but I haven't seen anyone who heard him. The attitude of Watson and Sewall is funnier than anything in Aristophanes. Watson wants to shoot, but doesn't quite dare to.

Gardiner
October 15, 1896

I have been putting this letter off on account of my book, which I supposed would be ready to send to you before this; but things are crowded at Riverside on account of the holiday and educational work they have on hand, so I shall have to wait a little longer. It was only through the friendly intercession of my Uncle Fox, the fat man, that they would undertake the job at all before December. As things are, I fancy you will receive it in about three or four weeks from the time of this writing. You will find a few poems that may surprise you a little, but I rather hope you will like them. You will like the typography, at any rate, and at the same time will have a chance to test my judgment in the matter of page arrangement and typographical art in general. If the book turns out, mechanically, as I think it will, it will be about the best piece of work the Riverside Press ever produced, which is not saying very much.

You make me uncomfortable with your talk about *Illumination*. I have not read the book, but, if I am to believe half that I read about it, it must be a bigger thing than I am ever likely to put my name to. If you do not know it already, you may be interested to learn that the author was five years in getting it together—almost as much time as Hawthorne spent over the *Marble Faun* and more than Hardy spent over *Jude*. I see by the *Critic* that Hardy is going to republish *The Pursuit of the Well Beloved*, that mysterious novel which ran through the *Illustrated London News* and then disappeared. I have a presentiment that it doesn't amount to very much, but I sincerely hope that I may be wrong. I am almost always, and so I feel encouraged for the author of *The Mayor* etc.

I have been gathering the phosphoric apple lately and have laid in a good supply of brain food for the winter. Professor James doesn't take much stock in brain foods—particularly phosphorus—but that doesn't make any difference to me when apples are the question at issue. Last night your mother took me down cellar to show me the Baldwins that she and her neighbor Hezekiah Dorn had gathered and the sight of them was gratifying. I only wish that you were to be here to play pitch and eat them.

Your father sat up for the first time yesterday and he reports the performance as worse than capital punishment. I can [see] that he is encouraged over it however, and feels that the worst of his long siege is behind him. He has been wonderfully cheerful through it all, but your mother is pretty well used up, nor do I wonder that she is. Of course I do not mean that she is anything more than temporarily tired out, but that is enough.

I had a surprise the other night in the shape of a letter from Saben. He is in Heidelberg now, but has been all over Germany to get there, and has done, according to his narrative, a bewildering amount of boozing on the way. It seems that he had letters of introduction to some of the leading wine men and they filled him up, regardless of expense, on the best they had. If any man but Saben had told the yarn, I might have doubted, but if he told me that he had put the Emperor to bed, I should believe him. I know him, and I recognize his personality and the impression it makes upon his elders. If you ever go to Heidelberg I hope you will hunt him up and have a smoke with him. After he has smiled on you once you will think you have always known him. He is posted on almost everything, but has to be "shut off" about midnight or he will go on till sunrise. His address is "Herr Mowry Saben" (he has dropped the "Israel") Uber Strasse 4, Neuenheim, Heidelberg. When he left this country he had about made up his mind to go crazy, but he seems to have changed his mind. Maybe the Johanissberger cured him. Here is a sentence from his letter which may be of vital interest to you. "My health is much better, and most likely I should have fully recovered but for my temerity in drinking some *water*—a very dangerous thing to do in large portions of Europe. I always drink wine or beer now."

I think your German life is developing your originality, or genius, or whatever you call it. If it develops your Greek to a corresponding extent, you are all right. I am glad, though, that you have got enough of brass buttons and that you no longer express any desire to see soldiers, for I was almost beginning to fear that you were going wrong. That, for some reason, makes me think of two books I want you to read before long: F. Marion Crawford's *Griefenstein* and Mark Twain's *Tramp Abroad.* You can get the Crawford in Tauchnitz but I don't know just where you will get Mark Twain. But you must get it, with the pictures, for I never read anything in my life that was so completely soaked with the atmosphere of the Vaterland. Perhaps you have already read it, but I don't think I ever heard you speak of it. As I remember it, it has more to do with Heidelberg and other picturesque parts of Germany than with the larger cities, but [that] won't make any great difference.

Whenever I feel out of sorts I take a look at that new schoolhouse on Plummer Street. I have a good view of about half of it from my window upstairs, and I tell you the sight of it gives me a feeling of spiritual encouragement. At times I am troubled to think of what the effect of so much hideousness may have [*sic*] on the children who inhabit it, but I have lately come to the conclusion that they will all be poets. If the building were not so completely hideous, it would not be a subject for humor, but, as it is, I think its very bleakness will be an inspiration. Still, it was a dangerous experiment on the part of the city fathers, and as for Architect Lewis—well, if I were he, I think I should find another profession. His work is not encouraging for the future of local idealism; and until a little of that sort of thing comes into existence, Gardiner will be pretty much the place that it is today. As such, it calls for no further comment. As I am situated, I do not feel that I am in a place to make too much talk about anybody or anything; but it does make me positively sick to see the results of modern materialism as they are revealed in a town like this. I cannot even joke over it as I used to; if I could, it would not affect me as it does. And when I add to this a vision of Trinity Church in Boston and a reflection of what it stands for, I begin to feel like breaking chairs, and wonder if a time is ever coming when the human race will acquire anything like a logical notion of human life—or, in other words, of Christianity. There is no Christianity in the Plummer Street Schoolhouse, any more than there is in Trinity Church. And now the discouraging truth has come to light that Rev. M. J. Savage left Boston because his parishioners would not build him a fancy doll's-house in Back Bay.—With things like these to consider, to say nothing of Parke, Davis, and Company's catalogue, no wonder the Christian Scientists howl.—This makes me think of Jones and the homeopathic confectionery that his boy brought with him from Chicago.

"Well, my son," said J., "suppose we throw this out of the window?"—"Wouldn't it be better, papa, to put it in the closet?" said the boy.—"Perhaps it would, my son," said Jones; and he turned on the water. That made the boy laugh, and he has been laughing ever since.

If you had been here last night, you might have seen the Royal Bengal Zouaves (Capt. W. D. Whitney) parade through Water Street. It was impressive.

Gardiner
November 6, 1896

That devilish book of mine has again been the means of delaying my letter, but I won't say anything more about it except to tell you that it has been put on the shelf for a while on account of the great rush. My uncle thinks it will be ready sometime about the middle of the month, so you may put it out of your mind for a while. It is reasonable to suppose that you will see it in the early part of December, but I can't make any promises.

Now I have elected McKinley, of course I feel better. I was hoping, though, that Bryan would get a larger vote, as I am coming more and more to look upon him as the greatest political figure in America since Lincoln. To tell the truth, I thought he would be elected. The idea was fixed in my mind, and I couldn't get rid of it till Wednesday night. Things are undoubtedly better as they are, for the country is in a condition where a politic man is very necessary; but all this does not alter my opinion of Mr. Bryan as a personality.—I will send you a bunch of newspapers by this mail, so you may read the accounts for yourself. The *New York Journal* gave the country to McKinley at eight o'clock Tuesday evening, and it is rumored that the blood went to McKinley's head a little when he read the telegram. I fancy his old mother is the most thoroughly tickled person in the United States, and I feel glad for her. I fear my own mother will never be tickled in any such way, though I may get to be a Common Councilman sometime if I am foxy. After that the White House is a matter of destiny.

On the night of the election (or rather the morning after) I participated in an impromptu torchlight procession formed for the purpose of routing out Citizen John Newell. We reached his house at about 1.30 a.m. and he joined the procession. He was very happy and very drunk and for some peculiar reason insisted on showing a remarkable affection for me. He put his arms around my neck and told me he hadn't been so drunk for fifteen years and that the country was saved. After that someone put a Zouave cap on his head and the procession moved on to ex-Mayor Spear's, where John made a boozy speech which was applauded with bells, yells and fish horns until the neighboring houses began to illuminate. I went to bed about three o'clock in the morning and woke up with sticks in my eyes. Elections are queer things, and I am glad that this one is over. There is to be a big time here next Tuesday evening, but I don't think I shall participate, though I may follow the crowd when the time comes. You know the guard in Antigone says,

> "Oh King, 'tis not for any man to say
> What things he will not do,"

and I am inclined to think he is about right.

Jones and I are reading *King Lear* together and I find it a great way to pass an hour or two. We think of going through Shakespere in this way, and I hope the plan will be carried out. Jones is rather visionary, but he is a mighty good fellow and his friendship helps me out amazingly. Of course he cannot be just like a fellow of my own age, but on the other hand the difference has an advantage. His familiarity with Shakespere makes me wonder what I have been doing with my time in past years. I know a few of the plays pretty well, but not as an intelligent man (speaking relatively, of course) ought to know them.—By the way, Jones has a great deal to say about the magnificence of Shakespere in German, and suggests that I tell you to watch the theatres. He despises France, and anything in it. Paris, according to his expression, is the foulest place in the world with the exception of San Francisco, which is a puzzle to him.

For some reason I have never yet acknowledged the receipt of the postage stamps which you have been good enough to send me at various times. I am always glad to get them, for the things have a fascination for me and I think they always will. Sometimes I wonder if my interest in certain trifles will be a help or a hindrance to my ambitions. You think it will be a help, but I am not so sure of it. After reading Browning's "Rabbi Ben Ezra," postage stamps are not very powerful things to consider. They are so obviously material and my ideas are getting to be so thoroughly ideal, that the collecting of anything but wisdom often seems like going back into ignorance and barbarism. Carlyle has given me a brush lately, and I am just beginning to see what he was driving at in his *Sartor Resartus*. If the book is anything it is a denial of the existence of matter as anything but a manifestation of thought. Christianity is the same thing, and so is illuminated commonsense. I made a materialistic jab at Mrs. Eddy not long ago and saw Jones twist his eyebrows. Then he asked me to read the book, and I did so to find myself astonished and at times amused. Mrs. Eddy has wheels, but they are turning in the right direction, though some must inevitably fly off. Epictetus and Socrates, Emerson and Carlyle, Paul and Christ (or Jesus, if you prefer) tell pretty much the same story from a more general point of view. This line of thought took hold of me when I was at Harvard, but my meeting with Jones was the first thing that set it fairly going. I do not agree with Jones in his theory of the immediate practicability of advanced ideas, nor do I believe in Christian Science as anything apart from the spiritual wisdom that is latent in us all; but I do believe in idealism as the one logical and satisfactory interpretation of life, and I am quite willing to give credit to Mr. Jones and Mrs. Eddy for some valuable suggestions. I also own my obligation to John Newell for a lesson in opposites. John is not a bad lot—he is only blind.

I don't much think you will agree with me in this matter, but that, of course, is your affair, not mine.—To conclude, let me give you a couple of definitions I worked out the other day while the pipe was breathing a little better than usual. I was thinking of the dangerous tendency toward asceticism which threatens a person nowadays who thinks, and all at once found myself defining asceticism (and disposing of it) as the resistance of the material, and idealism as the denial of it. I don't imagine this to be original, but it serves my purpose just as well.—Parke Davis and Co. have discontinued the manufacture of their compound extract of tomato. I do not say this to disparage medicines, but to congratulate the tomato.

Gardiner
December 7, 1896

Things have been going so like the devil with me for the past two months that nothing short of idealism would have kept me together; and a fortnight ago, to put a finishing touch to the whole business, my mother died of diphtheria. I am not going to say very much about it, because I do not believe in that sort of thing; and most of all because it would not do any good. She has gone ahead and I am glad for her. You see I have come to look on death as a deliverance and an advancement (*vide* "Kosmos," "Two Sonnets," etc.) and I am very glad to be able to stand up and say that I am an idealist. Perhaps idealism is the philosophy of desperation, but I do not think so. To me it is the only logical and satisfactory theory of life. It is a great mystery to me that you can call *Sartor Resartus* a great book when you read it from a material point of view, but I am not keen to quarrel with you. I think too much of your friendship to run the risk of arousing any possible feeling by starting a useless argument,— so you may think "as you damn' please" and I'll do the same. As for Emerson's Essay on "Compensation," I fancy I shall get a great deal more out of it when I read it again, and that is what I intend to do very soon.

I gave Jones a copy of that most remarkable book of poems entitled *The Torrent and the Night Before,* and he professes to like it pretty well. I do not make much account of the criticism of friends—that is, their friendly criticism—but of course it is pleasant to feel that they are sincere. So I was glad to have Jones tell me that he found himself "stuck" in "The Night Before."

"Nobody can read that," he said, "but yourself, and dog-gone (J. has a copyright on that) if I believe you can."—I was a little surprised at this, as I always supposed the poem was as plain as a man's nose; but I rather think the metre was what mixed it up. Metre is something he knows nothing about.

Speaking of the book, I received the whole thing (312 copies) the other morning, but did not take enough interest in them to open the package until evening. In fact, I feel as if I should like to kick them from here to Augusta and never see them again. They looked so small and so devilish blue to me that they made me sick; but now I am feeling better and am beginning to foster my same old ridiculous notion that they may amount to something some day. Blair and Jones (they have never met each other) both say the "Chorus of Old Men" is the best thing in the book, and I think you may agree with them. Personally I have nothing to say in regard to that matter. I cannot judge my own work at all. I doubt if anyone can who writes anything.

I haven't read anything lately—save scattered pages in different books—but the first half of Le Petit Chose, and A House-Boat on the Styx, which, to my surprise, proved to be an undeniably good thing. There are some personal touches in it that may as well be called genius, and done with it. Of course such a book must flatten some in places, but it holds up remarkably well. In fact, I think one may safely say that the book is worth reading. Peter Newell's pictures are also rather good.

Your ravings over the American abroad were no surprise to me. Butler sang the same tune (by the way, Butler is going to be married in February) after his return from Italy and I have heard the complaint from many sources. I don't know why it is that the average American has to be such a damned fool, but I suppose it is because he is young. Independence and ignorance make a most unhappy combination to a critical observer, but I prefer it to servility and ignorance, for all that. I wonder how much longer the German people are going to sacrifice the best years of their life to the army and Divine (!) right? The whole thing makes me fairly gag when I allow myself to think of it, and I cannot possibly believe that William over there can keep on as he is going for a great many years. There are going to be changes before very long, and I am inclined to believe that the man at Potsdam (is that where he lives?) will feel them. I hope so, at any rate.

Well, I must put on my old duds and clear the ashes out of the cellar. I used to think I was out of my sphere when doing that kind of work but now I think differently. Such things do a man a world of good, if he can only bring himself to think so.

When this letter reaches you, you will also receive three copies of my great book. One of them you will find inscribed, and perhaps you will be good enough to keep it. The other two you may dispose of as you see fit. Put 'em in the fire if [you] want to.

I have hardly held up my end in letter writing, but don't let that affect you any. Much obliged for the Olympian stamps, and the others. Send along anything that is odd or attractive, but I must draw the line at beer-labels. Posters are a puzzle to me, but beer-labels—well I won't say anything more about them. Give my best "respects" to Mrs. Smith, and drink something for me in the Three Lions. Wish I could be there with you, but I can't.

[P.S.] Won't you send me a copy of *Fliegende Blätter*? I enjoyed the others, but do not think them in any way comparable with *Punch* and *Life*. I couldn't read all of the jokes, but I could look at the pictures. Much obliged.

Gardiner
December 22, 1896

About a fortnight ago I sent you a letter and three copies of *The Torrent*. They must have reached Berlin about the time you changed your place of living and I am rather anxious to know if you got them all right. The books are all gone now and I am glad of it; only, of course, I want to feel sure that you have yours all right.

It is too early to tell you how the thing is coming out. I can only say that the book has been very favourably received by such as have taken the trouble to write to me. The only newspaper notice that amounts to anything was written by Mr. Chamberlin, the "Listener," in the *Boston Transcript*. I enclose what he has to say. Everything is all stirred up here at home and I am living on hope and faith, which, by the way, make a pretty good diet when the mind will receive them. I must [not] say anything now, however, about idealism, except to tell you that I got Jones to read me the essay on "Compensation" the other day. It is a greater thing than I fancied, but still from my point of view, it is painfully incomplete. It is merely a step in the right direction —toward the point that was reached, but not yet generally understood, in *Sartor Resartus*.

Jones, by the way, wants me to ask you to send him a bundle of Berlin newspapers and a *Fliegende Blätter* if you will. He hopes you are getting as much out of your German life as he did, and a great deal more; and he is a mighty good fellow. Devilish queer in many ways, I confess; but what good fellow isn't. Sometimes I wonder if I fully appreciate my privilege of dropping in on him whenever I like and hearing a man talk who doesn't think the universe is centered in himself and who doesn't preach the primal cussedness of things as I used to before I began to think. He is a glorious antidote for the Doctor—and the doctors, too,— perhaps.

I can't decorate the rest of this sheet with anything better than a few selections from some letters I have received. Don't mistake my motives, for I assure you I haven't the smallest symptom of "swelled head." The future looks as dark as ever, but I have a little better courage to look into it. Of course these things are only sent to you as an old friend, and one who is interested. Don't magnify them, for you may be disappointed.

"Although busy to the point of desperation I find . . . I have got to read it. Like Artemus Ward's Tiger, it is 'small but healthy.' "—John Vance Cheney.

"Very rarely, I think, does one find such work as yours—where every line that meets the eye proves itself at a glance real literature."—Barrett Wendell.

"I have read enough of it to recognize your debt of gratitude to the Muse for the gift with which she has enriched your life." —Charles Eliot Norton.

"I should like to know you. When you come to Boston, please let me shake hands with you and thank you by word of mouth for your book which I have read with unconditioned delight."—Nathan Haskell Dole.

"You have sound reason for writing and publishing."—Prof. H. Johnson. Bowdoin.

"I have read nearly all the lines, and read them with more interest, and enjoyment of thought and workmanship than I have found in any volume of new verse for a long time."—L. B. R. Briggs—Harvard.

"I call it unmistakable poetry—most of it, indeed, of the 'inevitable sort'; and in many of the lines there is a deep and moving music . . . 'Dear Friends,' 'Walt Whitman,' and 'Supremacy' seem to me completely vital . . . Your gift seems to me quite a certain thing . . . 'Boston' would not help you much; if you could go to England and stay there! [Word illegible] do you not come to town once in a while, etc."—Dr. Titus M. Coan (N. Y. Bureau of Revision).

"I know that I shall like your positively distinct touch in the poems. I am much impressed with them and already a little acquainted with your unique point of view. You certainly have a strong individual outlook, etc." J. J. Hays—Harvard.

Professor Chapman of Bowdoin is the only man who seems to care anything about "The Wilderness."

Tear this business up when you have read it.

[P.S.] Your mother wants me to tell you that she is tired and so won't write today. Everything all right, but going rather slow.

Your father walks more and more every day and has good courage.

W. Lindsey (*Cinder Path Tales*) picks out "Kosmos," "Walt Whitman," and "The Dead Village."

Gardiner
January 17, 1897

No, I don't think your criticism is rot, or anything of the kind; on the contrary I think it is, for the most part, sound and wise, though I must confess that I don't exactly understand what you mean when you say I have put too much of myself into my work. With the exception of an occasional sonnet and the obviously didactic—"damned didactic," if you prefer it so—pieces, I intended the book to be entirely impersonal. I fear you are inclined to make too much of my frequent use of the first person singular. I confess there is considerable of the "I" element in it, but that "I" is not always "me." This is bad grammar, but I like to be ungrammatical sometimes.

There is a man in Oregon who thinks "The Wilderness" is the best thing in the book. I was very glad to hear from him, as I had begun to fear the poem was "no good." Others like other pieces, but nobody out of Gardiner has anything to say about the "Old Men" or the dead men either. I think, however, you have a point there and I shall try to be a little less bloodthirsty in my next volume—if it ever appears. The "Two Sonnets" have also failed to draw out any individual comment. I guess they are too rank for these times.

I have just finished Daudet's *Le Petit Chose*. I began it a long time ago but dropped it at the end of Part Fourth when I ought to have stopped. The first half of the book is fine, but the second is a falling off. As a whole, I should say the book was hardly worth reading, though there are lots of fine touches in it. The style is choppy, and apparently laborious, but still it is strangely in keeping with the story. Daudet is always an artist in one way or another. I have not read much of anything else lately except the gospel according to Saint John, which I found an entirely different thing from what I used to find it. The popular misinterpretation of Christianity makes me sick. I think I have said as much before.

Your bundle of papers came all right, and I was very glad to get them. I couldn't do much with them myself, but they furnished Jones with a good deal of innocent amusement, so you need not feel that they were wasted. He wants you to go somewhere on the *Linden* and get a lobster and a pint of champagne and a black cigar. I don't remember the place, but as Jones was there about twenty years ago, I fancy it will make much difference [*sic*]. He also has tender recollections of a certain deepshelled oyster which you have probably found by this time if you have any predilection for bivalves.

I don't think very much of your standing for two hours to see the Emperor and his lackeys, but I might have done the same thing and then cussed myself. We mortals are all fools and most of us are damned fools; but the time is coming when we are going to be something else. My philosophy says so and you say "to hell with my philosophy"; but that's all right—we'll wait, and someone else will see. There's where the altruism of it comes in. There's a good deal in altruism—particularly when the pipe is drawing well.

Mr. Chamberlin of the *Transcript* has invited me to go to the St. Botolph club with him and meet some "bright men." I suppose I shall go—if ever I go to Boston again—but I shall feel rather out of place. It is gratifying, though, to realize that I have attracted the attention of certain people, and I am beginning to feel that I may possibly do something sometime that will bring me a publisher. Publishers are mysterious beings to me, and I am wondering what the process is by which they are captured.

At your request, I enclose a few more extracts from letters and things, which I copied off the other day. I have received a letter (4 pages) from an unknown female who seems to be in a very bad way over my verses.

Here are a few more notices which you may like to look over. I would not send them to anyone else, and I look to you to burn them up when you have read them.

". . . I could wish that the poems gave rather more of yourself and less of the men who have influenced you. But I hope that your next book, which I trust you will let me see, will show you standing firmly on your own feet and doing as good work steadily as you do at your best in this little volume."—Prof. Geo. P. Baker, Harvard.

". . . May I express my pleasure at poetry which has so much warm blood in its veins?"—Horace E. Scudder.

". . . If you are still young, your poetic future is most promising. I was chiefly impressed by 'Aaron Stark,' 'The Dead Village,' 'Dear Friends,' the latter part of 'Sonnet' (p. 8), 'Zola,' and not a few other pieces."—Edgar Fawcett.

". . . Perhaps I can say nothing of greater praise than that the other day I heard indirectly from Prof. Carpenter of Columbia, who is loud in praise of your song."—J. J. Hays, Harvard.

"I have read them with much appreciation, especially the sonnets . . . I like particularly the one on Crabbe."—Edmund Gosse.

". . . Particularly would I congratulate you upon the pieces entitled 'The World' and 'The Children of the Night' and upon your sonnets."—Clinton Scollard.

". . . There are poems in this little book that exhibit the finest taste in their making and whose standard is far above that of ordinary verse."—*Boston Courier*.

". . . And now the attention of lovers of striking verse is arrested by a little blue-bound pamphlet emanating from Gardiner, Maine . . . There are sonnets . . . full of strength and passion and—well, yes, perhaps pessimism (*sic*) though they are too healthy to be really pessimistic. They are vital, virile expressions of a wholly modern spirit . . . The little volume has only 44 pages, but I should not wonder if curiosity seekers should in future times pay high prices for it—especially if Mr. R. goes on in the same free, bold course."—N. H. Dole in *Bookseller, News-dealer, and Stationer.*

"From Gardiner, Maine, there comes a good thing, albeit a little one, etc." "Credo" quoted. *Time and the Hour*—Boston.

"'The Night Before' is highly dramatic."—*New Orleans Pic-ayune.*

"A man who can do the things you have done in *The Torrent* does not need the small praise of a small man like me . . . The world may not have it, but go on doing it just the same." Letter from J. E. Chamberlin ("Listener").

"I don't thank you for sending me a book, for I get books of poetry until I haven't shelf-room for them. But you have given me a rare sensation: you have sent me a book that I can read, and for that I thank you. I am a very busy man, but you have sent me a book I cannot help reading and for that I forgive you. I cannot find anybody in my circle who knows you—I find friends of good judgment who on reading your poems wonder and wonder how it is that you are unknown . . . Let a total stranger hail you with admiration, putting aside all flattering words of which you have no need, for which you have no desire . . . I have ventured to use some of the expressions in this letter in an interview to be published in February . . ."—Edward Eggleston.

"There is much in it that I like, particularly 'The Dead Village,' 'Kosmos,' 'Walt Whitman,' 'The Clerks,' and 'Dear Friends.' I think no man who has ever attempted any artistic work could fail to appreciate the last . . . I am quite sure your sonnet work is the best, and of them all, 'The Dead Village' I like best. It is a beautiful thing."—William Lindsey. (Which goes to prove that W.L. doesn't see what I am driving at).

"There's a hell of a lot of hell in it."—J. C. Barstow.

Gardiner
February 3, 1897

I am sorry to see you go back on your own good judgment, but as I know your last letter was nothing but the result of a temporary enthusiasm, I have not lost any faith in your solidity of criticism and intellect. It is not in the scheme of reason, if I may say it, that you or any other man should care for everything in the book, so don't lose yourself again but keep within bounds. In the meantime I fully appreciate the very friendly spirit in which your enthusiastic screed of January 5 was scratched off and assure [you] that I haven't a particle of doubt but that you are quite honest in your general appreciation of the verses I have written. Only, don't lay it on too thick. The mere fact that so many are relatively indifferent to the merits of the book is enough to prove that it cannot carry the weight of praise you would heap upon it. There is a man in Denver who has a kind of unconscious numerical sympathy with you in your estimate of my importance, but it is very clear to me that you are both all wrong.

The *Bookman* evidently takes me for a yelling pessimist, and that I must say that I am very much surprised. And the *Bookman* is not alone, either. The same man in Denver, Colorado, thinks I have blue devils, but I assure you I have not. I also make free to say that many of my verses [were] written with a conscious hope that they might make some despairing devil a little stronger and a little better satisfied with things—not as they are, but as they are to be. This is the point the critics will not see. Because I don't dance on [an] illuminated hilltop and sing about the bobolinks and bumble-bees, they tell me that my world is a "prison house, etc." Well, if the work is good for anything, and some good men seem to think it is, I am confident that all this will be corrected some day and that people will begin to see what I am driving at. Of course "The Night Before" is purely objective, and may be called anything from pessimism to rot. I must confess that I haven't the slightest idea whether it is good for anything or not. I printed it to find out; but the opinions I have received are so conflicting that I am not much better off than I was before. The fact that you and Hubbell speak so well of it convinces me that it is nothing to be sorry for, but I am afraid it is one of those unfortunate narrative pieces which require a second reading before it amounts to anything at all. Jones says this is the case, and Jones is not given to flattery. But a little time will settle the whole difficulty and perhaps dispose of the whole book by consigning it to that untroubled region where, as A. Lang once said, "the old moons go." One thing, however, is gratifying. The book is as big today as it will ever be, no matter what destiny may or may not do for it.

Well, I have drivelled about my *Torrent* long enough, and now will tell you that J. and I are reading up (J. is reading and I am listening) on Oriental Religions. I have been interested to find out that Christianity is in reality nothing more than Buddhism humanized; and that Nirvana and Heaven are from the idealist's point of view—which is to me the only point of view—pretty much the same thing. You will object to this; but if you ever take the trouble to look into those matters (and you must before you make anything out of Plato) I am sure that you will come around,—not to my way of thinking, but to my way—or if you prefer it, T. Carlyle's way—of looking at things.

I have just read Emerson on "The Over-Soul." If you do not know it, for heaven's sake get hold of it. In this I seem to find all that he was struggling to bring out in that eminently unsatisfactory essay on "Compensation"—which is no more a measure of Emerson's genius than a cloudy dawn is of daylight.

I am very glad to know that you have found so congenial a friend as Emery. I should like to meet him but for the present such a thing will be impossible. Send along a *Meggendorfer* when you happen to think of it. I like to look at the pictures.

I have not been out over the Iron Mine for three weeks, and am honestly ashamed to say so. Shall go some time this week, though I fancy the road is pretty tough.

[Comments on the *Torrent* enclosed with the letter of February 3, 1897]

". . . The result will probably repay the expenditure of trouble, as Mr. Robinson has a respectable knack of versification."—*Philadelphia Press.*

"I have read them all from 'The Torrent' to 'The Night Before' and they have given me pleasure—for their strength—for their kindness, and for their insight into the things of life. They have a certain unnamable quality all their own."—George Wharton Edwards.

". . . Forty-four pages of poetry which is poetry indeed."—*Christian Register,* Boston.

"I have read your little slip of a book and it is not weak and has promise, but not yet such fulfillment as it makes me believe you are capable of. I am a poor critic and sweat over whatever I write, keeping it for years and never satisfied. May I say this is the word you want and do not take it to be unkindly. You will do better if you are yet young. If you are not—I cannot be sure—you seem to have in you the fertile root. Nourish it."—S. Weir Mitchell.

The Bookman you will read for yourself.

"In this very limited space ('The Torrent') Mr. Robinson succeeds in shattering many remarkable and hitherto respected laws of versification."—*Chicago Record.*

"There are 43 poems varying greatly in form, subject-matter and merit, but all pervaded by a certain sober dignity that before long impresses the reader with its almost monotone. There are no bright gleams of either laughter or joy—what smiles there are bring tears close behind them and the joy is a grey sort of happiness at best. The queer uncanny poem entitled 'Luke Havergal' will illustrate the sombreness of them all . . . There is a helplessness, a hopelessness . . . that arouses a sympathy, which, upon investigation, we find is not asked. For the helplessness is a helplessness againt the inscrutable, not against the ordinary ills and sorrows of life . . . With this . . . is a fine, firm strength, borrowed perhaps from the cold hard winter nights and days that are the greatest charm of the northland where the book was born . . . To our mind 'The House on the Hill' is the finest in the volume . . . It is like a little bit of a human heart spread out in paper and print. (Then follows "The Wilderness") . . . An excellent bit is the 'Ballade of Dead Friends' with its reckless swing and hurry, sounding like Villon at his best . . . A sonnet that is simple and sweet and by comparison with the rest almost cheerful . . . is 'The Miracle.' Mr. R. often says things that startle with their vividness and truth. For instance a verse or two of 'The Children of the Night' . . . There are a few commonplace verses in the volume, such as 'Max Nordau,' 'The Night Before' (ach!) and 'For Calderon,' but it is unjust to judge a man by his worst traits or a writer by his poorest work. Mr. Robinson's best work is very good work—indeed so fine that this little book of his is one of the books of the year. Mr. R. is, we believe, a young man yet; if so, he is not only a y. m. of much promise, but a y. m. of great accomplishment. [Here E. A. R. draws a caricature of himself showing a tiny body and a hugely swelled head]; for to write verse on a plane with his is a task beyond all save some half dozen of our poets. And perhaps that is a too liberal estimate; just at present we can't recall that number to mind . . . Technically, they are well done . . . He can be unconventional without becoming undignified; he is often mystical, but never absurd. The attention of Mr. Bliss Carman is respectfully requested, etc."—*The Denver Times*.

"I am surprised to find such original and scholarly work being done by one whose name is so unfamiliar to me."—Charles G. D. Roberts.

Gardiner
February 11, 1897

I have just received a letter from a bank president in Vancouver, Washington, and as a result have taken a big chew of tobacco and drawn a picture of myself, which I trust will please you. I am not exactly an artist, but it seems to me that I have done this thing pretty well—particularly the "pants"—which are wofully faithful to the originals. The hair is slightly proleptic (if that word will cover the ground) and the nose is not quite my

Dr. Eggleston threw himself up with his kind review, in the Outlook to my most copious, and I am getting more affliction for non existing copies of my book that please me. This Baltimore man, however, must have got his enthusiasm from the Dial, or the Drama Times. The Dial, by the way, was very kind. Our old friend W. Morton Payne quotes the dedication and then kindly shows "the implication that constitutes an epigram" and goes on to quote "Oh for a pail &c." The rest of the notice runs something like this — "It would not be fair, at least relatively, to apply these roses to Mrs. T.'s own poems, which are far above the average in strength and expression. They struck many grateful notes, and particularly the note of austere reproach that is so rarely heard in contemporary song. A striking example of this note is furnished in the close of his sonnet to Verlaine ...... We are not quite prepared to say all this of Verlaine, but the doctrine is of

Harry de Forest Smith, 1891

own; but the general effect is good. The goatee (how the deuce do you spell it?) is a dream of what I sincerely hope may never come true. The eye is rolling in a very fine frenzy.

Dr. Eggleston stirred things up with his kind reference, in the *Outlook,* to my masterpieces, and I am getting more applications for non-existing copies of my book than please me. This Vancouver man, however, must have got his enthusiasm from the *Dial,* or the *Denver Times. The Dial,* by the way, was very kind. Our old friend W. Morton Payne quotes the dedication and then kindly ignores "the implication that critics are epicene" and goes on to quote "Oh for a poet, etc." The rest of the notice runs something like this:—"It would not be fair, at least relatively, to apply these verses to Mr. R's own poems, which are far above the average in thought and expression. They strike many graceful notes, and particularly the note of austere restraint that is so rarely heard in contemporary song. A striking example of this writer's workmanship is found in the close of his sonnet to Verlaine . . . We are not quite prepared to say all this of Verlaine, but the doctrine is of wide application, and gives pause to the professional belittler of great and shining names."—That means your criticism of "Here's the last rose" and "The Children of the Night."

Yesterday I received a very funny letter from Mr. S. J. Boardman of the *Bangor Commercial.* He wants my photograph and autobiography for publication. I appreciate his kindness, but I do not sympathize with his notions of human sanity. I do not deny that I am crazy more or less, but I haven't quite come to the Moses P. Handy condition. I hope I never shall.—I also received a copy of *Quo Vadis* from Jones and one of *Margaret Ogilvy* from Miss Whitmore. Such things are very pleasant, though there is a touch of sadness in the appropriateness of the last named gift. The book is a beautiful thing to read, though I am not quite ready to uphold the principle. It is impossible, though, to think of Mr. Barrie doing it in any other spirit than that of absolute and almost unconscious sincerity. I should advise you to read it while your mother is still with you. It may make you think of a few things, as it made me, before it is too late. No man can ever appreciate the debt he owes to his mother, but sometimes a little thing may come up to set him thinking. If I had read this little book (it is very small) three or four years before it was written perhaps I should not have to think of some things which I think of now—things that come back to me in spite of my conviction that everything is better as it is, and that my mother is to be congratulated. These things sound hard, but they are true.

I went over to see your father and mother yesterday afternoon and found them in very good spirits. Your father was in his chair, and said that he had just been travelling all over the house. He seems to be coming up all right, though the process is slow.

Please put it down to my credit that I have, for once in my life, written two letters to your one. I am going to Boston the last of the month and try to convince some publisher that he needs my stuff in order to keep him going.

[P.S.] I enclose a clipping from the *Cleveland Leader*, which is very different from the Denver man's opinions.

Gardiner
March 15, 1897

How long do you think a man can live in hell? I think he can live there a good many years—a hundred, perhaps, if his bowels keep in decent order—but he isn't going to have a very good time. No man can have a very good time—of the right sort, at any rate—until he understands things; and how the devil is a man to understand things in an age like this, when the whole trend of popular thought is in the wrong direction—not only that, but proud of the way it is taking? The age is all right, material progress is all right, Herbert Spencer is all right, hell is all right. These things are temporal necessities, but they are damned uninteresting to one who can get a glimpse of the real light through the clouds of time. It is that glimpse that makes me wish to live and see it out. If it were not for that glimpse, I should be tempted, as Tennyson used to be, to stick my nose into a rag soaked with chloroform and be done with it—that is, if I could screw up the courage. But now, thank God, that is not the kind of courage I am praying for; what I am after is the courage to see and to believe that my present life is the best thing for me, and that every man has it in his power to overcome whatever obstacles may be in his way —even that seeming obstacle we call by the name of Death. I have not said much about my life for the past three years—I mean the past ten—because with all its lack of anything like material hope and pleasure—it was tolerable. For all my long lean face, I never gave up; and I never shall give up. I can't do it; but I can suffer like damnation, which shows there is something wrong with me somewhere. The past three months of my life, however, are quite another thing. If they had come two years ago, or even one, I think they would have finished me. The book has helped me out a little—in fact, I was rather bewildered by its reception— but that counts (the praise, I mean) for very little. There are things here at home that are pulling me back, and I've got to look out for them. I can't get away, just now—I don't see how I can for a year—and the result is that all my best strength is required in keeping my thoughts in some sort of rational order. The one great pleasure of my life is the knowledge that my poor mother is out of it. I can't quite understand—yet—the laws of compensation that make a woman suffer what she did and from so many causes. We say she died of diphtheria. What does that mean? It means just this: she had endured all [she] could and was ready to die. I had been watching it for a year. If she had not had diphtheria, or membranous croup, or whatever it was that took her off so hellishly, she would have gone crazy. I am not going crazy, for I see some things she did not see—some things she could not see; but I am going to lose all those pleasures which are said to make up the happiness of this life and I'm glad of it. I'm glad to say that I am strong enough to do without them. There is a pleasure—a joy—that is greater than all these little selfish notions and I have found the way to it through idealism. Once I thought I was in a way to be a Christian Scientist, but that will be impossible. The system is too dependent on unsubstantial inferences. As it is taught and managed it is not Christianity, though the claim is that the two terms are synonymous. It is rapidly developing into a sect, and one that will have a tremendous power in the world; but it is only a stepping stone to the truth. It has proved the power, however, of even a partial recognition, and thereby proved the utter fallacy of all existing notions of religion—popular notions, I mean.

The great scholars of the world are for the most part spiritual imbeciles, and there is where the trouble lies. The willingness "to be a child again" comes hard—so hard that it will never come to many who are in the world today. That is not what they are here for. "The world was made in order, and the atoms march in time." It is a damned queer time to us who are here now; but it is all right and we are all going to hear it as it is—when the mortal wax gets out of our ears.

This, I fancy, is not the letter you have been looking for; but you will have to make it do.—Joe tells me that your father can get out of his chair now without any help, which is good news for all of us. I shall get out there some time this week. That is one of the few places in the world where I think people are really glad to see me.—I should like very much to have a letter from Emery, but hardly look for it.—I can give you unlimited "Robinsoniana," but if you depend on it for your future income, you'll get most grievously stuck.

[P.S.] Between your bicycle and *Sartor Resartus* you ought to fix your nerves all right.

Gardiner
April 4, 1897

Since I wrote my last letter I have been to Cambridge and Boston where I tried, without success, to find a publisher. Mr.

Lawson "thinks he may possibly do something with it in the fall," but that was said to "let me down easy."

I was treated magnificently and ought to have enjoyed myself; but somehow I felt out of place, and could not quite bring myself to believe that I cut quite the figure in men's eyes that they would have had me think. I was much lunched at the Colonial Club and A. S. Hill gave me a cigarette. I drank rum punch at the St. Botolph and talked with men who can stand on their feet and not feel as I do (no reference to the punch). My courage is all right, but to spend four or five years in getting a small book together and then to have it just fall short, "is a damned tough bullet to chew"—even though I am well aware that almost every author has chewed it. If I could convince myself that the stuff is the real thing, I should be satisfied, but I am slowly beginning to see that much of it is commonplace and that some of it is rot.

As I am situated now, I can't seem to do much of anything, and, on the other hand, I can't get away—not for the present, at any rate. I have had a golden opportunity this winter to study the possibilities of mental resistance, and it is the triumph of my life to know that I am good for something. My female correspondent has done wonders for me, and has proved to me that I possess the power of helping others, which, after all, is about the greatest thing a man, or a book, can do. She is infernally bright and not at all ugly and has something of a literary reputation. The best of it all is, she is too old to give me a chance to bother myself with any sentimental uneasiness. It's a queer experience for a man like me, but it has done me a world of good. I have made her over, so she says, and have cleaned no end of cobwebs from her brain. If ever I go to Wilkes-Barre, I can tell you more about her.

While in Cambridge I read and re-read *The Seven Seas*. At first the book was a disappointment to me, but now I think better of it. "For to Admire" is a wonderful poem, and is, to my mind, by all odds the best of them. The great fault of the book lies in the fact that it appeals to the nerves rather than to the intellect.

And I question if poetry of that sort can stand the test of years. I do not care at all for the "Three Sealers," but the "Song of the Banjo" is a work of genius. So is the last stanza of "L'Envoy" and the whole of "The Last Chantey."—At the same time I read Stevenson's collected *Poems and Ballads* and think I found in them a more permanent note. Stevenson does not make so much noise but he makes a deeper impression on the reader's better self. In Kipling, the words fascinate you; in Stevenson, the man attracts you and makes you feel better for knowing him. Men who have talked with Kipling tell me that he is a surprise; that neither his pictures nor his writings give any definite idea of him. Stevenson, they say, gives, or gave, the opposite impression. I don't know which is the better recommendation.

Zola's *L'Assomoir*, which I have been reading off and on for the past two or three weeks is growing tremendous toward the end. Taken as a whole I think this book is the most astonishing example of cumulative power that I have ever met with. There may be a certain element of smut in it, but the motive of the author and the general tone of the work put that all aside—that is, as smut. Zola is the greatest worker in the objective that the world has ever seen, and someday he will be recognized for what he is.

At last I have a down-town den to crawl into. Blair, Pope, Robbins and myself have engaged a room over Brown's store (up two flights) at two dollars a month, stove included and we find it most advantageous. I have always wanted something of the kind, but never could stomach the idea of a *club*. Village clubs are just a little the foulest things I know of in a way of social gatherings. Four shall be the limit. Three, ordinarily, would be much better and there is a great deal to be said in favor of two. —But we get along very well, Pope furnishing all the maxims. "What is the criterion of fatherhood?—It is, are the children glad when Father comes home."—Pope wants to get married, but hasn't any money or any job.

By the way, Butler and his wife seem very happy indeed. I

took dinner with them at the Bellevue and had a smoke with them (with him, I mean) afterwards. She is very fair to see, and thinks *Jude* is a great book—rather a remarkable combination—at least, it struck me that way.—Hubbell is likely to be a father any minute, and may be one already.

This is a dismal, dreary day, but that makes no particular difference. I think I have got beyond the point where the state of the weather makes any great difference with me. Of course I like to see the sun shining, but we can't always do that, so it's better to be decent whatever comes. I'm doing an *Octave* on "The Master of the Moment." If I get it fixed to suit me—that is, half suit me—I [will] send it along.

Gardiner
April 24, 1897

I suppose you have been looking for this letter for some time, and I would not be much surprised to learn that you were disgusted. I know I have been a most unsatisfactory correspondent ever since you went away, but there has been a reason for it all— not a very good reason, perhaps; but still a reason and one that has kept me in the very devil of a stew. Things are going to change someday, in the nature of things, but God knows when. In the meantime I am writing "octaves" which I fear won't amount to much. The form is too hard and the limitations too damnably exacting. It was for that reason that I thought they would best suit my purpose, but now I'm not so sure of it.

Professor Johnson doesn't think much of my *Antigone* scheme, and he says you are a good man. He professes to think a great deal of my stuff, and I rather think he does see something in it. I spent four hours with him and found him a very good fellow. Perhaps I told you so. I think I did. No matter whether I did or not.—His objection to *Antigone* is sound, but I shall have to finish it—sometime—all the same. He says I can't afford it, and I can't; but there are lots of other things I can't afford to do. And this is true of all of us.

My "unknown female" (she's a fixture) is going to send me

a copy of *Gaston de Latour.* She wants to send me something and thinks Pater will be good for me. She is a woman of brains, though her extreme admiration of my book may reflect a little on her judgment. Be that as it may, she's devilish bright, and I should like to know her.

Went down to Mrs. Richards' again last evening and had a pretty good time. I was invited, with a villanelle, to tea; but I couldn't stand that, so I told her I'd be down about half past seven or eight. I don't know whether that sort of thing goes down or not, but it went all right in this case. I had a good time, as I said, and the three [dogs] again to help me out. They put their heads up on my knees and give my hands something to do. I scratch their ears and they like it. When you get a dog, be sure to get one that likes to have his ears scratched.—There was some small literary talk (I can do that well enough) and then there was some good music. Hays Gardiner said all the pleasant things that were necessary between selections and I had a good time. I repeat this, because it has been such a devil of a while since I had the last one. That must have been the last sawdust ride. You see I'm still a little boy, though hardly anyone suspects it here in Gardiner.

Your *Forum* was a long time coming, but it is here at last and I'll send it right along. I also have some *Chap-Books,* which you are very welcome to call your own. The euphemistic spew on "Sentimental Tommy" is by my old instructor Mr. (now Professor) Gates, of Harvard. I told him I had read it, and he grinned. Gates is a pretty good fellow and thinks the new school of poetry consists of Francis Thompson. I don't exactly agree with him.

Did I tell you I saw Butler and his frau? Well I did, and they seem to be very happy. She must have a rather lonely time of it, but I suppose that is a good thing. It teaches a woman to entertain herself and to find out what she is good for. Solitude is the best means of getting acquainted with one's self, but if one gets too well acquainted there is likely to be trouble. Sometimes we get sick of ourselves, and that's bad. Nine tenths of the happiness in the world (if there is any) is due to man's ignorance of his own disposition. The happy people are they who never had time to think it over. It is only when I forget what an ass I am that I find life tolerable; but I am putting away the ass more and more—to my own mind at least—and recognizing my place in the scheme of things. It is quite a place; so is yours; so is G. Swift's. There's a good deal to live for, but a man has to go through hell really to find it out. The process is hard, but the result pays. If it didn't there would be no universe. This may sound obscure, but it isn't.

I haven't been out to see your father for some time. Think I'll go this afternoon. When I saw him last he was getting on first rate and was able to get up alone. Now I expect to find him running.

Frank Avery blew his bowels out with a shot-gun. That was hell. I suppose you read about it in the paper.

Don't get mad, but write just the same. I'll try to do better after this.

Gardiner
May 17, 1897

In reply to your letter, received this morning, I fear I haven't very much to say, more than to tell you that I am very glad to hear that you have accomplished so much and that you are coming home so soon. You may or may not get the Kenyon College place; but whether you do or not, you are all right. I know that, and I have known it all along. One day when we were coming out of the woods I told you what I thought of you and I have never changed my mind.

Life is all hell with me now, and I don't pretend to remember anything. I don't even remember whether or not I have answered your letter of three or four weeks ago in which you asked about the Wilkes-Barre *inconnue*—the invisible female who has taken such a fancy to my idealism and my "Two Sonnets." Yes, her name is E—— B—— [*sic*] as you think, and she is an almighty

bright woman as I have said before. This much I remember.—
Some day I hope to meet her and have a talk with her. She is
distinctly a rare bird and I am anxious to see what she is like in
the life. In the picture she is not repulsive. Her friendliness
toward me is a god-send just now; nothing silly about it—nothing
sentimental;—but just plain honest good sense and frankness.
The eternal feminine is much in evidence in her letters and that
is why I like her. She knows a good deal more than I do about
books and things but I have partly straightened out some of her
ideas—which is in itself a thing to live for. The fact that I have
done a little spiritual good in the world is what keeps me going
now. How many times have I said this, I wonder?

I got lonesome the other evening and went down to Mrs.
Richards', where I found two daughters and a dog. I tried to
make myself pleasant and entertaining to the daughters and I
think the dog understood my position. At any rate he came up
and let me scratch his ears again, and looked at me in a way that
implied, "go ahead—you're getting along first rate." After that
there was some more music, but I didn't quite have the nerve to
ask for "Mandalay" again, as the *pater* had a visitor in the next
room. The only trouble with that family is they are too abnormally happy and unconscious of the damnation that makes up
nine tenths of life. This world is a grind and the sooner we make
up our minds to the fact the better it will be for us. That, to my
mind, is the real optimism. The world is as good as it can be,
but God knows that's bad enough.

Did you ever read Mérrimée's *Lettres a une Inconnue?* They
are rather good to browse through—one or two a day—and there
is a good deal of human nature in them, together with the same
dry sarcasm that makes *Colomba* readable—if anything does.
The essential smallness of the French nature is forever cropping
out, though, and there is nothing in the book that suggests real
greatness.—Yes, I wish you would bring me a copy of Johannus
Ambrosius—to give away. I can't read German myself, but I

know someone who can and I'd like to give her that book. She doesn't live in Wilkes-Barre.

A thing in the book line that pleases me a great deal is Augusta Webster's *Portraits*—a most remarkable book of poems—better read them sometime. Some parts of the book must go home to everybody. *The Torrent* has stopped running but I'm going to start it again in the fall, with a little additional water. If it's anything stronger than water, so much the better; but just now I'll call it water. Everything I have made seems thin now. I want to go to New Zealand. Ever since I lied so like the devil about "my northern pines" I have had visions of Auckland. I think if I buried myself there for five or six years I could write a sonnet. I can't get over the feeling that I'm going to write a poem some day—a poem that will live even though it kills me.—Go ahead and be as Greek as you can. You are going to do big work—in fact, you have done it already without knowing it.

Gardiner
June 17, 1897

I have been trying for a week to answer your last letter—last, I suppose, in two senses,—but somehow have not got down to it till this morning. The first thing I have to say is that I am very much pleased with your book-plate. Today I cannot think of any I have seen that I like as well. Did you think it out for yourself, or did Herr Otto do it for you? At any rate you have a good thing and I congratulate you. One reason why I am not more enthusiastic on the subject of book-plates is that I very seldom see one that in any way appeals to me. Most of them are unsatisfactory and many of them are ugly—not to say hideous.

It will be good to have you here again. The apple tree has gone pretty much to the devil, but we can make a place under the other one, down by the barn, I think. We'll have to make one somewhere.—Your father is getting along about the same. I won't lie to you and make things out better than they are, but will tell you right here that he will not be able to do much for himself this summer. His general health is all right, but his legs are all wrong. And that's about all there is to say about him except that he is counting the days between now and the time you are coming home. He has had a wicked winter, but one that cannot be repeated unless he has another fall. If that happens, it will go hard with him.

My Pennsylvania friend is going to Zurich tomorrow, for the summer. I told her that the western world would be lonely and uninteresting without her, and she called me down for saying so on the ground that the Eternity of my philosophy does away with the limitations of time and place. She is the most sagacious female that I ever ran across, and I have to be very careful how I express myself when writing to her. Any information you may give me in regard to her personality will be thankfully received. I only know that she has dark sharp eyes, dark hair (gray on the forehead) and that she stands five feet six in her stocking feet. She doesn't eat any meat to speak of, but subsists for the most part on bananas and graham and the elixir of her own thoughts. She also rides a bicycle.

I'm reading *Gaston de Latour* and am getting a great deal of pleasure from it. Just what it is that gives me the most pleasure I cannot say, though I must confess that the style is a great deal. The boy (Gaston) is evidently getting ready for the ideal truth of Christianity, but whether the book goes far enough to take him to it, I cannot say. I've only read four chapters. Some day I must get hold of *Marius* and find out what Pater really stands for.

We have had most diabolical weather this spring. Many of the farmers (myself included) have hardly planted anything and here it is past the middle of June. The devil only knows how it will turn out, but I fancy there will be no great trouble unless the frost comes early. Maine is getting to be the meanest corner on the face of the earth to live in, and I am waiting for a chance to get out of it. I have permission to go to Wilkes-Barre, but fear that isn't much better. I may go to New Zealand after all. The great objection lies in the uncertainty of getting back. I don't quite like the notion of making a life-exile of myself.

Gardiner
November 1, 1897

I was rather surprised to learn that you had been to Boston and New York, but I suppose you have the right to go where you choose. I am going over the same ground myself before long but cannot say just when. Probably I shall leave here about the tenth of this month. Sometimes I feel a little queer about going, but I know it is the only thing for me to do. I have lived this kind of life about as long as I can and my system—physical, intellectual, and spiritual—demands a change. Everything may go to pot but I don't believe it. I have an incurable feeling that I am going to do something though I never expect to make much money. If I make a living after a couple of years of brain shrivelling I shall feel that I am doing well. From the *Children* I do not expect much, if anything, in the way of direct remuneration but I shall always feel, even if I starve to death someday, that the book has done a good deal for me. Perhaps the knowledge that I have done a good deal for the book has something to do with this feeling. When I think of the hours I have spent over some of the lines in it I wonder if it is all worth while; but in the end I cease wondering. If anything is worthy of a man's best and hardest effort, that thing is the utterance of what he believes to be the truth. Of course I like a joke, and I like art for its own sake; but those things in themselves are not enough. Just as deliberate pathos in literature—that is, pathos for "effect" alone—is almost always a mistake, so, I think, is mere objectivity (I'd use some other word if I could think of it) at the best unsatisfactory. So I hope you will like my "Octaves," "Calvary," "L'Envoi," etc. better than "The Night Before."

To change the subject, when are you coming to Gardiner

again? I should like very much to see you once more before I go, but of course I do not expect you to come for that alone. Only if you think of coming soon, try to bring it about in the course of a fortnight and let me know three or four days ahead. Kindly remember me to Mrs. Smith.

* IV *

THE TOWN DOWN THE RIVER

(December 17, 1897 ~ August 30, 1905)

Harvard Club
27 W. 44th Street
December 17, 1897

I am here after some extra delay and find myself very well contented with things in general, though I feel that it will be a week or two before I get settled down to do the work I have laid out. I have very good quarters at No. 135 West 64th Street where I shall be glad to see you at any time.

The book seems to be making a rather favorable impression wherever it goes and I cannot but feel that something will come from it. How much, of course, I have no means of knowing. Perhaps the fact that it has put me already in the way of meeting some people who are supposed to be worth knowing is something, but I am afraid I shall never be one to take the best advantage of that sort of thing. Last evening, or rather this morning, I was at the Author's Club, where the stomach seemed to be in evidence rather more than the mind. There were no startlingly famous people present, though I had the honor of pressing the illustrious cuticle of Hamlin Garland, who seems to be a very good fellow.— I also have entry to the Century Club, though I fear I shall take no advantage of it. Meeting this or that man is nothing to me. I must have a chance to know him, and that chance I cannot make; it must come about of its own accord.

I sent a copy of the *Children* to your friend Mr. Emery, but have not yet heard from him. Find out if you can what he thinks of the new poems—somehow I have a good deal of faith in his opinion, even if I know he is over enthusiastic.

Write whenever you feel like it and I'll try to let you know how I am getting on.

I've been conscious of my shortcomings for many days past and have intended to sit down and write to you time and again; but somehow I haven't done it till now, and now I can only send you a few words to let you know that I have not forgotten your existence.

I shall begin to do better before long and make up for my past faults.—I've just settled down to real work—did 24 lines this afternoon beginning "George Annandale"—a long thing in blank verse which is either good or bad and half a dozen stanzas of a lighter thing which I may or may not take the trouble to finish. I feel, however, that I have got "down to it" and that this town is the place for me at present. Some time before very long I'll try to get down to see you, though as you know, I am not much for travelling. The devil of it is to get started. I don't hear anything about the book except that Badger sells a copy once in a while—which is all I really expected. It is too early, though, to tell anything about that.

I trust your family is doing well and that your father and mother are doing the same. Sometimes I've thought of writing to your mother, but never got to it. Dinner time now. Wish I could live without eating—to me it is a damned big bother—what Mulvaney would call a "shuperfluous necessity." Perhaps it is partly because I have known so many men who seemed to live for nothing else. Write.

New York
February 4, 1898

I don't feel much like writing, but I send you a few words out of common decency.

For the past two weeks I have been sick with the grip and am just beginning to feel a little like myself again. As for going to Philadelphia next [week], I'm rather afraid I can't do it but I'll manage to get there later. I was in Wilkes-Barre about a month ago, over Sunday, and thought of working you into the same trip; but the more I thought of it, the more I thought it would be better to make a separate job of it. Had a good time and found a good friend, which is not a combination to be laughed at.

Don't hear very much from the *Children* except that 300 copies have gone somewhere. What notices have come in are very good. The long (second) notice in the *Transcript* was written by Gardiner. Don't know who wrote the first one. I am very well satisfied with the way things are going—didn't expect any howling success. Phillips is getting a big boom and I think he has done something to deserve it. Perhaps a bit too much straining for effect.—I appreciate all of your friendliness in calling people's attention to my book and take much satisfaction in the knowledge that you have found a place that suits you.

135 West 64th Street
New York
February 21, 1898

For reasons that I'll not take the trouble to explain now it will not be easy for me to go to Philadelphia for two or three weeks to come. When I see you I'll tell you all about it, or try to. It is nothing at all serious, but still enough to keep me where I am. Mostly my incurable damned foolishness, no doubt. Things go on pretty much the same way. I'm doing some work but it is all in the way of an entirely new departure and I cannot bring myself to feel anything like sure of it. New York is doing me good, but not in the way I anticipated. I am not meeting many people for the simple reason that I can't adapt myself. I have never realized before what an ass I am in this way, but I realize it now, and any remark on the part of a friend to the effect that I'll get over it, or I'll come to like it, causes a kind of sickly grin to spread over my face. The devil only knows what is coming of it all, but I have a persistent idea that it is something. Just now I am in a transition stage and realize that I ought not to print anything for five or six years, but it rather looks as if I should get out another book in about a year from now. It is in my system and must be expelled somehow.

Burnham has just come in to lug me out to dinner so I'll stop here.—Don't buy so many postal cards.

New York
April 14, 1898

I have not been very friendly this winter in the way of correspondence, but I hope you will not think too strangely of it. This has been a queer sort of winter with me and my chief occupation has been to give my nerves a chance to settle back to where they belong. When I came here they were like the E string of a fiddle.

I shall come to see you sometime before very long. Just when, I cannot say, but not for a fortnight or so. I am undecided as to where I shall spend the summer. Sometimes I think I shall go to Winthrop, Mass. and again to Dallas, Pa. I feel quite certain I shall not go to Gardiner. In a year from now I ought to have a good lot of work turned off, and I must find some quiet place to do it in. The first book seems to strike pretty hard wherever it goes, but as yet it is not a great traveller.

Things are going on very well with me, but the times are so damnably out of joint that I don't like to look ahead too far. I am almost beginning to lose faith in our modern progress. From my present "jaundiced" point of view it looks as if the whole so-called civilized world would have to go back and get a new start. If it buries "divine right" and three or four priest-ridden, rotten monarchies in the process, perhaps it will be worth while. In spite of the fact that you have been to Berlin I still believe that the gulf between England and America and the rest of the world is immeasurable and incomprehensible to the people at large. America is proving its crudeness and craziness just now, but things will right themselves—even in Congress and the White House. I wonder if Cleveland and Olney write letters to each other.

I have been waiting, as a matter of course, to hear from you, but today it occurs to me that you may have been doing pretty much the same thing and that you may have the better excuse for not writing. At any rate, I'll write and let you know among other things that Professor William James doesn't know anything about Herbert Spencer. I've just been reading *The Will to Believe* along with the *Data of Ethics* (after *First Principles* and enough of the *Sociology* to make a kind of mental scaffolding for the rest) and have come to the conclusion that James is not a man to take wisdom with him when he dies. Read the book for yourself sometime and tell me what you think of it.—Just now I am not working. Everything has stopped for the time being and I am chiefly occupied in trying to figure out how long I can hold myself up on a foundation of abstractions. After this winter (I shall give the next six or seven months to the book, and then let hell do its cracking, if necessary) I shall have my choice between this, the graveyard and the place where men and women sing to the moon. I have acted tolerably well during the past year, but not so well but that a few have seen through it,—and I fancy I can keep it up for several years yet unless things get too nasty. If I get the Cambridge job I shall make what they call a living and be able to keep my trousers creased; but I shall find it an almighty job to keep Alcibiades out of U. 5 or myself out of hell. You see there is no man on earth who can tell me, to any purpose, that I do not know my methods and the demands they make on my time; and as this is a matter I cannot talk about without seeming to be [a] mass of mere self-conceit, I have only to chew the rag, as the good phrase goes, as little as possible and try to think that I have thirty or forty years ahead of me. To be born with just one thing to live for, and that thing a relative impossibility, is to be born with certain disadvantages; and when you add to this an unusually slow and complex method of doing that one thing, the idealization of a job becomes difficult indeed. So, if I prove a fizzle after all and ultimately develop into a semi-respectable nonentity, you will still remember that I once had aspirations and that I shall always use tobacco in every form but cigarettes and snuff. Today I am remarkably good natured, but tomorrow I may be reading *The Ring and the Book.* I keep that for those occasions and find it excellent tonic. Do you know I have a theory that Browning's life-long happiness with his wife is all humbug? The man's life was in his art, but he was big enough to make the world think otherwise.—I'm also reading *Little Lord Fauntleroy.* —Write whenever you happen to feel in the mood and remember me to Mr. Johnson and Mr. Emery. I say Mr. Emery because I feel somehow that I know him. I have an impression that he is what Schuman would call an Otto, which is the analogue of Rock and the patrician correlative of Bon Zig.

14 *Oxford Street*
Cambridge
January 5, 1899

I have done a little more than usual this time in the way of writing, or not writing, but I'll send you a word now if only to let you know that your ancient Xenophon is all right—I have it with me here. The other books are safe at home.—I wanted to see you in Brunswick but everything came at once and I had no time. I was in Winthrop all through the holidays except for a day or two, and when I was in Gardiner I could find no evidence that you had been there. If I had, I could have done no more than rush out to your house and back again.

I am here, as you see, and I am at work just now overhauling the graduates' application business which is an eternal job. After that I shall probably have something a little more stimulating. The office of a big college is a new thing to me and I ought to find something in it—something human and interesting. The only trouble is with my eyes, which are likely to go back on me and so put an end to what otherwise might be a final solution of the bread and butter problem—which is an asses' bridge to all who are not hungry. To me, it is getting to be something different. If I don't hold this job, I am more than likely to hold a shovel. In the meantime Pegasus is in a box stall; he pulls the halter if I tie him up.

How is everything with you? And how is the prodigy? Write and let me know that you are alive and if you have read *Cyrano de Bergerac*. It isn't quite great but it is nearer to it perhaps than anything in the shape of a metrical play since *Faust*.

Everything is very natural here and it is good to see the place again. I wish you were here, but possibly you do not. John William White has a particularly smooth trim on his whiskers today, and Dean Briggs remains unchanged. Did you see his article in the last *Atlantic?* If not, read it: "Fathers, Mothers and Freshmen." It ought to do some good. Possibly it might if it were in the *Boston Globe*.

> *Harvard University*
> *Cambridge, Mass.*
> *June 29, 1899*

I am mighty glad to know that you are fixed for next [year] and that your garden is growing. Mine has not come up.—I shall leave this place at the end of the week and after that I may be a tramp or an evangelist—if there is any difference. I have two things under consideration, but whether anything will come of either of them, I cannot say. If things fall through I shall have [to] dig. It will be entirely unnecessary for you to ask me if I am not hasty in coming to this decision. Three months more of the life I have lived for the past half year would make an imbecile of me if not a corpse. I don't know but something has been done already in the way of both.—Don't think from this that I am finding fault with the office—the fault is my own, and I know it. I had a possible chance—though I was handicapped in [a] queer way that I could not easily make another understand—to do something and I found that I had not the brains—the right kind of brains, at any rate—to do it. So I have to credit myself with an-

* 299 *

other failure—which is no novel sensation—and go for something else. I have now got to the point where I can not feel at ease with fellows who make a living and that is bad.—My schemes are still rampant and I manage to do a little almost every day—enough no doubt to take me a little farther every day from a respectable living, whatever that may be. I do not expect anything from my friends, but impatience and perhaps disgust, but there are a few things that my friends do not know—things that I have known ever since I was four years old or whenever it was that I began to think rationally—and these things act as a kind of sorry prop for my shortcomings—of which I have more than you have ever dreamed of.

Yesterday I [had a] note from Butler telling me that his wife has blessed him with twins. It beats the devil how this world is increasing and how all of the little devils who are making their appearance at the rate of several a minute are going to be virtuous and happy. I am beginning to feel more and more that the only hope for me lies in my chance in getting away from the sight of every face that I have ever known. I do not fancy that there is a great deal of time left for me anyhow and I must manage to crowd something into it. I know this consciousness and prearranged pressure is mostly wrong and likely, or possible, to blow over; but for all that I am not omnipotent and so must yield to human weaknesses. It is not the expectation of doing big things, but rather the necessity of doing something, that keeps me stretched. If I were a big man, I should do this and that—manufacture ten-penny nails and get into the common council; and in my old age with a competence and plenty of time, I should write and study Spanish. The big men can do this, perhaps, but I can't. Some of my friends think I am a good deal bigger than I am, but I do not feel sure that I am wholly to blame for that.

All this sounds like growling but it is not really that. I feel dissatisfied with myself, of course, but there is no man on earth with whom I can find fault as far as his dealings with me are concerned. Perhaps a persistent gnawing consciousness that I have been so damnably overrated by those who know me is the cause of half my uneasiness. I have an almost morbid feeling of responsibility toward my friends and another that I cannot meet them half way.

I don't know just where I shall be in two weeks from now, but will let you know. I shall enjoy the *Philoctetes* and I am glad you are going at it. Palmer's *Antigone* is, I am sorry to say, utterly wooden and inexcusable. I say inexcusable, for it would be insulting the man to [say] that the faults of the thing were not largely the result of a deliberated scheme of what we might call rhetorical phlebotomy. The result is neither a literal translation nor a poetical one; and there are places where the Professor's lack of taste is almost ludicrous. Read it, and judge for yourself.

I'll try to write a little oftener and in a little better frame of mind in the future.

1716 Cambridge Street
Cambridge, Mass.
September 21, 1899

I am not paying you back for your long vacation—I am merely letting things go, according to my custom. My letters of late have been short and few, and I, like you, have played golf, which is damnably surprising, no doubt. I am not an artist in the business but still I can tear up the turf and occasionally send the ball whizzing for as many as fifty or sixty yards. I read the other day of a man in Newport who drove two hundred and ninety-five and I congratulated him. I like to see people succeed. I am succeeding myself in writing a kind of book which may or may not be good for something. I'll send you a copy when it is between covers, though I don't know just when that will be. If things go well it ought to be sometime in the first quarter of the twentieth century. I'm reading *Vanity Fair,* Emerson, Marion Crawford, Ibsen, and Aristophanes—in Pliocene prose. I get something out of the giant humor of the stuff, but can't say just what.

I leave this house on Monday next, but anything sent here will reach me. I'll send you your Xenophon before I go to New York.

I hope to spend a few days with Gledhill in Plymouth on the way. Gledhill has been shooting deer in the Adirondacks and thinks he is a devil of a hunter. This makes me think of Joe. What is he shooting nowadays—or is he still on the boat? The earth is still turning on its axis and I am in fairly good condition. Remember me to Mrs. Smith, and to your father and mother when you see them.

71 Irving Place
New York
November 16, 1899

I don't know whether you remember me or not; but you sent me a letter a long time ago, and you may possibly keep in mind the elongated anatomy of a certain irresponsible architect in natural stone. I should have written to you long before, only I didn't.

I am here. I have been here for a month. The town is all around me and Henry Irving is playing Shylock at the Knickerbocker Theatre. I tried to see him—stood in line nearly an hour to learn that I could get nothing under two dollars for any performance and a poor seat at that. Consequently I didn't see Mr. Irving, though I have blown myself on eight dollars worth of wind and horse-tail. Music hath charms to soothe the tired head —particularly after six months in the Harvard office. Just what that business did for me, I don't know, but it did something— beneficial, I think. If I believed in an orthodox hell I should have no more fears, but it can't be that, for I am not orthodox.

I am slowly giving birth to a book and have been—off and on— since January, though I did [not] get really down to it until July when I got my temporary freedom. For sandwich just now I am reading *Wilhelm Meister*. If by any chance you don't know it, take it up at the first opportunity. It is as indispensable as it is formless.—Did you get the Xenophon all right? Let me hear from you again before you are a grandfather and tell me something about things. Remember me to Mrs. Smith, and to your father and mother when you see them.

* 302 *

When I told you that I had sent the Xenophon book, I told you something that was not exactly so. I meant that I had left it in Cambridge tied up and stamped, for my friend Henderson to send, supposing that he would exercise his usual promptness. It seems, however, that he grew lazy after I left him, and let the book stay on his desk until about ten days ago, when it was sent and, I trust, received. Let me know if you got it all right.

I have done a big lot of work since I came here and I hope to have something between covers before very long. There will be nearly two-thousand lines of it and I fancy it is rather a queer sort of thing. I call it blank verse, but you may call it what you please as long as you don't have anything to say about "misplaced emphasis." That is the one thing that makes me raw.—Have you read Stephen Phillips? He is just out with a new book, a tragedy on the always available subject of Paola and Francesca. I shall be disappointed if it is not more than an ordinarily good thing, though I fear it will be too flowery. Do you know where I can find Kipling's *Absent-minded Beggar?* I understand that it is rot, but I should like to see it all the same.

I have said nothing, I believe, about your translation of the *Philoctetes,* but I have been interested in it all along. Whenever it is most convenient, I want an opportunity to read it, and I have hopes that you see fit to have it typewritten. Not that your handwriting is hard to read, but nothing save a personal letter is satisfactory unless we have it in some sort of type. Of course I shall be glad to get it anyway; but if it is typewritten I shall get a great deal more pleasure from it and a better notion as to its worth. All this sounds as if I expected you to get it copied for my particular delectation, but that is not what I mean.

Christmas has come and gone, and I—to speak selfishly—am glad of it. The season always gives me the blues in spite of myself, though I manage to get a good deal of pleasure from thinking of the multitudes of happy kids in various parts of the world. This year I have received some unexpected reminders of certain existences and they have somehow inflamed my desire to go to New Zealand, or to some other impossible place, where I [can] work out the things that are in me—provided they are there—without the paralyzing consciousness of being watched by my neighbors. This confesses a kind of weakness on my part, and I fancy I may exaggerate my sensibilities somewhat;—but the fact remains that I do get rather uneasy at times, and have a half-feeling that I am intellectual offal—which is bad. In a day or two I hope to [be in a] reasonable frame of mind again and at work once more at the one thing I seem, even in my way, to be able to do.

71 *Irving Place*
April 8, 1900

Your last letter was not so cheerful as it might have been, and it made me feel that you were giving rather too much time to the study of your own shadow. You will think of me as a past master, no doubt, in this particular study, and probably you will laugh when you read this: but no matter how guilty I may be in the shadow-business I refer to, you are to find, if you can, a grain of wisdom in my words and be mighty glad that things are no worse with you than they are. If the big wheel does not turn to suit you, you have at any rate the satisfaction of knowing that your friends have no ghost of a chance, or of an inclination, to doubt your ability to do whatever might come your way; and as long as you have that, you have something of more significance than you realize. As long as you do not realize it, I suppose it doesn't mean very much to you; but if ever you come to the feeling (and you will not) that you are studied [?] as something between a doubtful issue and a damned fool, you will understand a few things better than you do now. I do not mean by this to give you the faintest suspicion that I have lost faith in myself—for I am a veritable volcano of assurance; I mean only to let you know that I see what others have lost, and to add, though not without any venom [sic], that it will give me no great satisfaction if the time comes for me to know that they have regained it. Friendship that has its roots in the expectation of what a fellow is going to write rather than in the fact of what he is—or is not—may be valuable, but I do not know that it is indispensable. So I peg along, wishing very often that we might go down in the woods and build one more fire. Then I realize that I have not earned the fire, and I peg away again. Yesterday I packed off twelve hundred lines of *Captain Craig* to the typewriter, and I shall send the remaining six or seven hundred in a week or so. My scheme of hurrying did not work, and I fear it never will. My method, or rather my nature, gives me the appearance of being the laziest organism on earth, but I am not quite that.—Make the most of your work where you are and the bigger things will have to follow. It is only your lack (for which you are finally to be congratulated) of superficial flourish and conventional hypocrisy that makes the process a slow one. In the meantime you are building your foundation four feet thick; and I have no fear but that the proper sort of edifice is coming. Keep at it and write me a letter once in a while.

71 *Irving Place*
June 2, 1900

I have delayed writing to you in the hope that I might have something to tell you in regard to the book; but as there seems to be no prospect of anything of that sort, I'll say merely that the thing has been in the hands of the Scribners for the past three weeks and that I have heard nothing from it. I can't say that I expect to hear anything favorable, for I doubt very much if it is the kind of work that they are after; when the word comes, however, I will let you know. If it were not for the fact that I am in a place where I must make everything, big and little, count for all there is in it, I should not care very much: my thirst for "fame," as a thing in itself, is not very strong, and I am too thoroughly convinced that a book with the germ of life in it cannot be killed to spend much time in worrying [about] the lack of immediate approval. If the stuff that I have written is good for anything, if it is as good as some rather intelligent people seem to think, it is merely in a long trance from which it will get up some day to do a small saraband in the public place. I don't think it will ever make a big noise or a big show, but I don't, on the other hand, think it is entirely dead. As for this new book, which is a rather particular kind of twentieth century comedy, I have nothing to say except that I did it as well as I could and that I am not altogether displeased with it. I can see how it will repel a good many delicate readers, but I don't see [how] it can fail to make them a little more sensible in their attitude toward the sentimental of life and death [sic]—and, incidentally, of funerals. I am half inclined to think that the whole thing was suggested, indirectly enough, as you will see when you read it, by the alarming pageant on the day when E. R. Protheroe was "carried to his final resting place"—and I am sure that you will see that I am talking now about the principle of the thing, not about Protheroe: there is not so much as the ghost of him in the poem, but I fear there is rather more of old Mr. Louis (you have heard me speak of him) than I first intended there should be. There is not very much of myself, but there are pages of what certain people take to be myself: it is to these people, in fact, that I ought to dedicate the book, for they are responsible for its existence. I should never have written it, as it stands, if I had not passed through those six months of hell in the College Office; and I should never have written it at all if I had not got out of that same hell at about the time I did. Book three is on the ways, and will be done—if I have any kind of a chance to do it—before many months. In the meantime it is hotter than the devil here. Remember me to your father and mother, to Mrs. Smith, and to anyone else you happen to see.

I have been thinking lately about your *Philoctetes* and I have come to the conclusion that you might do well to think twice before including your division of the play into acts, episodes, etc. It seems to my untutored mind that the thing would be more satisfactory printed straight along without any interruptions. To anyone who knows the structure of ancient tragedies such a division would be superfluous, and to one who does not it might be rather clumsy—maybe irritating. This is only one of my suggestions, and of course you will take it for no more than it is worth.

I am getting along in a sort of way, peculiar to myself, and I am [doing] more or less work—rather less just now. I am gradually forming another book, making sundry amorphous attempts to maintain the editorial dignity of New York newspapers, and wondering now and then what the devil Small Maynard and Company are doing with *CC*. I heard once that Carman had recommended the old gentleman for publication, but that was in the middle ages and I have heard nothing since. If ever I emerge from my present condition we will contrive to have a dinner somewhere and drink to numerous vanities of splendor. Pope is happy, and I really think he has found his place. I think strongly of going there myself next year, but there is so much time for me to go to other places, including hell, in the interim, that I don't say much about it. Remember me to Mrs. Smith and keep your eyes on the stars.

I should have enjoyed that afternoon with you and the Doctor, but unfortunately I wasn't invited. Besides which, I doubt if I could have made connections. Seriously, there is no spot of earth

* 307 *

that means more to me than that same bit of woods behind your house. It is that, and the Doctor's offices that were, that makes me wish sometimes to go back there for a season. I shouldn't have the offices, to be sure, but I could lead him into the forest and that would be just about as good. I had already heard through Emma, Herman's wife, that I had stirred the sleeping fires in A. Bailey, Esq. Don't, for God's sake, think this is a matter for mirth. I think of it as the first authoritative response that I have yet received. My only regret is that nothing was said about the opinion of Wm. Ward and Sumner Soule. And Fred Berry.—The Scribner's are likely to bring the book out before long, and then we'll have a chance to see what the public makes of it. Anyhow, I shall feel secure and not have the distressful experience of looking longer on my own offspring as orphans of the night.—I don't know whether I deserve anything or not, but I have been through enough to feel that it is about time for something in the way of a change. I can't yet say anything definite about this job. Unless I can contrive to get some time for myself —time that I earn, I mean—it merely [means] that I shall remain here a little longer than I should otherwise. I often wonder if there's any reason why I should remain, after all. The best of me is on paper—and God knows how much or little it is worth.

Yours sincerely,

E.A.R.

NOTES

NOTES

A Note on the Text

In the Houghton Library at Harvard are 191 letters written to Harry Smith between 1890 and 1932; most were written before 1900. From this edition I have omitted a few letters, most of them brief notes, which it seemed needless to print. Those I include are printed in full and, I hope, with proper fidelity to somewhat difficult manuscript. When I have made conjecture or have supplied omitted words, I indicate the fact by using brackets. Parentheses are Robinson's. Manifest slips of the pen I have silently corrected, but I have retained persistent errors—e.g., "I" for "me." Robinson occasionally commented on his own mistakes. Writing "too," he makes it look like an ampersand; in a note he adds, "That 'too' was an accident, but I rather like the look of it— don't think I could do it again." I have deleted a few such comments as requiring more explanation than they are worth. Robinson did not consistently write full headings for his letters; I have therefore occasionally supplied the name of a town or a street address. But when I have changed or supplied dates I have indicated the fact by a note. For the reader's convenience, I have here and there clarified the punctuation, have italicized all titles of books and all foreign words. Titles of poems, etc., I have enclosed in quotation marks.

Notes and Index

The following books are most frequently referred to in the notes:
Collected Poems of Edwin Arlington Robinson (New York: The Macmillan Company, 1937). Hereafter referred to as *Poems*.
Selected Letters of Edwin Arlington Robinson (New York: The Macmillan Company, 1940). Hereafter referred to as *Selected Letters*.
Edwin Arlington Robinson, A Biography. By Hermann Hagedorn (New York: The Macmillan Company, 1938). Hereafter referred to as Hagedorn.
E. A. R. By Laura E. Richards (Cambridge: Harvard University Press, 1936). Hereafter referred to as *E. A. R.*

Except as it is indicated otherwise, quotations from Robinson's other letters are made from unpublished manuscripts in the Houghton Library.

In order to avoid needless repetition, I have placed minor notes in the Index. Persons casually referred to (e.g., Poll, p. 86) are there identified. Books are listed by title, with a reference to the name of the author, under whose name I have listed all the books mentioned by Robinson. Such a method may be thought to give a comprehensive view of his reading.

INTRODUCTION

Page xiii. *Harry Thurston Peck.* See note on letter of February 3, 1897.

Page xiv. *T. K. Whipple. Spokesmen* (New York: D. Appleton and Company, 1928), page 57.

Page xvi. *Rosalind Richards. A Northern Countryside* (1916), page 55. The Smith family is there concealed under the name Drew.

Page xix. *"I wonder more and more . . . "* Rollo Walter Brown, *Next Door to a Poet* (New York: D. Appleton-Century Co., Inc., 1937), pages 62-63.

Page xix. *"about one-fourth as pleasant . . ."* To Arthur Gledhill, *Selected Letters*, page 10.

Page xx. *"It was there that I met . . ."* To Gledhill, June 8, 1894. *"a good friend or two here in Gardiner."* September 29, 1894.

Page xxi. *"a young lady."* The young lady was the sister of one of Robinson's friends. Mr. Hagedorn's information, placing this incident some six or seven years too early, led him to regard it as a "tenuous and evanescent" high school romance (page 49).

Page xxii. *English novelists.* To Gledhill, May 24, 1891.

Page xxiii. *T. K. Whipple. Spokesmen*, page 57.

Granville Hicks. The Great Tradition (New York: The Macmillan Company, 1933), page 245.

Page xxv. *Professor of Greek at Amherst.* Some account of Smith's career may be found in *The Amherst Graduates Quarterly* (November 1939), pages 1-9.

Page xxvii. "The Miracle" appeared in *The Children of the Night*, published by Charles Scribner's Sons, 1905.

THE LETTERS

1890

September 27. *when you left Gardiner.* Smith had returned to Bowdoin College (about forty miles south of Gardiner) for his senior year.

River Survey. On the same day Robinson wrote to his former schoolmate, Arthur R. Gledhill, to say that he would earn fifty dollars for the month's work.

business be damned. To Gledhill, December 7, 1890: "What would life be worth if it was all absorbed in this feverish drudgery of business?"

October 12. *"Tis ignorance that makes . . ."* Cf. Robinson's development of this idea, and figure, in "Tasker Norcross," *Poems*, page 507.

November 9. *A strayed reveler.* Cf. Matthew Arnold, "The Strayed Reveler."

The Bros. Barstow. Nathaniel, George, Joseph, and James Barstow, of Gardiner, were among the close friends of Robinson's childhood and youth. George and "Joe" are most frequently mentioned in these letters.

"Behind the clouds." In the poem entitled "The Rainy Day."

the Inferno. Translation by John Jay Chapman, LXI, 649-651.

December 5. *since I came home from Brunswick.* On December 7, 1890 Robinson wrote to Gledhill: "Three weeks ago today I spent Sunday with Smith at Bowdoin. It was a new thing to me and awoke all my latent desire for a taste of college life. For the past two or three months I have been harboring an idea that I may take a year's course next Fall in something (I have not decided what) at Harvard. You may remember that I was 'contemplating' three years ago. Of course this may never come to pass, but I can see nothing now to hinder it." On September 27 of the same year he had told Gledhill, "I have entirely given up all ideas of going to college."

"The Island." Byron. Canto II, 448, 454-455.

"The Future." Matthew Arnold's poem of that title. See the letter of March 22, 1891.

1891

January 25. Robinson dated this letter, after the common error, "1890," but the reference to Harvard indicates that it belongs in the later year. On September 27, 1890 he wrote to Gledhill: "If I had not made the mistake that I did in supposing it would be impossible for me to take a college course on account of 'home rule' things would probably have turned out in a different manner. Father always talked down colleges and claimed they did more harm than good."

Blackmore. In a letter to Gledhill (March 11, 1891) Robinson reversed the lines:

"The less we have in hand to count
The more remains to hope for."

March 10. *Atwood.* Willis P. Atwood, of Gardiner, a high-school classmate of Robinson's and the subject of one of his early poems. See Hagedorn, page 43.

"was ever a gentleman so ill-used." There may be significance in Robinson's misquotation. The text reads, "was ever worthy gentleman so used!"

recent criticism. Atlantic, LXVII, 276 said of Saltus' *Love and Lore:* "an alertness of movement and occasionally a penetration of life which interest one, but the light cast on the subject is mainly a cigarette light."

Scrofulous novels. Browning, "Soliloquy of the Spanish Cloister":

"Or, my Scrofulous French novel
On grey paper with blunt type."

April 30. *You had been in the store.* During the vacations Smith occasionally worked in a haberdasher's shop in Gardiner.

Kipling. Many years later, Joyce Kilmer quoted Robinson as saying, "I am always revising my opinion of Kipling. I have changed my mind about him so often that I have no confidence in my critical judgment."—*Literature in the Making* (New York, 1917), page 267. Still later (August 15, 1932), Robinson wrote to Laura E. Richards, "There is a certain superjournalistic touch [in Kipling] that no one else could quite produce, but most of it is pretty hard going and with not too much in the Cart . . . In 'A Matter of Fact' he says 'once a journalist, always and forever a journalist'—and he has proved himself sorrowfully right."

Hardy. Writing to Gledhill on April 20, 1891, Robinson spoke of having read *The Hand of Ethelberta, Far from the Madding Crowd,* and *Under the Greenwood Tree.* The first he thought "a poor thing," the others, "masterpieces." Hardy, he thought, was not, "all things considered," so great a novelist as Blackmore, "but in his own quiet way it seems to me that he stands without

* 313 *

an equal." In another letter to Gledhill (May 24, 1891) he praised *Desperate Remedies*.

May 21. *Schuman.* Alanson Tucker Schuman(n) (1846-1918), a homeopathic physician of convivial habits and small practice, who delighted to write "ballades, rondeaux, villanelles and rondels by the score, as he wrote sonnets by the hundred." Schuman, who acted in these earlier years as Robinson's adviser and critic, was all his life a friend of the poet, who honored his memory with an obituary notice in the *Boston Evening Transcript*, March 30, 1918. See the letter of October 5, 1893. For a more extensive account of Schuman, see Hagedorn, pages 33-37, *et passim*. See "Ballade of Broken Flutes," *Poems*, page 77. Schuman's one volume of verse, *The Man and the Rose*, was published by Richard G. Badger (Boston, 1911).

the ode of Horace. The Eleventh Ode of Horace's First Book: *"Tu ne quaesieris, scire nefas, etc."* *Poems*, page 91. Horace's ode to Leuconoë with changes from this version appeared in *The Children of the Night* (Scribner's, 1905), page 59.

Bulwer says. Edward Bulwer-Lytton, *The Odes and Epodes of Horace*.

June 10. *as Coleridge says.* Robinson alludes to the last lines of a sonnet by Hartley Coleridge:
> ". . . can a drop of the eternal spring,
> Shadow of living lights, in vain be made?"

See note on letter of March 11, 1894.

June 21. *One of the higher grade of newspapers.* A few years later he refused a position as literary editor of the *Kansas City Star*. See Hagedorn, pages 159-160.

friends are scarce. A letter to Gledhill (July 24, 1890) says "Sometimes a week or ten days goes by without my seeing one of the boys or girls." *Selected Letters*, page 4.

MacLeod of Dare . . . The closing . . . is magnificent. The final paragraph of the novel by William Black invites comparison with the closing lines of *Tristram*:
> So fair shines the morning sun on the white sands of Iona! The three days' gale is over. Behold! how Ulva—Ulva the green-shored—the *Ool-a-va* that the sailors love—is laughing out again to the clear skies. And the great skarts on the shores of Erisgeir are spreading abroad their dusky wings to get them dried in the sun; and the seals are basking on the rocks in Loch-na-Keal; and in Loch Scridain the white gulls sit buoyant on the blue sea. There go the Gometra men in their brown-sailed boat to look after the lobster traps . . . The new, bright day has begun; the world has awakened again to the joyous sunlight; there is a chattering of the sea-birds all along the shores. It is a bright, eager, glad day for all the world. But there is silence in Castle Dare.

September 13. *you are not in town.* The summer vacation ended, Smith had taken up his new duties as a teacher in the public schools of Rockland, Maine.

October 6. *717 Cambridge Street.* Of this room, Robinson wrote on the same day to Gledhill, saying that it cost him $180.00 "and is not a palace at that."

October 11. *Sic itur* . . . Virgil.

October 18. *Hubbard.* Henry Vincent Hubbard, Harvard '97. Houghton Library possesses a copy of *The Children of the Night* inscribed "To H. V. Hubbard, Oct. 17, 1899."

the last Advocate. "Ballade of the White Ship" appeared in *The Advocate* of October 16, 1891, page 22.

speaking of ears. Robinson suffered necrosis of the bone, perhaps the result of an injury inflicted by an impatient teacher at the grammar school in Gardiner. See Hagedorn, pages 20, 61, *et passim.*

November 2. *working on the ice in Gardiner.* Robinson had worked as a timekeeper for the Oakland Ice Company in February 1889. The job meant getting up at 5 A.M. and staying all day on the windswept river; "working on the ice" thereafter stood for him as a particular symbol of torture.

my "dear friends." Robinson's acute sensitiveness to the opinions of his townspeople is everywhere apparent. To Gledhill he wrote on January 10, 1892: "When my dear friends ask me what I am 'studying for' at Harvard and 'what I propose to do, Mr. Robinson,' I say 'go to.' I have fits of dreaming wherein I kill hundreds in buckram." See the sonnet "Dear Friends," *Poems,* page 83, and the letter of October 1, 1893.

November 7. *Canton "University."* Glendhill was at this time a student of theology at St. Lawrence University, Canton, New York.

poem by William Vaughn Moody. "Dolorosa" appeared in *Scribner's* for November 1891, page 62.

November 15. *that youthful prodigy.* "Freddy" was the precociously mischievous son of Giles A. Stuart, principal of Gardiner High School.

the settee business. Gledhill and Robinson, finding the high school laboratory too cold for one of their evening gatherings, broke up a settee and burned it in the stove (Hagedorn, page 42). Robinson characteristically refused to put the affair out of mind. To Gledhill, on February 13, 1893, he wrote: "Perhaps the most sinful act I ever did was to lie to his erudition, G. A. S———t [sic] once in a time concerning a certain settee. At least, that is the thing I felt the cheapest for." Billy Gay, who "blew," was the son and assistant of the school's janitor.

"uttered nothing base." Tennyson, "To the Queen," March, 1851.

November 29. *that story in the Century. The Naulahka,* by Kipling and Wolcott Balestier, was serialized in *The Century.*

Crawford's new serial was *Don Orsino.*

Mrs. de Sumichrast's reception. Professor de Sumichrast wrote in his diary on November 26, 1891: "evg. reception to Harvard and Annex students and Faculty: we had over a hundred present and the evg. was a success." At this party Robinson met James L. Tryon. See Tryon's pamphlet *Harvard Days with Edwin Arlington Robinson* (Waterville, Maine, 1940), page 4.

December 8. *"In Harvard 5"* appeared in the *Advocate* of December 11, 1891.

my cousins from Cambridgeport. The daughters of Edward Proby Fox.

this declination put a slight "damper" on me. Mr. Lovett, reviewing Hagedorn's life of the poet, said, "The present reviewer, who sat on the board of the

Harvard Monthly which rejected some of Robinson's early verse at a time when publication would have meant much to him and the *Monthly,* here does public penance for the unpardonable sin." *The New Republic,* XCVII (November 30, 1938), 108.

Advocate with Villanelle. "Villanelle of Change" appeared in the *Advocate* of November 25, 1891.

December 13. *Barnard.* Leonard M. Barnard, of Gardiner, was at this time a student of engineering and architecture at the Massachusetts Institute of Technology. He later returned to Gardiner, where he became City Engineer. He was a casual member of the club established over Brown's dry-goods store in 1897.

1892

January 18. Robinson dated this letter 1891.

Whitney. William Dexter Whitney, a handsome Gardiner youth, was at this time a student in the School of Law at Boston University.

Johnson from Kentucky. Shirley Everton Johnson, of Louisville, Harvard '95, author of *The Cult of the Purple Rose.* On March 29, 1892 Robinson wrote to Gledhill: "I have just written a French composition and my friend Johnson from Kentucky has copied it for his own benefit. There is nothing like associated effort in college."

"There was an old soldier." Carl Sandburg prints a slightly different version of this favorite Civil War ballad in *The American Songbag* (1927), page 432.

February 3. Misdated 1891.

February 21. *Saben.* Mowry Saben. See Hagedorn, *passim.*

March 18. *only grand opera . . . that ever interested me much.* For Gledhill (March 29, 1892) Robinson adopted a less sophisticated air. "I went to hear Patti last Saturday evening in *Traviata.* Never realized what Grand Opera was before."

April 17. *I make no measure.* This poem appeared in *The Globe* (New York City) for May 1896, pages 143-144. It is reproduced by Charles Beecher Hogan in *A Bibliography of Edwin Arlington Robinson* (New Haven: Yale University Press, 1936), page 173.

There is a drear and lonely tract. "Supremacy" appeared in the *Advocate* of June 16, 1892.

May 2. *Hamlin Garland. Arena* was serializing *A Spoil of Office* and *Century, Ol' Pap's Flaxen.*

May 23. *Latham.* George Warrington Latham, Harvard '93.

October 9. The passages from Kipling are reproduced by permission of Mrs. George Bambridge, the daughter of Rudyard Kipling, and of the publishers Methuen & Company, Ltd., of London, the Macmillan Company of Canada, and Doubleday & Company, New York.

October 19. *I am reading Blackmore's Alice Lorraine.* Robinson's devotion to the romancers (Black, Crawford, Blackmore, etc.) was constant. Disparaging reviews of *Alice Lorraine* angered him. "I like Black myself," he wrote Gledhill (March 21, 1893), "and hate to hear him slandered."

November 21. *"The old lost stars . . ."* "L'Envoi," *Barrack-Room Ballads.*

Reprinted by permission of Mrs. Bambridge and of Methuen & Company, Ltd., The Macmillan Company of Canada, Ltd., and Doubleday & Company, New York.

November 29. *Prof. Norton's lectures.* For Robinson's later comments on Norton, see Rollo Walter Brown, *Next Door to a Poet* (New York, 1937), pages 27-28. Houghton Library possesses a copy of *The Torrent and the Night Before* inscribed to Norton "with compliments (and apologies) of E. A. Robinson. 10 December, 1896."

December 11. *Kipling's poem.* "The Gypsy Trail," *Century Magazine,* December 1892, pages 278-279.

Wilkins' pastel. "After the Rain," by Mary E. Wilkins, *ibid.,* page 271.

1893

January 13. Misdated 1892.

Butler. William Edward Butler (1874-1912), the son of a Boston merchant, was one of Robinson's closest friends at Harvard and for several years thereafter. See Hagedorn, *passim.* Butler took his own life on November 1, 1912. *The Man Against the Sky* is dedicated to his memory.

January 23. Misdated January 22. The 23d was a Monday.

the paragraph in the Critic. The *Critic* of January 14, 1893 (page 26) ascribed *Tess of the D'Urbervilles* to Richard Blackmore, saying: "His *Tess of the D'Urbervilles* has produced a deep impression in Russia . . . Lists of the unfamiliar words in dialect . . . have been sent to Mr. Blackmore for paraphrase as the work progressed."

inconsistent for him to live in America. "The Rhyme of the Three Captains" is an anti-American account of the activities of John Paul Jones.

February 5. This letter is undated. On February 13, 1893 Robinson wrote to Gledhill that he had been "laid up" for the past ten days with shingles. The reference to the gathering in Saben's room and the remark that he did not go to Boston as usual on Saturday evening indicate February 5 as probably the correct date.

Perry's Eighteenth Century Literature. Thomas Sergeant Perry, *English Literature in the Eighteenth Century* (New York, 1883).

enclose a list of the questions. The questions have not been preserved with the letters.

March 7. *"Seven men from all the world."* Cp. Robinson's "Ten men from Zanzibar," *Poems,* page 164.

March 13. *Pursuit of the Well-Beloved.* The *Well-Beloved* was serialized under this title in the *Illustrated London News* (1892).

March 19. *the new school.* Smith, who had been teaching in the Rockland High School, had been made principal of a newly erected grade school.

May 7. *Meredith's sharp sayings.* An intimate of Robinson's last thirty years recalls that the poet aspired to talk "like a character out of Meredith." Gawaine, in an early version of *Lancelot,* was made to talk in that fashion but the concerted protest of friends made Robinson sober him down.

June 21. *the best thing I have ever seen by Kipling.* Robinson remembered this story for many years. To Joyce Kilmer he said, "many of Kipling's worst poems are greatly overpraised, while some of his best . . . are not appreciated . . . The poem beginning 'There's a whisper down the field' has never been properly appreciated . . . One of his greatest poems, by the way, 'The Children of the Zodiac,' happens to be in prose." Joyce Kilmer in *Literature in the Making* (New York, 1917), page 267.

June 21. (*a gift*). In the *Mark Twain Quarterly* (Spring 1938), page 19, G. W. Latham tells of receiving this book as a gift from Robinson.

October 1. *hug my own particular phantoms.* See Bryant, "Thanatopsis," lines 63-64

> . . . and each one as before will chase
> His favorite phantom.

Aldrich's lines. Robinson slightly misquotes the sonnet "Enamored Architect of Airy Rhyme," *The Poems of Thomas Bailey Aldrich* (Boston, 1897), II, 182. He quoted the same line to Gledhill in a letter of March 21, 1893. Houghton Library possesses a copy of *The Torrent* inscribed "Thomas Bailey Aldrich, with compliments of E. A. Robinson, 13 December, 1896."

"Supremacy," with many changes from this version, appeared in *The Children of the Night* (Scribner's, 1905), page 70.

October 22. *Uncle Joe.* Joe Barstow.

Longfellow's "Kéramos." See "Partnership," *Poems*, page 222, originally entitled "The Wife of Palissy." The poem appears to have originated in Robinson's reading of "Kéramos," where Palissy's story is mentioned.

Tryon. James Libby Tryon, of Portland, Maine, was at this time a student in the Episcopal Theological School at Cambridge. See his *Harvard Days with Edwin Arlington Robinson*, a pamphlet privately printed at Waterville, Maine (1940). See Hagedorn, pages 66, 72, 80.

November 5. *perpetual state of discontent.* See the letter of October 28, 1893 to Gledhill, *Selected Letters*, pages 9-11.

November 11. *I sent you the "Ballades."* In the Public Library at Gardiner is a copy of *Ballades and Rondeaus, Chants Royal, Sestinas, Villanelles, etc. Selected with Chapter* [sic] *on the Various Forms*, by Gleeson White, London 1887. An undated penciled inscription on the flyleaf reads "A. T. Schuman from R."

Life is my job. See letter of May 23, 1893 to Gledhill, *Selected Letters*, pages 8-9.

November 19. *M.C.R.R.* The Maine Central Railroad.

December. The letter of November 5, 1893 indicates that Smith visited Gardiner over the weekend of October 9; presumably Robinson read "Marshall" to him then. In the letter of February 11, 1894 Robinson speaks of Lowell's *Biglow Papers* in a manner that indicates an earlier reference. This undated letter therefore seems to belong to late 1893.

1894

January 27. *tutor a young lady.* Hagedorn (page 48) places this incident some half dozen years too early. See the letter of May 1, 1894. The young lady was admitted to Wellesley in September 1895.

February 4. *the stone house on the hill.* Robinson and Smith schemed to build a cabin of field stone on the Smith property at Iron Mine Hill. They gathered a few boulders but never completed the project. See Hagedorn, page 48.

February 18. *"To stay at home is best."* Longfellow, "Song":
"Stay, stay at home, my heart, and rest;
Home-keeping hearts are happiest"
that persistent presentiment. Robinson lived in constant apprehension that his diseased ear might suddenly take his life or impair his reason.

my friend Ford. Joseph Sherman Ford, 2d, Harvard '94, was now (and for the remainder of his life) a master at the Phillips Exeter Academy, Exeter, New Hampshire.

Sir John Lubbock's book. The Pleasures of Life.

February 25. *"The House on the Hill."* This version of Robinson's best-known villanelle appeared in *The Globe*, September 1894, page 828. A revised version was printed in *The Children of the Night* (Scribner's), page 34.

translating Virgil. Robinson's translation of Eclogue III, "Palaemon," is printed among the notes to *Selected Letters*.

March 11. *my uncle.* Edward Proby Fox, of Cambridge, Massachusetts was an employee of the Riverside Press. *Tristram* is dedicated to his memory.

Hartley Coleridge's sonnet. Poems by Hartley Coleridge (London, 1851), II, page 6. See note on letter of June 10, 1891.

Mr. Moulton's book. The Ancient Classical Drama, by Richard Green Moulton (Oxford, Clarendon Press, 1890).

March 18. *the rough sketch I enclose.* The sketch has not been preserved with the letters.

April 15. *Mr. Mosher's book-making.* Thomas Bird Mosher (1852-1923) of Portland, Maine, distinguished for chastely classical models of book-making and for discriminating choice of texts for publication.

"Ballade des Pendues." By Théodore de Banville. The translation is entitled "The Ballad of the King's Orchard."

Sharp's collection. In the Public Library of Gardiner, Maine is a copy of *Sonnets of this Century*, ed. William Sharp, London, n.d. It is inscribed, "A. T. Schuman from Robinson—Dec. 1897."

April 22. *my life is infinitely larger.* See the letter of October 28, 1893 to Arthur Gledhill, *Selected Letters*, page 10.

the wood-cutter and his dog. The Task, V, 41-57.

"Don Quixote." In the volume *At the Sign of the Lyre.*

May 6. *"this my town of banishment."* To Gledhill Robinson wrote on September 29, 1894: "A good friend or two here in Gardiner would make all the difference in the world, but as things are, I have to do my talking in letters—that is, most of it. Of course there are one or two fellows here who help things along to a great extent but they are not the kind I most need."

May 13. *those who ask for little.* "Those who want little get nothing." Chapter IX. This melodramatic little novel concerns an intellectual, withdrawn young woman and a surly young man who meet at a Swiss sanitarium, reluctantly fall in love, and thereby learn kindliness and tolerance. The contrived ending is false pathos, but the theme of love late found and soon lost seems to have appealed to Robinson's mood. The characters of the novel discuss a philosophy not vastly unlike that expressed in Robinson's earliest poems.

May 20. *Adela.* Adela Hill Wood became Mrs. Harry de Forest Smith on June 19, 1895.

you must not ask me to come to your wedding. To Gledhill Robinson wrote on Dec. 26, 1894: "Smith hopes to get married in June, but I tell him that he had better wait until fall so as to give me one more summer with him in the pines behind his house . . . There will be a great hole made in my life when Smith gets married. He is my last really intimate friend within my call. When he goes I shall be alone—except for letters, which are more than they sometimes seem."

May 27. *Dean.* Horace Dean Robinson (1857-1899), the poet's eldest brother.

Phipter. That is, E. H. Plumptre.

June 3. *"The Night Before."* A dramatic monologue, one of the title poems of Robinson's first volume. A man about to be hanged for the murder of his wife's lover recounts to a priest the circumstances of his action and the torture of spirit that impelled him to it.

June 10. *Mr. Scudder.* Horace Scudder, editor of the *Atlantic.*

Deming. Philander Deming (1829-1915), author of stories in the *Atlantic* which later appeared as *Tompkins and other Folks* (1885).

a little poem in blank verse. "To H.R.H. Princess Beatrice," *Tiresias and other Poems* (1885).

Barrett Wendell's book. A reference in the letter of June 9, 1895 suggests Wendell's *William Shakespeare* (1894). *Stelligeri and other Essays* appeared in 1893.

June 17. *my great poem.* "The Night Before."

Critic . . . one of my sonnets. "Oh, for a poet" appeared in the *Critic* of November 24, 1894, page 12. See the letter of December 4, 1894.

September 29. *Sharp's "Vista."* *Chap-Book,* I (September 15, 1894), pages 224-228.

The Yellow Book, I (April 1894). Henry James, "The Death of the Lion"; Arthur Waugh, "Reticence in Literature."

October 7. *the last McClure's.* The stories to which Robinson refers appear in *McClure's* for October 1894: Doyle's "Sweethearts," Barr's "A Deal on 'Change," and Harte's "Young Robin Grey."

The Globe. "A quarterly of limited circulation and unlimited impudence" published in New York by William Henry Thorne, "A frothy adventurer." See Hagedorn, page 103. Mr. Hogan's bibliography lists eight of Robinson's poems as appearing in the non-paying *Globe* from 1894 to 1897. The issue of September 1894 printed "The House on the Hill" and "The Miracle."

Thorne's nonsense. Volume four of the *Globe* (1893-94) carried a series of articles entitled "The Wreck of the Mayflower." The passage to which Robinson refers appears on page 801 in a postscript: ". . . and Mr. Robinson—a much younger person [than Judge Webster]—bids fair to outshine all competitors in his native state." Thorne is said by Hagedorn (page 168) to have been one of the prototypes of "Isaac and Archibald."

October 21. *Marjorie Fleming.* Robinson doubtless read the account prepared by Dr. John Brown for the *North British Review*, November 1863, and later published as a small volume. Robinson refers to Marjorie's poem on the subject of three young turkeys who were eaten by rats:

> A direful death indeed they had,
> As wad put any parent mad;
> But she was more than usual calm,
> She did not give a single dam.
> She is as gentil as a lamb.

Also:

> Very soft and white his cheeks;
> His hair is red, and grey his breeks;
> His tooth is like the daisy fair:
> His only fault is in his hair

Marjorie Fleming died in 1811, in her ninth year.

"The Passion Flower." *The Passion Flower of Magdala*, by Walter Kennedy, occupied the entire issue of *Chap-Book* for October 15, 1894.

October 28. *Nothing is there more marvellous.* Robinson typed these lines on an undated sheet, but they seem to belong with this letter. Some of the lines were incorporated into *Captain Craig, Poems*, pages 117-118, 140. They are a rendition of *Antigone*, ll. 332-333, 334-347 (James A. Notopoulos, *The New England Quarterly*, March 1944, page 109).

November 4. *to say nothing of Franklin.* Thomas Francklin (?), whose translation of *Antigone* appeared in 1766.

the last McClure's. November 1894. The stories of which Robinson speaks are Doyle's "De Profundis" and Barr's "The Doom of London."

Bowdoin Art Museum. "Someone who has just come from Bowdoin College tells me that the new art building, for which Elihu Vedder did the decorations, is one of the most satisfactory pieces of architecture done of late years in America . . . In painful contrast the art building at Harvard stands out. For I hear that Prof. Charles Eliot Norton has already given it his qualified condemnation." *Chap-Book*, November 1, 1894, pages 353-354.

November 11. *article on the poets.* *Outlook*, L (October 20, 1894), pages 620-622. "The Poets of the Bodley Head," by Katharine T. Hinkson.

Mr. Le Gallienne's adulterous nightingales. Robinson refers to the following lines from "Tree Worship":

> Some Rizzio nightingale that plained adulterous love
> Beneath the boudoir-bough of some fast-married bird . . .

The Yellow Book, I (April 1894), page 59.

November 19. *the kids.* The children of Robinson's brother Herman.

The Simpletons. *Harper's* first serial installment of the novel later called *Jude the Obscure* appeared under this title and was subsequently altered to *Hearts Insurgent*.

November 26. *"Ballade of Dead Friends."* *The Torrent and the Night Before*, pages 18-19.

December 9. *my Sonnet.* "Oh, for a poet . . ." *Poems*, page 93.

Songs after Sunset. The correct title of Saltus' volume is *Dreams after Sunset*.

experimental quatrain. *Poems*, page 75. Experimental quatrain. These lines appeared in *The Children of the Night* (Scribner's), page 13.

Robinson enclosed with this letter typed copies of Andrew Lang's and C. Kegan Paul's translations of Ronsard's sonnet, *"Quand vous serez bien vielle . . ."*

1895

January 12. *the first chorus in Aegeus. Poems*, page 97.

"Aaron Stark." Poems, page 86.

Kipling's Jungle Story. "Letting in the Jungle," *McClure's*, January 1895.

the article on the novel. "The Novel," by Margaret Field, *Munsey's* (January 1895), pages 371 ff.

good thing by Frank Chaffee. "So Runs the World," a short story. *Ibid.*, pages 389 ff.

January 20. Kenneth Grahame. *Chap-Book* (January 15, 1895).

my request for posters. Smith, who was collecting the placards used to advertise current magazines, had enlisted Robinson's help. The *Chap-Book* spoke frequently of this popular hobby, and devoted to it almost the entire issue of October 1, 1894. The collecting craze soon died away as the quality of poster art declined. (*Boston Transcript*, December 12, 1896).

January 28. *The Celibates.* In the Public Library at Gardiner is a copy of George Moore's *The Celibates* inscribed "To E. A. Robinson from W. E. B. Nov. '96." W. E. B. is William Edward Butler.

February 3. *a check for seven dollars.* For the sonnet, "For a Copy of Poe's Poems," which was not published until August 1906, page 243.

Julia Ward Howe and her daughters. Laura E. Richards, of Gardiner, was the daughter of Julia Howe. Mrs. Richards later became a close friend of the poet. See letters of April 24, 1897 and May 17, 1897; see *Selected Letters, passim*; and *E. A. R.*

February 10. Robinson dated this letter "1894" but the envelope is postmarked 1895.

Ouida's article. "Literature and the English Book Trade," *North American Review* (February 1895), pages 157 ff.

February 24. *The Bibelot.* A periodical pamphlet reprinting choice passages of literature, issued monthly by Thomas B. Mosher for twenty years, beginning in 1895.

O. B. Clason. Sometime mayor of Gardiner.

March 10. *Garland's little obstetrical story. The Land of the Straddle-Bug*, serialized in the *Chap-Book*. See letter of February 3, 1895.

March 17. *Minto . . . his English Prose. A Manual of English Prose Literature*, by William Minto, 1872.

I enclose a quotation. Robinson wrote the passage on a separate sheet, with the date and his signature.

The Master of Balliol's Advice in All Undertakings
First make your arrangements;
Then trust in Heaven;
And in no case worry.
Quoted by "Q" in *McClure's Magazine*.
March 17, 1895   E. A. Robinson

Mr. Mabie's contribution. "A Comment on Some Recent Books," by Hamilton Wright Mabie, *Chap-Book* II (March 15, 1895), pages 367-371.

Old World Lyrics. A little volume of translated lyrics, published by Thomas B. Mosher, 1893.

April 28. The envelope of this undated letter is postmarked "Apr. 29, 1895, 8:30 A.M."

Chatteris Bridge scene. At the end of chapter 14.

my Hardy sonnet. "For a Book by Thomas Hardy," *The Critic* (November 23, 1895), page 348. See letter of April 14, 1895.

May 5. The envelope of this undated letter is postmarked "May 6, 1895, 8:30 A.M."

article . . . by Maurice Thompson. "Nuts from Perigord," *Chap-Book* (May 1, 1895), pages 473-478.

poem by Bliss Carman. "Little Lyrics of Joy—V." *Ibid.*, page 478.

Lamia. II, 46-47.

May 12. "The Children of the Zodiac" in *Many Inventions;* "Georgie Porgie," in *Life's Handicap;* "The Limitations of Pambé-Serang," *ibid.;* "The Mutiny of the Mavericks," *ibid.;* "The Bridge Builders," in *The Day's Work.* *Richard Fénigan.* The hero of *La Petite Paroisse.*

May 20. *damn a man for one short piece.* See letter of March 17, 1895.

my quatrain. See letter of December 9, 1894.

May 26. *wholly out of the mood.* Robinson's letters to Gledhill during the summer of 1895 indicate a long period of the blues. On August 20, 1895 he wrote: "I have been so miserable and down at the heel generally this summer on account of my ear, which has been going like the devil, and some other things which have not been going at all, that I have had small heart for letter-writing."

my six hens. Cf. the hens in *Captain Craig, Poems,* page 140.

October 6. Smith, now doing graduate work at Harvard, was living at 53 Trowbridge Street, Cambridge.

one of the really great sort. The *Harvard Crimson* of Oct. 1, 1895 reports that the freshmen were addressed by (among others) Professor Charles Eliot Norton. See letter of November 29, 1892 and note.

Lombroso's article. "Nordau's *Degeneration*: Its Value and Its Errors," by Césare Lombroso, *Century,* N.S. XXVIII (October 1895), pages 936 ff.

November 10. *Schuman's sonnet.* Schuman's ballade, "When William Shakespeare Wrote His Plays," appeared in *Bookman* II (November 1895), page 190 and was reprinted in *The Man and the Rose,* page 80.

since I got back. Robinson wrote to Gledhill on November 7 that he had just returned to Gardiner after two weeks in Boston and Cambridge.

this scheme of mine. Robinson had turned away from prose and was now planning the volume of poems which later appeared as *The Torrent and the Night Before.*

November 26. The envelope of this undated letter is postmarked "Nov. 26, 1895, 8:00 P.M."

Jamie. James S. Barstow.

December 14. *The Philistine.* A periodical pamphlet issued by The Roycrofters.

The sonnet translation of Horace's ode to Leuconoë was printed in *The Children of the Night* (Scribner's, 1905), page 59.

the *"Tavern" part of my book.* The title originally planned was *The Tavern and the Night Before.* See letter of March 7, 1896.

1896

February 19. *Jones.* Hagedorn (page 95) speaks of Jones as "a Christian Science practitioner," but his name does not appear in the records of The First Church of Christ, Scientist at Gardiner, nor is there any memory of him among the poet's surviving acquaintance. I have been unable to learn his full name.

March 7. *Kelley.* W. W. Kelley, a job printer in Gardiner.

May 22. *Sonnets to Paul Verlaine. Poems,* page 96.

"The Dead Village." *Poems,* page 88.

June 7. *"The gold men."* A phrase commonly applied to the supporters of McKinley in the presidential campaign of 1896.

enclose a sonnet. "The Clerks" appeared in the *Boston Transcript,* June 4, 1896. *Poems,* page 90.

September 11. This letter and all letters through June 17, 1897 are addressed to Germany, where Smith was studying at the University of Berlin. *"The Chorus of Old Men." Poems,* page 97.

September 27. *Watson's Armenian Sonnets. The Purple East,* reviewed September 1, 1896, page 120.

December 7. *"Two Sonnets." Poems,* page 89.

Blair. Arthur Blair, a high school classmate of Robinson's.

December 22. Robinson enclosed with this letter a clipping from the *Transcript,* December 16, 1896:

> Speaking of personal expressions, a remarkable thing of that sort has come to the Listener in the form of a very little unbound book of verse by Edwin A. Robinson of Maine. His personal expression [*sic*] carried almost to the point of literary pamphleteering. But pamphleteering or what not, is it not a pleasure to get hold of a man who knows something on his own account, and isn't measuring the world according to somebody else's system? One who can praise and see into the very heart of and reason for George Crabbe and Paul Verlaine, Matthew Arnold and Emile Zola, getting at the kernel of real thought that makes each one of these a force, is not an ordinary echoer of others and judge of things according to pedantic systems. But it is desirable that one who puts out verses, even at his own expense, should be able to write verse. Can this man do it? The Listener is not a critic of poetry, but he rather likes things like this, about one Aaron Stark . . .

John Chamberlin, author of the article, thereupon quotes the sonnet "Aaron Stark."

Titus M. Coan. See Hagedorn, pages 110, *et passim.*

1897

January 17. *"The Wilderness." Poems,* page 99.

An unknown female. Miss Edith Brower, of Wilkes-Barre, Pennsylvania. See letters of April 4, 1897, February 4, 1898. Miss Brower was hereafter a life-long friend of the poet. See Hagedorn, *passim.*

an interview to be published in February. "Edward Eggleston: An Interview," appeared in *The Outlook* of February 6, 1897.

February 3. *takes me for a yelling pessimist.* Harry Thurston Peck wrote in the *Bookman* of February 1897 that E. A. R. saw the world as a prison house and elicited the famous reply: "The world is not a 'prison-house,' but a kind of spiritual kindergarten where millions of bewildered infants are trying to spell God with the wrong blocks."

The Christian Register. Vol. LXXVI (January 21, 1897), page 43.

Chicago Record. January 23, 1897.

The brief notice in the *Chicago Record* reads as follows:
    " 'This book is dedicated to any man, woman or critic who will cut the edges off it—I have done the top.' With this modest foreword one's interest is stirred to effort; opinions may differ according to mood whether it is worth the while. In this day there are so many oddities in versification that one hesitates over his own conviction and is at a loss to know whether the fault is his or the poet's.
    "This is Mr. Robinson's picture of 'The Torrent': [the critic then quotes 'The Torrent'].
    "In very limited space Mr. Robinson succeeds in shattering many vener-able and hitherto respected laws of versification."

February 11. *The Dial . . . was very kind. Dial,* February 1, 1897, page 92. Robinson makes a few inadvertent and unimportant changes in the text.

implication that critics are epicene." The Torrent was dedicated "to any man, woman, or critic who will cut the edges."

Margaret Ogilvy. Sir James M. Barrie's biography of his mother.

clipping from the Cleveland Leader. This undated clipping reads:
    In spite of the modest appearance of *The Torrent and the Night Before,* and that it was printed for the author, and its too simple dedication, one finds in Edwin Arlington Robinson's paper-bound volume of poems a large degree of merit . . . There is a remarkably striking resemblance in the story of 'The Night Before' to D'Annunzio's 'Episcopo and Co.' . . . but it is entirely permissible for poets to choose their subjects from prose works, and whether it was intentional or not does not detract from the commend-able character of the blank verse production of Mr. Robinson. One does not have to read far in 'The Night Before' to discover its merit.
The reviewer then quotes about fifty lines of that poem.

March 15. *the willingness to be a child again.* See "Octave VII," *Poems,* page 102.

"The world was made in order." Robinson quotes from stanza twelve of Emer-son's "Monadnock."

April 4. *Mr. Lawson.* Houghton Library possesses a copy of *The Children of the Night* inscribed to Ernest Lawson, September 1906.

"damned tough bullet to chew." Kipling, "Soldier an' Sailor Too."

L'Assommoir, which I have been reading. On June 19, 1929 Robinson wrote to Laura Richards, "When I wrote that rather pinfeatherish Zola sonnet [*Poems,* page 85], I had read only *L'Assommoir* and I have read only one of his books since then." *E. A. R.*, page 14. But these remarks to Smith suggest that Robinson had not read *L'Assommoir* before the appearance of *The Torrent*. See letters of April 17, 1892 and May 11, 1892 for other references to Zola.

down-town den. With Arthur Blair, Seth Ellis Pope, and Linville W. Robbins, Robinson had hired a room on Water Street in which the friends gathered for talk and pipes. See *E. A. R.*, pages 31-32 and Hagedorn, pages 92-94. This letter makes it clear that "the quadruped" (a term not mentioned by Robinson) was not for very long a feature of his life in Gardiner. "Aunt Imogen" was begun in this room. See Daniel Gregory Mason, *Music in My Time* (New York: The Macmillan Company, 1938), page 125.

"The Master of the Moment." "Octave XXII," *Poems*, page 107.

April 24. *down to Mrs. Richards'*. Mrs. Richards' account of these visits appears in *E. A. R.*, pages 47-53.

Hays Gardiner. John Hays Gardiner, a cousin of the Richards', was from this time until his early death a friend and benefactor of the poet. See Hagedorn, pages 125-126. *Captain Craig* was dedicated to Gardiner's memory.

Nine tenths of the happiness in the world. This idea never left Robinson. See his development of it in "Tasker Norcross," *Poems*, page 503:

> "Blessed are they
> That see themselves for what they never were . . ."

May 17. *Yes, her name is E—— B——.* In the same Berlin pension with Smith were visitors from Wilkes-Barre who were acquainted with Miss Brower. *lied about "my northern pines."* In the poem "Boston," *Poems*, page 83.

June 17. *whether the book goes far enough.* Pater did not finish *Gaston de Latour.*

November 1. *The Children.* *The Children of the Night*, published by Richard G. Badger (Boston, December 6, 1897).

"Octaves," *Poems*, pages 100 ff. "Calvary," *Poems*, page 83; "L'Envoi," *Poems*, page 108.

December 17. The envelope of this undated letter is postmarked "Dec. 17, 1897."

1898

January 13. *beginning George Annandale.* This letter corrects Hagedorn's assumption (page 177) that the poem was begun in 1901.

February 4. *working you into the same trip.* Smith was at this time teaching at the University of Pennsylvania.

The . . . notice in the Transcript. By John Hays Gardiner, December 24, 1897. "The first one" appeared on December 18.

February 21. *Burnham.* George Edwin Burnham, whom Robinson had known at Harvard where Burnham was a member of the Law School from September 1891 to 1894.

October 12. *William James.* See Robinson's letter of November 2, 1898 to J. H. Gardiner, *Selected Letters*, pages 14-16.

the Cambridge job. Gardiner was seeking a clerical post for Robinson in the administrative offices (University Hall) at Harvard.

January 5. Robinson dated the letter 1898 but there is no doubt of his being in error. He was in New York City during the first few months of 1898.

I was in Winthrop. See Hagedorn, page 146. Robinson's friend Arthur Blair was now working in a bank in Winthrop, Maine, a few miles from Gardiner. Robinson seems to have visited him between November 1898 and January 1899. See Alice Frost Lord, *Lewiston (Maine) Journal,* Magazine Section, January 4, 1941.

the prodigy. Smith's daughter Barbara, born November 15, 1897.

June 29. *shall leave . . . at the end of the week.* On the contrary, Robinson spent the entire summer in Cambridge, living in his old lodgings at 1716 Cambridge Street and writing *Captain Craig.*

some of my friends. Daniel Gregory Mason was now in Cambridge and saw much of Robinson. See *Music in My Time,* by D. G. Mason. Robinson had also met Josephine Peabody, who gave him encouragement. See Hagedorn, chapter XI, and *Selected Letters.*

Philoctetes. Smith's unpublished translation.

September 21. *writing a kind of book.* Captain Craig.

November 16. *71 Irving Place.* Robinson had returned to New York in October and was now living with George Burnham in a "little box room." William Vaughn Moody a year later lived in the same house. "I am pretty lonely here [he wrote to D. G. Mason on November 14, 1900], as Robinson has gone to Hoboken or Spuytenduyvil or somewhere to live with the goats, and I only see him once a week. For a few days I thought the noise would drive me wild . . . There are three hundred and twenty-three hand-organs and ninety-seven pianos on our block, and every hour thirty-five thousand drays loaded with sheet-iron pass the house. Irving Place, you know, is a quiet old-fashioned neighborhood, so we are justly proud of these slight evidences of animation." *Some Letters of William Vaughn Moody,* ed. D. G. Mason (Boston, 1913), page 130.

December 17. *my friend Henderson.* Lawrence Henderson, whom Robinson had met at the Richards' and later in Cambridge.

June 2. *old Mr. Louis.* Alfred Hyman Louis (1829-1915), an aged, scholarly vagabond whom Robinson had met and befriended in New York. For an account of Louis' character and career, see Denham Sutcliffe, "The Original of Robinson's Captain Craig," *New England Quarterly,* XVI (September 1943), 407-431.

Book Three. Robinson's third volume was *The Town Down the River* (1910).

November 22. *maintain the editorial dignity.* See Hagedorn, page 172.

CC. Captain Craig.

drink to numerous varieties of splendor. See "Three Quatrains," *Poems,* page 75.

Pope. Seth Ellis Pope.

August 30. Robinson was now working in the New York Customhouse.

A. Bailey. See Hagedorn, page 155.

Scribner's . . . likely to bring the book out. A second edition of *The Children of the Night* was published by Scribner's on October 14, 1905.

INDEX

INDEX

Refugees, The (Doyle), 190
Religio Medici (Browne), 124
Renan, Ernest
    Vie de Jesus, 226, 228
Return of the Native, The (Hardy),
    16, 17
Reviews, low quality in America, 93
Rhetoric (Hill), 32
Richards, Laura E., xxv, 284, 286,
    322
Riley, James Whitcomb, 43, 196, 200
Ring and the Book, The (Browning),
    298
Robbins, Linville W., 282
Robert Helmont (Daudet), 212
Roberts, Charles G. D., 276
Robinson, Edward, xiii, xv
Robinson, Edwin Arlington
    Scorn of business and of "prac-
tical" men, 4, 107; sense of his own
impracticality, 20, 53, 111, 154,
246-247, 254; sense of failure, 112-
113, 125, 228; shame at not earning, 117, 119, 133, 230-231, 246;
jobs not salvation, 21; works on
River Survey, xv, 4; ward clerk,
254; works in Harvard office, 297-
299
    His loneliness, 22, 24, 149, 151,
156, 191, 210, 211, 244, 250, 284-
285, 314; sense of social inade-
quacy, 31, 42, 44, 57-58, 295; dependence on letters, 22, 50, 55, 76,
119, 121, 150, 319; dependence on
friends, 154, 246; fear of disappointing them, 300-301, 304-305;
his unsmilingness, 135; chronic
grouch, 205; trouble with eyes, 30,
32, 90, 99, 108, 189, 190, 230,
239, 298; diseased ear, xvii, 33, 73-
74, 231, 315, 323; shingles, 83-85;
death of his mother, 264, 278-279;
impatience with Gardiner and sensitivity to public opinion, 9, 15, 36,
57, 103, 115, 129, 149, 236, 287,
289, 315; "life is all hell," 154,
264, 279, 283, 285, 299; despair,
66, 80, 115, 145, 149, 150, 154,
159, 166, 297-298, 300, 304, 323;
idealism, "optimistic desperation,"

244, 246, 252, 263, 264, 267, 270,
274, 279, 280, 285; fatalism, 24,
53, 61, 113, 138-139, 162, 246; religious doubts, 145, 148; materialism, 260, 278, 296; his sympathy
with men, 108, 134-135, 137; denial of sympathy, 135
    Plays fiddle, 239; postage stamps,
242-243, 262-263, 266; plays golf,
301; visit to Exeter, 230; "down-
town den," 282, 326; goes to New
York, 293, 302
HARVARD
Anticipation of, 8-14 passim; 312-
313; application accepted, 23; leaves
for, 25; registration, 29; fear of failure, 33-35; growing confidence, 38;
opinion of undergraduates, 40; de-
mocracy at, 47; wish to know literati, 37; expenses, 49; elective system, 50-51; special student, 50;
schedules, 30, 68; examinations,
36-37, 39, 52, 53; grades, 46, 51,
57, 61, 86; athletics, 40, 41, 62, 74-
75; on leaving, 42, 102-103; effect
of Harvard, 66, 101, 144-145; patriotism for, 18, 191, 216, 247-250;
nostalgia for, 116, 152, 235
    Sense of dedication to literature,
120, 187, 247; despair of writing
well, 151-152, 163, 170; precision
of language, 6, 16, 18, 30, 38, 44,
52, 59, 89, 91, 95, 114, 115, 128,
152, 167, 198, 206, 229; interest in
verse forms, 7, 112, 133, 140-141,
146; speed of composition, 122,
161, 176, 187, 202, 205; writing
short stories, 120, 124, 162, 167,
190-191, 194, 196, 219; receives
his first check, 203; sonnet printed,
192; prescribed writing at Harvard,
34, 37, 43, 55, 58, 60-61; fondness
for music, 131; composing music,
196, 200, 233; pleasure in well-
made books, 69, 76, 102, 142, 181;
his illegible penmanship, 10, 12,
25, 31, 33, 63, 66, 89, 90, 112,
118, 123, 126, 137, 195, 206; immorality in literature, 3, 13, 14, 44,
54-55, 94-95, 220-221; naturalism,